# In Search of Happiness

# In Search of Happiness

## James Houston

A LION BOOK

Oxford.Batavia.Sydney

Copyright © 1990 James Houston

Published by
**Lion Publishing plc**
Sandy Lane West, Oxford, England
ISBN 0 7459 1907 3
**Lion Publishing Corporation**
1705 Hubbard Avenue, Batavia, Illinois 60510, USA
ISBN 0 7459 1907 3
**Albatross Books Pty Ltd**
PO Box 320, Sutherland, NSW 2232, Australia
ISBN 0 7324 0240 9

First edition 1990

Copyright of Bible quotations
*The Holy Bible, New International Version,*
copyright © 1973, 1978, 1984 by International Bible Society
Anglicization © 1979, 1986 by Hodder & Stoughton Ltd
Used by permission of Hodder & Stoughton Ltd

Printed and bound in the United States

# Contents

*In memory of my friend and colleague*
*Klaus Bockmuehl*
*and in tribute and gratitude to*
*Regent Alumni*
*who have taught me so much of the experience*
*of happiness*

# Introduction

'Writing a book on happiness? You must be joking!' Such was the response of a friend who knows me well. You see, I am not one of those bouncy types, nor would many ever see me as an extrovert. For those who define happiness as 'having fun', and who seem to have ginger ale instead of a blood circulation, I am definitely not their type. Thrill, novelty, romance, speed and games are not on my agenda. I have never measured myself for my Happiness Quotient with a Euphorimeter.

In fact, my wife has stated rather bluntly that for her, happiness means having a husband who is not writing a book on happiness! My children, who have now grown into friends of mine, have found me to be rather too serious about the matter of living and relating. So it is rather a family joke that in my old age I should be writing about happiness. So why am I doing it?

This book is partly written because I have not been happy in many phases of my life. No one is born happy, though we may all achieve a measure of happiness. When the fruits of happiness begin to enter our lives, it is a time for rejoicing, and we want to share it with our fellow-sufferers. This book is also written with a passionate concern for the quest for integrity in personal well-being. My motive is also partly auto-biographical. Writing it has reminded me of where I don't want to go wrong again, in turning down blind alleys and getting lost in life.

This book is also an expression of gratitude for the students that I have encountered, first as an Oxford don, and then for the past twenty years in the pioneering environment of Regent College, Vancouver. Here, many wonderful young men and women have blessed my life by their sacrifices and their quest for God. I discovered, as you will, through the stories of my friends in this book, how rich the shared tapestry of life can be. Our lives truly open up when we give, relate and share each others' stories, instead of possessing, controlling and manipulating others for our self-interest.

Happiness is no laughing matter. It is the serious business of humanity. It is made all the more serious in our drug culture and with the threat of global extinction, if we do not find the right prescription for the well-being of the human race. Fortunately, this is the era of glasnost, and of a more human, personal approach in business and industry. All of us need a new honesty, to recognize that the world-views and mind-sets of our past are no longer adequate to cope with the issues of our times. Only by taking on this honesty can we provide a habitable, happy future for the generations after us.

The main argument of this book is that happiness is not a product, nor even a personal achievement. It is this commodity mentality that underlies the drug culture as well as the consumerism that threatens to destroy our world. The commodity mentality breeds self-interest, turning us against each other in suspicion and selfishness. Instead, happiness is the fruit of a gifted life, of goodness received from others, and love given and shared. Happiness can only come our way when we have a strong life in relationship with others.

If God is love, then he is the ultimate source of all friendship. It is therefore worthwhile overcoming any religious prejudices we have, to find out how we can become truer persons, more real with ourselves and with other people. We need a religious glasnost to transform the unhappiness of our lives.

I am especially indebted to the sacrificial love of my wife, my companion of thirty-eight years of married happiness, for her willingness to spare me as I have been closeted in writing. Many of my students at Regent College have contributed their stories to illustrate aspects of this book, and I am grateful for their permission to have their stories recorded. For confidentiality, their names have been changed. Friends and family enrich my own life with happiness, so I thank them for their loving support to write as I have done.

However, no one but I can alone be responsible for any errors or weaknesses of this book. I am deeply grateful for the generous help of my friends Miss Jean Nordlun and Mrs Elizabeth Buckmuehl who have helped with the index and correcting the proofs. My editor, Robin Keeley, has been consistently encouraging and helpful in getting this work published.

Jim Houston
Advent 1989

# 1
# How are you Happy?

*Do not go outside yourself, but turn back within;*
*truth dwells in the inner man; and if you find your*
*nature given to frequent change, go beyond your-*
*self. Move on, then, to that source where the light*
*of reason itself receives its light.*

*When you enter your room, you enter your heart.*
*Happy those who delight to enter their hearts and*
*find no evil there.*

**Augustine**

Happiness does not fall into our lap by chance or accident. It is the fruit of a particular way of life that includes discipline, self-reflection, influence upon others, personal contentment, security and inner peace. So happiness is not just a fad, nor is it a god, although in our society it is often pursued as if it were one or the other. Nor is it a destination, but a journey still unfinished. Happiness is certainly not the absence of pain, or otherwise it would be confused with pleasure—as is often the case in our culture. So what is happiness? Happiness is everything that gives well-being to one's self; harmony and assurance to others; depth and perspectives to the spiritual realities around and above us.

However, happiness can be deceptive. It can be a temporary state of affairs, or longer lasting. Happiness can be true or false. Of all the emotions, happiness is perhaps the easiest to identify, the most elusive to find, and the most difficult to define. It means so many things to different people, and the conditions for happiness can even be different for the same person at differing phases of their life.

In our culture, happiness tends to be identified with personal security, such as having enough money in the bank, or having a secure job, or a well mapped-out career. It means to have significance given to us by our standing with other people, especially with those close to us, whom we love. It means having the confidence to share with a soul friend, who really understands us and whom we can trust in spite of our weaknesses. Happiness, too, reflects our sense of assured identity. It is touched off by little things such as the smile of our boss, in something well done, or the approval of a satisfied customer. On another level, environmental influences can help us to be happy, such as awakening from a good night's rest, the glorious technicolor of a rising dawn, living in a place of beauty, or enjoying the music we love best.

All these are examples of moments of happiness. However, they need more permanence and substance actually to make us 'happy people', especially if others are going to recognize this in us. Over the years, at least some of us learn to look into the faces of others and discern the drawn tensions and deadpan masks of those who have pain and unhappiness in their lives, even if they try to cover it with laughter. In contrast, we can also recognize people whose contented and serene expressions show us that they have a deep inner peace and joy. People like this stand in marked contrast to those who are frankly bored, who are exhausted emotionally, who are opaque to others, or who are plainly sad and tragic.

## The motive for this book

'How happy are you?' This question is probably the most serious question we can ask, or be asked. The question takes us to the roots of ourselves. It searches out our values, the way we have chosen to live, the quality of our faith, the depth and character of our relationships with others, the inner feelings we have about ourselves, and the impact or lack of it in the lives of those closest to us.

In the modern world, the question is trivialized a million times each day. People ask each other 'how are you?', expecting an instant summary of the other's feelings before they hop out of the elevator at the next floor. We barely allow each other enough time for a polite response, let alone an honest one. The goal-oriented person, living and working in a culture which worships success, will probably hate this question, because he or she has already destroyed much of the possibility they might have for being happy.

On the other hand, those who have been robbed of childhood, through cruelty, neglect or poverty, may find the subject of happiness quite alien. As far as they are concerned, happiness belongs to another planet. Either we talk of happiness in superficial or even false ways, or else it probes us too painfully to allow us to expose our wounds to it.

The widely felt sense of alienation in our culture has come about because we settle for cheap generalizations about each other. We are not truly prepared to get to know each other, because handling our own pains and burdens may be more than enough. We have been trained to believe that our emotional life is too messy to spend time on. So we naturally divert our attention, and the attention of others, away from it. This is why we are suspicious of this question: 'how happy are you?' It gets us too involved in ourselves, and adds complication to our lives. We feel we should simply stick to being practical people, and get on with the business of living.

However, we know that this approach will not do. We know that an unexamined life is not really worth living. This book is intended to help us understand what happiness is, why it has declined in our culture, and how we can rediscover happiness for ourselves. The central purpose of the book is to find the true source of happiness, and to ask who it is that we can praise for our happiness. The contralto singer, Kathleen Ferrier, was holidaying in the Swiss Alps when she was dying of cancer. Marvelling at the beauty and grandeur of the Matterhorn, she reflected sadly that she had no one to thank for the happiness this beauty gave her. This shows that happiness can only be complete when it is given to others. This is one of the great keys to understanding happiness. It can never be grasped selfishly for our own sake, but must be shared. We simply cannot hold on to happiness. We have to give it away before we, and others, can truly enjoy it.

This is an ideal that many of us do not experience. We live in a crazy world, where unhappiness is the norm. Our century has probably seen more unhappiness than any previous century. As we look beyond the year 2000, we can pray that it will be a turning point for the human race; turning from darkness to light. So many people long for the world to become a happier place. Perhaps we need to reflect on how we could begin by making our world happier if we ourselves learnt to be happy within our own hearts first.

## What makes you happy?

Attempts are made by sociologists and others to measure how happy we are. Yet it is obvious that we tend to have a wide spectrum of attitudes, motives and events that make us happy. A young couple fall in love and seem very happy. Then disillusion sets in, followed by loss of confidence in each other, and much mutual unhappiness. A business-woman enjoys a highly-successful career. But then a breakdown occurs in her marriage relationship, and she loses the sense of well-being she had in her job, and even in her whole career. Events such as this reveal the instability in what we thought originally might give us happiness. This is why we need to shift our focus from asking ourselves, 'how happy are you?' to asking, 'how are you happy?' This is a fundamental question, and our answers to it will reflect the type of personality we each have.

We speak loosely of having 'a temperament', behaving 'temperamentally', being a certain 'personality' type, and of having 'character'. We need to examine what we mean in greater detail. The ancient categories of human temperament were formulated in the fifth century BC by Hippocrates, who has been called 'the founder of medicine'. He saw four temperamental types: the melancholic, sanguine, phlegmatic and choleric. Today, there are many other ways in which human personality is understood.

Personality expresses inter-personal relationships, showing how we have learned to respond and to relate to others with their very different temperaments to our own. Character speaks of our individual traits that have become stabilized, giving us firmness, consistency, and moral strengths that are freed from addictive or compulsive behaviour. However, the sober truth is that we are dominated not by a freed self, but by a compulsive self. For this reason, our personality is more accurately defined by our compulsions than by our strengths and abilities.

We can escape from facing these inner weaknesses by relating to objects rather than to people. Since the world of objects does not engage us relationally as people, we can happily continue to ignore our addictive behaviour. So an artist can go on painting, or a gardener happily engage his temperament with plants, or a business person or a scholar can pursue their career and express their temperamental strengths. However, we also live in a world of other people. It is in our relational conflicts with each other that we come into conflict with ourselves, as our addictions cross the contrary addictions of others. This is where we are likely to experience most unhappiness.

If we major upon our strengths and abilities, as many personality tests do, we may become blind to the fact that our defects cause our own types of unhappiness. This is why it is helpful to look at those areas of our personality where we act compulsively, and where our way of behaving tends to be unbalanced. It can also be helpful in dealing with other people to learn about their compulsions. We will then be able to understand them better, make excuses for them in kindness, or show them true compassion. How much human misery we might alleviate if we understood each other more wisely and sympathetically. Then we could begin to discern how we too affect other people, in unhappy conflicts.

If, for example, a young man appears distant and suspicious of older men, even when they treat him kindly, then I should suspect that he has a negative image of his own father. Or if a girl has trouble relating comfortably with older women, I may wonder how she gets on with her own mother. This shows how our relationships can be soured by parental factors quite outside the relationship itself. We all tend to over-react to other people who consciously or unconsciously remind us of people who have hurt and offended us. We can also violently over-react to people because they unwittingly touch the deeper wounds of our past, not yet healed.

This is why ignorance of other people's personalities can be a dangerous thing. Ignorance of others tends to exaggerate the negative in our relationships. When we say we do not like or trust other people, it is often not because they have offended us or let us down, but because they are not 'our type', or because we are ignorant of how they 'tick'.

Awareness of our own personality type awakens us to the situations we set up for ourselves that produce both happiness and unhappiness. This self-understanding can help us to live more wisely—and more humbly. It will make us more sensitive to the negative impact we make on other people. None of us can afford to be complacent in our relationships, when we live with so many hurting people all around us. Nor can we remain ignorant about ourselves, if we are seriously searching for more happiness and contentment in our lives.

We will now look at nine types of personality. You may be able to identify yourself immediately; or you may feel that you are a combination of more than one type. Each type highlights compulsive aspects of our personalities.


## 1: The perfectionist

This type of person seeks to avoid anger, to be a good little boy or girl, and to live as the most reasonable and self-righteous person possible. Later in their life, they discover a great deal of anger within them. They may suffer from depression and feel terribly let down by other people, though they may get glimpses of themselves as being the real pro blem. All their life they have done 'the right thing'. If only other people had been the sweetness and light that they have been! Bothered by seeing so much that is wrong with other people, they become like a smouldering underground fire, even though they will not admit it is they themselves who cause their own unhappiness.

The irony of perfectionists is that while they believe in the values which can make them truly happy, they can also destroy themselves if they allow resentment, nostalgia for the past or bitterness with the status quo to get the upper hand. The perfectionist will recognize that the following statements about happiness are what rings true for him or her:

☐Being happy means living up to my ideals.

☐Happiness is not what I want most consciously. I prefer to

do what is right than to be preoccupied with what is plea-surable.

☐ I get frustrated when other people do not do things pro-perly. This makes me unhappy.

☐ I do not know when I am angry. I believe that my emotions are on a level keel.

☐ I am critical of others. Other people rarely reach the stan-dard of performance that would give me happiness.

☐ As a child it was very painful for me to be criticized by others. I now see that my own sense of happiness really lies in being more forgiving of others.

☐ I admit that I tend to get attracted by worthy causes, and throw myself into them to gain happiness. At first I thought I was being selfless in doing this.

## 2: The giver

This type of person avoids acknowledging his or her needs, while yearning to be accepted and approved by others. Giv-ers find it hard to admit that in helping others they are really seeking happiness in being appreciated. Givers are really try-ing to buy love or win it. They need to be needed. This can lead to constant disappointment when others, who they want to help, do not respond in the ways they would like to dictate.

Givers can be very popular socially, if they learn to sup-press their more manipulative tendencies. Happiness for the giver means taking on the identity of being 'the power be-hind the throne', or someone who works 'behind the scenes'. Givers will identify themselves in the following statements:

☐ Being happy is being with and helping other people.

☐ Unhappiness is often caused by never seeming to have long-established friendships. My relationships are intense while they last, but they tend to be short-lived.

☐ I suppose I feel happiest when I am being nurtured by the affection of others. I love to be loved.

☐ I do not feel that I have many needs. I would much rather be useful to others.

☐ Flattery is a vice I have to guard against because I do tend to put myself in the limelight.

☐ As a child, I believe I was much loved. But I also learnt to perform, to make sure I was loved even more.

☐ Seeking love, I can act manipulatively, so my motives for being a helper need to be checked and challenged by those I trust.

## 3: The performer

Modern life approves of performers, because they are desperate to achieve. Failure is sin to them. They try to avoid failure by whatever means are open to them. Performers have been described as chameleons, because they will fit into whatever environment will enable them to succeed, even at the cost of their integrity. Their self-worth is highly dependent upon what they do, and so their performance, or lack of it, rates very highly indeed.

For the performer, happiness lies in being an activist, and love is expressed through action. Jobs have to 'succeed', marriages have to 'work', and all relationships are really functional. The following statements ring true for the performer:

☐ Being happy means being busy.

☐ Happiness means getting into the right job or profession where I can generally run my own show.

☐ I fear failure. Having put so much effort into what I do, I cannot imagine what it would mean to fail.

☐ I don't think too much about myself. I just get on with the job. Introspective people complicate things too much.

☐I am a great talker, and I live enthusiastically. I do keep myself on the go. These things do give me happiness.

☐As a child, I was often praised for the things I did, and for good grades at school. I remember best my teenage years when I really began to see how important it was to do well in all I had to do, or enjoyed doing.

☐First impressions count for a lot, so personal happiness is helped

## 4: The romantic

Some people feel particularly the need to be 'special', perhaps because of emotional deprivation in childhood. They avoid being 'ordinary' at all costs, for their sense of self-worth is bound up with an awareness of personal tragedy. The romantic may frequently feel depressed. However, the strong sense of a melancholic past is balanced by the anticipation of a romantic future. This fills the lives of romantics with a deep desire for an exciting, even extraordinary, future. The romantic is familiar with the following statements:

☐I cannot be truly happy until my past has been completely healed.

☐I am most happy when my dreams come true.

☐Depth of feeling really means more to me than 'mere happiness'.

☐I have a deep desire to be authentic and real.

☐I am impatient with the flatness of ordinary living. I need to do dramatic things, to heighten my imagination with intensified feelings, and to fantasize about situations I will never experience in reality.

☐As a child I felt abandoned. Because of this, I expect people to come into my life and then leave me. I become angry with the people who constantly let me down. I do not have much respect for authority.

☐ I readily fall into fits of depression. Sometimes these depressions seriously affect me, leaving me paralysed. Happiness is not my normal state. Happiness is too elusive for me to say that I am a happy person.

## 5: The observer

Independently-minded, the observer stands back from life. Observers are happiest living in a castle, high above the town, from which they can view all that is going on in the world around them. Aloof from interactions with others, they prefer not to get involved, but observe others from the window of their lives.

Observers can live quite simply. They do not expend great amounts of emotional energy and are not attached to others. Instead, they are attracted to systems and to abstractions generally. They make good engineers or computer experts. The following statements reflect on their outlook on life:

☐ Happiness is to avoid emptiness in my life.

☐ Being happy is having a correct judgment of what is observed. In that way, I am never ignorant.

☐ I am suspicious of emotions. They may have a place, but they are always secondary to correct thinking.

☐ Life is best handled by putting things into separate compartments. I am most happy when I can sort things out and handle them separately.

☐ It is true that I am often lonely, but I try not to think about myself. I am happiest when I am figuring out some problem. I love puzzles, and enjoy doing crosswords and other word games.

☐ As a child, I loved solitude. I would creep off to be by

myself in my own hiding place. Sometimes I was afraid of being in a crowd, or even of getting pinned down in a conversation in front of others.

☐Privacy means a lot to my sense of well-being, so I struggle to have happiness in intimate relationships.


## 6: The responsible

The responsible are dutiful people. They have lost faith in authorities, and feel that they need to uphold the world like Atlas himself. It is important to them not to make mistakes, so are often indecisive, certainly cautious, and not risk-takers. The responsible prefer to repeat a winning formula rather than to experiment with an untried one. They would rather deal with the familiar, in which they can excel, than take a new initiative. The responsible are actually afraid to change. Because of this, they live careful lives. They seek safety in guidelines, in loyalty, and in hiding behind institutional and professional roles. The responsible express themselves in the following statements:

☐Happiness lies in being a middle-of-the-road person.

☐Being happy is knowing the limits in which I can operate.

☐I am suspicious of authority. I have often seen it abused by others, and know how untrustworthy other people can be.

☐Life is best handled by taking time to see all the options, and then acting carefully, responsibly and dutifully.

☐I am very aware of the pitfalls and dangers of life. For this reason, I have to live cautiously, and I do not tend to take initiatives. I much prefer having secure guidelines.

☐As a child, I suffered much abuse from my parents. This meant that I felt powerless as a child, and grew up afraid of getting hurt. I became uncertain because of the unpredictability of my seniors.

□Prudence is a very important virtue for me. Happiness lies within emotional safeguards all the time. I hate any form of deviance.

## 7: The fun-lover

The childhood fear of pain leads the fun-lover to appear sunny, fun-loving and lighthearted. This type of person acts like Peter Pan, the eternal youth, or like Narcissus, engaged in self-absorption. The desire to 'feel good' makes the fun-lover playful, bubbling, talkative and excitable. Work is unattractive unless it can be made 'fun' to do. Duty is tedious to the fun-lover, who can often appear unreliable and fickle.

For the fun-lover, happiness is very much in the mind. They tend to assume that there are very few things in life you cannot enjoy if you only have the right attitude. The fun-lover will agree with most of the following statements:

□Happiness is what you can expect out of life, if you only put your mind to it.

□Being happy is getting excited about things.

□You can always talk your way out of a situation if you have your wits.

□Life is best handled by always being nice, and seeing the good things in other people. I always try to look on the bright side of life.

□I like other people to think of me as a happy person, because I really am. I have to admit that I do like being adored. I am very enthusiastic about the present and I feel even more optimistic about the future.

□As a child, I have the happiest of memories. I have no memories of fear at all. I have always had positive memories.

□I may be a glutton for novelty, but I am very sober about

making good choices in my life. I prefer to brainstorm than
to take up the drudgery of daily tasks.

## 8: The strong boss

The avoidance of any evidence of weakness makes this type
of person watchful, tough and aggressive. The strong boss
likes to 'have it out' with others, to set things straight. They
hate to be taken advantage of, or to let others see any sign of
weakness. Life may be a struggle, but strong bosses are de-
termined that they are going to win through whatever the
cost.

This means that strong bosses have a tendency to pull
down others who are on a pedestal. They can be cruel, and
can take revenge if they feel the need. Their motive for living
is self-preservation, which they exert forcefully. If they have
strong moral or religious convictions, they can become crusa-
ders. As a child, the strong boss had a tough upbringing.
Their world was dominated by a strong father, and by bul-
lies who had to be faced and beaten if need be. The following
statements frame their mind-set:

☐ Happiness lies in looking after yourself, and not becoming
a doormat to anyone. I believe in justice and see when there
is injustice very clearly.

☐ Being happy is also in protecting others under me, so that
they get a fair deal. I enjoy serving others.

☐ I am not afraid to confront other people. In fact, I rather
like the challenge when it comes.

☐ I think of myself as an 'earthy' type of person, because I
value realism. I have very little patience for those who have
their heads in the clouds.

☐ I admit I can be ruthless towards people who intrude on my
territory.

☐ As a child, I had to struggle against unfair odds. I took

pride in not showing my feelings when I was unfairly treated. I was only respected when I appeared strong.

☐ Truth and innocence are important virtues for me. I seek the truth in a fair fight to get at what is right. Getting mad really does clear the air, and if the innocent are treated unfairly, then a fight for them is also well justified. After all, there is nothing wrong with getting angry.

## 9: The mediator

The mediator works hard to avoid any kind of conflict, and to live in an atmosphere of harmony. Mediators lack emotional energy, which leads them to identify with other people's interests and to keep the peace at any price. Because of this, they are available to others. Mediators enjoy routine, do not get excited about things, and can be lazy. They have a poor sense of distinguishing the important from the unimportant, although once a value is established they can be very stubborn in holding on to it. As a child, the mediator felt overlooked, ignored and found him or herself in the middle of tension on many occasions. He or she learnt to cope with this by withdrawing and emotionally going to sleep. The mediator will tend to agree with the following statements:

☐ Happiness lies in avoiding conflict.

☐ I am most happy when I am not having to face challenges and choices, but am secure in my familiar routine.

☐ Getting upset is not worth it. Some people think that I am too easygoing. I don't get too enthusiastic, but then I hate to waste energy on anything. Why let anything bother you too much?

☐ I think of myself as a stable character. I keep a low profile and have no great ambition to stand out in anything.

☐ I get 'stuck' sometimes, and then I need outside help to get me on the road again.

☐As a child, I realized that it was 'damned if you do, and damned if you don't', so I found the best way was to lie low, and keep out of sight. After all, I was the middle child, so I let my elder and younger siblings face the firing line instead.

☐I admit that I am laid back, but I can also be a completely loyal friend. For me, happiness is to love another person with all my being.

The passions that confront each of these personality types are based on the seven deadly sins that medieval Christianity struggled to overcome. Two other categories have been added: the deceit of the performer, and the fear of the responsible. The sequence of passions that fit each personality type is as follows:
1. anger; 2. pride; 3. deceit; 4. envy; 5. greed; 6. fear; 7. gluttony; 8. lust; 9. sloth.

The emotional traps that lead to an addictive way of life are in the same sequence:
1. perfection; 2. activism or service; 3. efficiency or success; 4. romanticism; 5. knowledge; 6. self-security that hides fear; 7. idealism that leads to gluttony or over-indulgence; 8. lust that is arrogance; 9. sloth or laziness.

These passions seduce us into drawing up our own lopsided terms for personal happiness. Later in this chapter we will look at the balancing virtues which can help to transform our experiences of happiness.

## Dynamics of personal happiness

The quest for well-being and happiness is clearly very different for each type of person. We can distinguish three major types of response to the outside world in the personality types. The first response is aggression. The perfectionist, the performer and the strong boss are aggressive types who seek happiness in moving out against other people. The aggression of the perfectionist is expressed in seeing what is wrong and putting it right. The performer is also aggressive, but the aggression is in appearing to be a success in the eyes of other people. Performers are happy when they have achieved a positive image, and look good. The strong boss tries to control people and situations, and it is the use of power that makes such people happy. Strength is the secret of their happiness. Their fallacy is to assume that they are bigger than the world, and that they can handle things on their own. All three forms of aggression reveal that there is a gap between what each of these personalities prescribe for their happiness, and the reality outside their own emotions.

A second type of response is in acceptance of the outside world. This is characteristic of the giver, the responsible, and the fun-lover. All three types have to adjust to the outside world to gain their happiness. They move towards other people, and seek their happiness in the approval of others. The giver takes the initiative with others, by caring for them, to the point of needing to be needed by others. Givers seek happiness in the appreciation of other people. The responsible achieve happiness by carrying out the demands placed upon them. However, their happiness is tempered by apprehension and a subdued fear of failure, so that happiness is very much a mixed emotion. Fun-lovers feel that the world is too big or too much for them to handle. They can only hope to live cheerfully in it, and then they will be happy. They attempt to view life optimistically by screening out all that is unpleasant and painful.

A third type of response is to withdraw from the world. The world is too big or too complex to handle, so defence is the only appropriate response. This is expressed in the romantic, the observer, and the mediator. Romantics feel that they have already missed the bus, so they wait for another opportunity to get on board. As they wait, their happiness lies in anticipation. They believe that their own uniqueness will somehow make their future 'special'. Such personalities tend to see themselves in unrealistic ways. The observer enjoys tidiness, as if the mind were a filing cabinet and everything was studied and sorted out accordingly. Observers react defensively when others intrude into their mind-set, upsetting it all with another way of looking at life. The mediator seeks harmony rather than correctness, and is prepared for peace at any price. They realize that others think their view of happiness is rather dull and unattractive, but they have concluded that it is the best deal they can achieve for themselves. Happiness for them is a rather detached affair.

Carried to excess, all these types of personality can lead to an imbalance in our attitudes and relationships with others. For the aggressive types, the more aggressive we become, then the deeper the presumptions grow. This in turn intensifies false hopes and their accompanying illusions. When aggressive types move from aggression towards presumption, then their withdrawal from others will eventually lead them into black despair.

There is a similar trap for the second category of dependent types. They begin to sense that they are living with false hopes. This can force them to move towards a more aggressive form of relating, only to discover that presumption has now compounded their problems and left them with unsubstantiated self-confidence.

The third category of withdrawing types also compound their problems when they try to overcome their despair by moving towards greater dependence on others. However, false hope leaves them in a worse condition than before.

Our childhood origins give rise to our fundamental motivations, then, and these in turn only provide us with partial pictures of what human happiness is fully intended to be, in all its wholeness. Our sense of self is always limited by our own impaired experiences and perceptions of our inadequate relationships with others. The big question about happiness is therefore: how can we break out from the the straitjacket of our own personality type to find the fullness of true happiness? We will pursue this later in the book, but first we need to examine some of the influences of our culture, and its historical roots, which still have an abiding impact upon our perceptions of what it means to be happy.

# 2

# The Pursuit of Happiness in the Street

*Of all the different purposes set before mankind, the most disastrous is surely 'the Pursuit of Happiness', slipped into the American Declaration of Independence, along with 'Life and Liberty' as an unalienable right, almost accidentally, at the last moment. Happiness is like a young deer, fleet and beautiful. Hunt him, and he becomes a poor frantic quarry; after the kill, a piece of stinking flesh.*

Malcolm Muggeridge, Conversion: A Spiritual Journey

Singing is one of the most spontaneous expressions of human emotion. People sing in the shower, whistle while they work, and tune in to the music they love best while they jog. Modern popular music, such as jazz, pop and rock'n'roll have helped us to understand the pulse beat of the street, revealing the values and quests of our society. If we begin our pursuit of happiness in the contemporary world, then the lyrics of the street have a lot to tell us.

## The lyrics of the street

In a mass culture, people may no longer make up their own songs, but their popular choices reveal the general attitudes of society as a whole. Love, which is easily the dominant theme of most pop songs, is held up as the solution to our problems. However, pop songs also communicate a number of unintentional messages about our culture: the exploitation of sex and women, for example, or the way in which people spend most of their lives chasing rainbows.

Romantic music creates its own distorting illusions, leading to what has been called 'IFD disease'. This is made up of the Idealization that makes impossible demands on life, which leads to Frustration (since the demands can never be met) and which then results in Demoralization or Despair. So we enter the street through its lyrics in pursuit of happiness. We will see that it is a self-defeating game.

Rock singer Bruce Springsteen is one of today's most popular expressions of the belief that ordinary people can find real things for themselves. Although he is a superstar, Springsteen appears as our friend, someone who is 'on our side'. He has the persona of a nervy, gauche youth exploring life for the first time. For many people he represents 'authenticity', standing for the core values that they crave to have. He is critical of the effects of capitalism in our unhappy world, and he celebrates the 'ordinary' rather than the special. He sings about the commonplace and the dreariness of living in the deserts of ordinary existence.

Talking about his hard-working, poor parents, Springsteen once said that they wanted him 'to get a little something for myself; what they did not understand was that I wanted everything.' That comment captures today's mood: not just a piece of the pie, but all of it for myself.

The prevailing experience in the pursuit of happiness in the street is that at first freedom and love seem to be quite compatible. But then reality strikes. If my girl also has freedom and love, then her quest for freedom may enable her to fly away, leaving me without freedom or love. As Springsteen's albums progress, the disillusionment deepens. First he saw what had happened to his father, and hated it. 'He had been so disappointed, had so much stuff knocked out of him, that he couldn't accept the idea that I had a dream and I had possibilities. The thing I wanted, he thought was just foolish.'

> *Daddy worked his whole life for nothing but pain,*
> *Now he walks these empty rooms,*
> *Looking for something to blame.*
> *You inherit the sins, you inherit the flames;*
> *Adam raised Cain.*

The answer is to get out into the street. Walking the sidewalks and driving away in a powerful car are the symbols of escape to freedom. Certainly the back seat of the car, on a lonely lane, symbolized for many in the sixties the beginning of sexual freedom.

> *You can hide 'neath your covers,*
> *And study your pain;*
> *Make crosses from your loves,*
> *Throw roses in the rain.*
> *Waste your summer praying in vain,*
> *For a savior to rise from these streets.*
> *Well now, I'm no hero,*
> *That's understood.*
> *All the redemption I can offer a girl,*
> *Is 'neath the dirty hood*
> *With a chance to make it good somehow;*
> *Hey what else can we do now?*
> *We got one last chance to make it real,*
> *To trade in these wings on some wheels,*
> *Climb in back,*
> *Heaven's waiting down the track*

But the excitement of racing the camaro, the easy catch that's easily lost, when 'all her pretty dreams are torn' and 'she stares into the night', leads into greater risks of desperation. 'Born to run', sings Springsteen, 'in the day we sweat it out in the streets of a runaway American dream, at night we ride through mansions of glory in suicide machines.' But 'The highway's jammed with broken heroes on a last chance power drive'. For 'You spend your life waiting for a moment that just doesn't come. Well, don't waste your time waiting.' Individuals can make decisions that influence the course of their lives, but they must also take responsibility for them as well:

> *You make up your mind, you choose the chance you take.*
> *You can't walk away from the price you pay.*

The impressions deepen in Springsteen's later albums that ordinary people have little to live for. Yet they hang on mysteriously in the belief that somehow, somewhere, there is something to believe in. In the end, violence, crime, jail and broken lives become the dominant themes in his songs. High hopes are now crushed in the face of oppressive forces of life, and dreams are pushed aside by the anguish of mere survival.

The message becomes clearer. First sexuality is interpreted as the expression of personal freedom. Then the eagerness for sex becomes addictive, utterly without commitment. That leads in turn to the irresistible demands of the flesh. This turns out to be bondage, not freedom after all. So helplessness and despair are then the vulnerable condition of a drug-hungry world.

## The indictment of a drug-hungry society

Dependence has become one of the major social problems of our times, while drug abuse has become a massive health hazard. Yet much confusion covers this whole realm of addiction and its treatment. We cannot begin to talk seriously about the quest for happiness without trying to understand the issue of drugs. Despite its central place in the issue of happiness, it is remarkable that so few churches are concerned about drug abuse and addiction. The same can be said of colleges and universities. Philosophy, which has traditionally focused its attention on the meaning of happiness and its importance in human life, is also strangely silent about the drug crisis of our times. Such silences reveal where the real problems of addiction lie: in our refusal to face up to the human condition, with all of its needs and fears.

We tend to think of drug addiction as a modern phenomenon, popularized first in the sixties by such campus leaders as Timothy O'Leary, and then more massively impacted by American troops in Vietnam. But the truth is that humankind has always experimented with drugs. In the ancient Near East, heroin is referred to in Sumerian tablets of 3,000-4,000 years ago. The ancient Greek poet Hesiod, in the eighth century BC, mentions the town of Necome, near Corinth, which means 'the town of the poppy'. Herodotus and Hippocrates speak of the therapeutic use of opium in the fourth century BC. Paracelsus, the Swiss physician, prepared laudanum as a medical opiate in the sixteenth century.

Opium smoking dates at least from the seventeenth century, and the Opium War of 1840-42 was over China's ban of this import, lucrative as the trade was for England at the time. Freud became a strong advocate of the use of cocaine (known to the Incas at least since its widespread usage in the Andes after AD1230). Peyote has long been known to the American Indians, while cannabis spread from China into India in the early centuries of the Christian era. The use of these and of other hallucinatory drugs is ancient.

What is modern is the sheer scale of drug-trading and addiction. Tragically, there are millions of addicts in the world today, and the figure continues to rise with new methods of production and crime. Previous civilizations used drugs within their religious rites, but secular, western civilization (the first attempt to build a civilization without religion, as the French novelist André Malraux pointed out) uses drugs for their own sake. So while dependence upon drugs is not new, the modern world is filled with the most drug-conscious of all cultures in history.

## A child of the wider culture

Much of the confusion about drugs today stems from the way in which we suppress our emotions in our cold, calculating, technological society. We use opiates in the widest sense of the word: tea and coffee drinking, tobacco smoking, alcohol, sexual addiction, and the more serious forms of drug addiction. We have also become a pain-suppressant society, assuming it is our right not to suffer, to have health, and to have the further right to enjoy pleasure. It has become socially acceptable to be seen as dependent on a whole range of activities: doing the crossword puzzle, watching or performing sports, television viewing, gambling, taking pain-killers and alcohol, using amphetamines, and taking more dangerous risks with hallucinogens and narcotics.

Seeking pleasure is one of the fundamental motivators of human behaviour, and this is entirely normal. The search for pleasure helps us in the fight against boredom, lethargy, and indifference. However, when pleasure is cultivated intensely as part of our everyday behaviour, then it can distort human emotions. Like everything else, pleasure has its price. If we assume it is a right, then it can readily become an abuse.

Why do drug addicts enter the drug scene in the first place? The main reasons given by addicts is that they do it for 'kicks' and enjoyment, or out of curiosity, or because their friends do it. Other factors are rarely mentioned at first, but once the misery and damage caused by addiction become apparent, all the misery of life pours out: personal loneliness and alienation; the crumbling of family support; deep distrust of other human beings. This is only the beginning of the agony. Addicts face the many problems of being forced to enter into a career of crime to pay for their habit, and as time goes by the pleasures of the drug experience fade. Finally the addict has to face severe emotional side-effects, and the mounting nightmare of withdrawal.

What is not usually understood by the addict is the original personality disorder which triggered off such intense pleasure-seeking. We all tend naturally to 'normalize' our home backgrounds, not realizing the full impact of being unloved, the lack of intimacy with parents, the absence of emotional shelter and security, and much else. Nor do we realize how profoundly television and the mass media generally bombard us with an overload of stimuli.

The drug culture is a direct response to the wider culture. We have learned to accept uncritically the idea of 'doing your own thing', experimenting with life and developing our own private world. These ideas lead directly from the general, amoral culture in which most people live to the entrapped culture of drugs.

We hunger for contact with what is 'real'; we thirst after an expanded sense of consciousness; we insist on greater freedom; we become impatient in our 'instant society'; we assume that there is deeper potential in our own selves. All these aspirations contribute to the making of the modern drug culture.

## Responding to the drug culture

There is no simple explanation for drug addiction. There is no single cause. Nor can there be some single measure to prevent drug abuse. In fact, the louder the alarm is sounded, the

greater the problem becomes. Even the research and literature used to try to prevent drug abuse may inadvertently increase the obsession in our society.

We may even have to admit that the modern faith in techniques to solve our problems gives rise to another faith—that
drugs can solve anything too. We believe that, given the tools,
we can all as individuals 'fix' our own needs and desires. This
in turn implies that every individual has the right to do their
own thing, to solve all that is necessary. Just as we have the
fundamental conviction that we can change everything with
the 'right techniques', so the promise is offered that drugs
too will change things. When this world is viewed as impossibly demanding and painful, then the prospect of another
world, chemically induced, is an attractive alternative.

If the drug culture has been spawned by the wider culture, then the wider culture must change before we see a diminishing of drug dependence. The whole climate of
commercial advertising, television, and political propaganda
must be called into question if we are to see a resolution to the
drug scene. For drug addiction is clearly an indictment of the
whole of western life and thought. It is also an indictment
against a worldly and superficial religious life.

However, instead of the radical change that is needed,
western culture responds to the problem of drugs in a typical
way—it looks for the 'right tools' to do the job. Governments
naturally opt for political solutions, and the most obvious
way is to target the sources of drug production and distribu-
tion. This happened in Turkey in the sixties, the 'Golden
Triangle' of south-east Asia in the seventies, and in Colom-
bia, Peru and Bolivia in the eighties. Other agencies spot-
light the breakdown of families, and the role of the family in
society. Others attack the more difficult task of attempting
to change attitudes towards smoking, diet and health in
general.

However, none of these methods get to grips with the root
cause of addiction. They fail to face up to the basic problems

that urbanization, technological power and our competitive greediness inflict upon us all. As long as the pursuit of pleasure, the belief in narcissistic freedom, and the loss of concern for the underprivileged continue, so the addictions of our society will intensify.

## Taking the brakes off

Perhaps one of the deadliest elements of our contemporary plight is permissiveness, compounded by loneliness and the absence of love. This poisonous mixture is the direct cause of today's drug culture. Permissiveness means that 'anything goes', and the feeling of being a cosmic orphan in an inhuman world can lead to intense desperation. All the boundaries that mark out normal human conduct begin to disappear.

The first to go are the boundaries of personal conduct; they crumble away with each new impulse to sin and sin again. Then the boundaries of what gives basis for meaningful discussion melt away leaving us unconnected, floating around with the sense of weightlessness, like astronauts beyond the pull of gravity. Then the boundaries of personality come under attack. We experience a separation of body, mind and spirit as if we are truly 'spaced out'. Our rational understanding becomes disconnected, and we feel out of touch with our own emotions. Other people begin to seem pseudo-real, and their commitments appear hollow. Gloria experienced exactly this profound sense of becoming a stranger to herself and all around her:

*I am bewildered by the state of my own self. I am bewildered by myself. Conflict between who? Self and self. Two separate identities. How can I explain that? Which self is really me? There is constant conversing, debating, struggling for power between these two. One will suggest*

*one thing, the other will try and stop it. One is obviously
'good', the other is not. The most irritating thing is that
although it is all inside me, concerning me, I am without
significant control. How then can I achieve unity of self?
How can I cope with two duelling minds in one body?*

*Then the pain of my utter worthlessness comes over me in
floods. My tears exhaust me, and I despise my tears.
People deserve so much more than I can give them.
Sometimes I want so much to do something worthwhile,
to be something great, that I ache with longing. At other
times I wonder why I am so introspective, when the sun is
shining and the day is great. Then once more I plunge
into those moods of inexpressible gnawing feelings of
restlessness, dissatisfaction, humiliation and displacement, that cause me to feel hopelessly inadequate, help-
lessly imperfect, like a blundering invader into human
existence. For I can do nothing right.*

*Even the most precious experiences of love turn to ashes,
and intimacy becomes a violation. I'm so frustrated with
my struggle between a goal of righteousness and purity,
and the temptation of the pleasures of evil. Why must I
remain chained to imperfection?*

For most people, thoughts like these are never articulated so
clearly, nor are they entered into a journal. Instead they are
contained within, without even being thought, in states of
confusion, anger, longing and despair. All the time they
smile, perform, and act as if these feelings were not their
own. They play games with other people, often in the awareness that others are doing the same thing with them. Occa-
sionally, the mask cracks, and a new one is put on to replace
it.

## The quest for absolute pleasure

In the sixties, the new mask was absolute love. The sixties sprayed love around like a deodorant. There were 'love-ins' in an orgy of sex, or there was the tribal love of extended 'families' and communal arrangements. Alongside love was absolute liberty: 'doing what you want, when you want, where you want, with whom you want'. With absolute love and liberty came absolute indolence, breaking off contact with the clock, sleeping when you wanted, nibbling when you felt like it. Following all three came the experience of absolute destitution, the return to nature, to nudity, to survival beyond the safety net of Daddy's American Express Card.

This demolition of boundaries opened up the gates to the quest for absolute pleasure. Education was abandoned, morality dried up, and the new powers of sensation were wondrously opened a paradise of pleasure, by the 'miracle of chemistry'. This drug-induced 'miracle' led to the discovery of the 'sixth sense', so that normal consciousness was now viewed as blindness in comparison.

It was as if another Copernican revolution had taken place; another Columbian discovery of a new world. The revolution was termed the 'expansion of consciousness'. What many drug addicts did not realize, as many tragically still do not, is that this is really a displacement of consciousness, rather than a true expansion, which eventually leads to atrophy and death. It is destruction through excess.

Kevin entered this path into the drug culture, not with the excesses of the hippies just described, but much more moderately. In Sunday School he had heard about Jesus Christ, and as a child of twelve he had a conversion experience. However, the model of Christianity he was given let him down. He followed a dull, middle-class lifestyle that was shallow, unreflective, and organized by his 'betters'. It was too superficial to bear inspection.

As a result, Kevin started to explore other religions. They

certainly seemed to have greater depth than what he had been
served up in church and home. He immersed himself in ex-
istential literature. Hermann Hesse's book, *Siddharta*, led
his curiosity into Buddhism. He left his secure job as an en-
gineer and went east. In Afghanistan he became part of the
drug culture, and then spent time in a Hindu ashram, learning yoga and meditation. What did drugs do for him?

> *They opened up to me a world of psychic reality that be-*
> *fore had been closed. Many fellow travellers at that time*
> *were seeking a spiritual meaning to life that was so lack-*
> *ing in my background. I remember being surprised to see*
> *brilliant young minds, absorbing 'spiritual truths' sitting*
> *at the feet of gurus, hearing stories like those of the Bha-*
> *gavad Gita which were fantastic and pre-scientific, thus*
> *hardly credible, while totally rejecting the Bible as sheer*
> *myth.*

This inconsistency alerted Kevin to realize that there were
boundaries he would not cross. He added, 'Others who
lacked those limits are not alive today.'

Through LSD, Kevin had spiritual experiences, 'God-
consciousness', that became a common theme among many
of his friends. Yet even then, 'I was aware that perhaps it
was a counterfeit key, one that should not be used. Either
the person was not ready to receive such experiences, or not
prepared spiritually to enter that inner world.'

Later still, Kevin began to see that the transition from the
use to the abuse of drugs was itself a shift from being a door of
perception to an escape from reality. Through wise friends,
already committed to a deep walk with God, he learned that
the pilgrimage to God was a far more reliable journey
through true friendships in ordinary life, than by the chemical journey with all its perils of self-abuse. When he was restored to the Christian life, Kevin had certainly gained a
new level of sensitivity, a deepened realism of life, and a

greater integrity to his faith. He was one of the few who emerged safely from the other side of the drug experience.

## Happiness and the human body

The delusion of Kevin's adventure with drugs is that truth can be discovered by poisoning the brain! It is a mark of our utter confusion if we say that truth can only be uncovered through a chemical delusion. Yet there is a connection between the exercise of the mind, the involvement of the emotions, and the experience of happiness. The ingredient that all unhappy people lack is involvement. We receive happiness in a relationship, or from an experience, when we are emotionally involved. The more we pay out in emotional involvement, the more we will get back. The less emotionally involved we are, the less satisfied we will be. If we withdraw from our family, or our work, or our other activities, we will become unhappy. No wonder that the detached, technocratic spirit leads to deep unhappiness.

Unhappiness is not the opposite of happiness. Unhappiness and happiness are not the flip sides of the same emotion. Feelings of unhappiness and happiness can exist side by side, much as love and hate live together. So if we avoid the things that make us unhappy, we will not automatically become happy. We may well lessen our unhappiness without achieving any increase of happiness.

Many people are born unhappy, and identical twins often have closer levels of unhappiness than fraternal twins. This suggests that there is a genetic component to happiness. However, no one is born happy. Happiness is an acquired sense of well-being. It is more closely related to social interaction than to any other environmental control. Our happiness or our unhappiness also seems to be self-fulfilling. People who are in a good mood tend to socialize more, increasing their level of happiness. In contrast, the unhappy tend to isolate themselves from others, deepening even further their loss of well-being.

This leads us to a related question: is there a physiological basis for happiness? Recent studies suggest that there is indeed a chemical basis for feelings of well-being within the human body. This lies in endorphins, the body's own natural opiates, which are produced in the pituitary gland and have a chemical structure similar to morphine. The difference is that they can be up to one hundred times more powerful.

Pain and exercise can trigger off the release of endorphins in the body. This is why physical fitness (especially after strenuous exercise) is associated with a mood of well-being. It explains the addiction to exercise which some people cultivate. Creative thought can also trigger off endorphin production. People who know what they want out of life, and who have creative, positive attitudes, can enjoy a deepening sense of well-being.

The nerves in the human body communicate both pain and pleasure to the brain. There are no erogenous zones of pleasure, as the sexual revolutionaries believed. Sexual satisfaction and pleasure can only result from a combination of many factors, brought into play by both partners. These factors include timing, an absence of stress, and the emotional responses that are needed at the time. The indirect access to the interior of the mid-brain, where pleasure is experienced, is chemically short-circuited by the use of drugs. But the physiology of the human body was never constituted for us to have direct access to this focus of pleasure. It is like cheating at golf by going from the first hole directly to the last one. All the contributory sensations, emotions, and feelings are short-circuited. Pleasure is naturally a by-product of activity which is in harmony with the physiological well-being of the whole individual.

When that sense of well-being has been reached, an excess of the same stimulus will not generate further sensations of pleasure. A hungry stomach finds the taste of food delicious, but when it is full it has no further need for taste. Ten ice cream sundaes will never give ten times more pleasure than one! Prolonged sexual activity decreases, rather than increases, in pleasure. Over-consumption, in all its forms, does not increase happiness, and the over-production of pleasure ends up by being plain boring.

This is why drug addicts have to step up dosages of the drug to maintain their levels of previous pleasure. This experience becomes more and more physiologically damaging to the body and mind of the addict. In C. S. Lewis's *The Screwtape Letters*, the archdevil Screwtape advises his apprentice: 'an ever-increasing craving for an ever-diminishing pleasure is the formula.'

## The pursuit of happiness: self-defeating?

All of this indicates that happiness is not an end in itself. Instead, it is a by-product of other human activities. Good things do not come out of the blue, but as the result of conscious actions on our part. Attitudes to life, emotional intensity and involvement, intimacy in relationships with other people, bodily well-being, altruism in self-forgetfulness, intellectual satisfaction, worthwhile work and, above all, a meaningful faith that overarches all our existence—these are what enable us to become happy people.

It is often said that those who hit the highest highs also bottom out with the lowest lows. Experiments have been carried out with rats which have had electrodes inserted into the part of the brain that stimulates pleasure. The rats are placed before three levers: if they press the first, food is released; if they press the second, they get a drink; if they press the third, they activate the electrodes to give them a short sensation of pleasure. The rats quickly learn to distinguish between the three levers. After trying them all, they eventually go on and on pressing the pleasure lever, until they die of starvation and thirst. The stimulus of pleasure has literally killed them! Why should they respond to the pains of hunger or thirst, when they had direct access to pleasure? This is the basic mistake behind the direct pursuit of pleasure. To pursue pleasure single-mindedly means to neglect the fullness of human personality.

To target solely upon pleasure is to miss out on so many other aspects of what it means to be truly human. In sexual neuroses, patients are thwarted from obtaining sexual pleasure precisely because they seek to obtain it directly. Yet this is exactly what the modern commercialization of sex does today. It cheats people of the glory of their humanity. The pursuit of happiness for its own sake amounts to a self-defeating exercise. It is a self-contradiction.

This self-contradiction is the great illusion of today's culture. We believe that self-fulfilment is a marketable product, something which we can buy along with the 'right deodorant', the 'right career', the 'right mate' and the 'right car'! However, all this does is to accelerate the vacuum experienced by Gloria earlier in this chapter. If we concentrate on pursuing happiness, it will vanish before our eyes. It is only as we withdraw ourselves from the tyranny of self-preoccupation that we can truly become happy. Only then can we have an authentic mode of existence.

Living for others appears a much more reliable recipe for happiness than living for oneself. So where then did this myth about the necessary pursuit of happiness come from?

## The right to pursue happiness

Curiously enough, it was Thomas Jefferson who taught us that the pursuit of happiness was our birthright. That was how it was written into the American Declaration of Independence in 1776. In a letter, Jefferson mentioned that this idea was not original to him. George Mason in the Virginia

Declaration of Rights had said something very similar. Further back still, John Wise wrote that the main business of the state was to attend to 'the happiness of the people'. So the 'right to pursue happiness', was originally the responsibility of government, rather than of the individual as the saying has been interpreted.

In 1774, John Wise argued that the whole purpose of the political compact was 'to ensure and to increase the happiness of the governed. The consequence is that the happiness of society is the first law of every government.' This led directly to the concept that democracy is 'government that advances the greatest happiness of the greatest number'. This, in turn, was based upon other unspoken assumptions which we need to examine.

The first assumption was that the world of the eighteenth century was no longer medieval. No longer dominated by the church and the state, people were free to think for themselves. They were free to 'dare to know', as the philosopher Immanuel Kant put it. This revolution of thought fostered the new concept of 'the rights of man', which the French Revolution was to spell out in terms of 'Liberty, Equality, Fraternity'. In the vast spaces of America, the 'rights' were spelled out in terms of happiness, freedom and property, with the anchor being property. Everyone had the right to own land as a pioneering settler.

'Let these truths be indelibly impressed on our minds,' declared John Dickinson in 1776, 'that we cannot be happy without being free—that we cannot be free without being free in our property'. In the thought of leaders such as John Locke, a man's property was the extension of his personality. As a result, the condition of a man's property was the index of his happiness. This popular belief is as strong as ever today: what we possess is an index of our happiness. In the eighteenth century, happiness lay in owning property. Today it lies in consuming material goods. Through both of these interpretations, the prevailing view of modern society is that happiness is to be equated with material prosperity.

The second assumption was that everyone knew what 'happiness' meant. In fact they didn't. Chancellor Kent, speaking in the New York Constitutional Convention of 1821, argued that American prosperity was itself the mark of God's approval, sufficient in itself to achieve happiness. He said:

> *Discontent in the midst of so much prosperity, and with such abundant means of happiness, looks like ingratitude, as if we were disposed to arraign the goodness of Providence. Do we not expose ourselves to the danger of being deprived of the blessings we have enjoyed?*

The moral was clearly to build bigger barns, live merrily, and in this way show your gratitude to Providence who provides with such generosity. In fact, this way of thinking contradicted Jesus' teaching in the parable of the Rich Fool. He too made himself comfortable and settled down to enjoy his riches, only to be told by God:

> *You fool! This very night your life will be demanded from you. Then who will get what you have prepared for yourself?*

Gradually then, throughout the nineteenth century, the pursuit of happiness became an individual right, to be interpreted individually as everyone thought fit. In the Middle Ages, rights had existed alongside duties, but now rights and duties became detached from one another. The problem is that if in democratic society everyone is free to pursue happiness as he or she sees fit, then the state eventually becomes ungovernable. This is where democratic society is now heading, towards a fragmentation of vested interests that often confront each other in clashing contradictions.

If we reflect on this modern emphasis upon 'my rights', we see that no other society has ever attempted to live like this, with such intense individualism or self-concern. The idea of 'human rights', as now interpreted, is quite unintelligible to societies as diverse as Europe in the medieval era, the worlds of classical Greece or Rome, or the Hebrew, Arabic, Hindu and Chinese cultures. This insistence on rights, with a happiness that is left to each person to seek after, can only lead to greater and greater confusion and chaos in the world today.

The third assumption in the eighteenth century was that it was the government who provided the people with happiness. However, this arose only as the Age of Reason displaced God. Without God, there is no ultimate purpose. The secular faiths which replaced God were belief in progress or, in the nineteenth century, in evolution. This had fateful consequences in this century, when totalitarian dictatorships interpreted their own futures as they saw fit. Hitler's Germany and Stalin's Russia did exactly this, with appalling consequences for the human race.

Meanwhile, in the capitalist world, if God is not allowed to rule, then mammon quickly takes his place. Just as Newton's law of gravitation governs the motion of the planets, so the law of avarice rules the market-place. Human greed, we fear, may one day send the world's markets crashing disastrously. If, however, every leader of government is also in pursuit of happiness, defined as each thinks fit, then is not democracy itself liable to extinction? Will we all end up like the rats who eventually starved, because we too have become addicted to pushing the pleasure lever all the time?

## Happiness: beyond ourselves

We have seen that the pursuit of happiness is a dead-end. Happiness is not like a commodity we can grasp and hold on to. It never becomes our property. Nathaniel Hawthorne, the American author, likened happiness to a butterfly. It flits away when chased, but it will come and alight on your hand if you only sit quietly, occupied in doing something else. Happiness is not naturally a permanent state; it is an exceptional gift. We have seen why this is true, both in the way our bodies and emotions work. If we persist in believing that happiness consists in having more and more, we will only perpetuate the social climate of our drug-addicted culture. There is a long historical tradition which shows us that luxury is the death of society. This is how it was with the Roman Empire, and how it will be with the modern West, if it persists in the folly of luxury.

It is clear, then, that we have no right to happiness. Instead, we gain our sense of self-worth by looking outwards in relationships: our obligations to others; the duties we perform well; the responsibilities we carry on behalf of others; the emotional involvement we have in the well-being of others. It is precisely when young people feel uncomfortable in their relationships that drugs become an attraction to alleviate the pain of alienation. Self-preoccupation only intensifies the experience of loneliness, turning us into the lonely person in the lonely crowd.

'Do your own thing' leads ultimately to despair, as we lose all grasp of who the self is. This advice turns out to be as vague and aimless as living perpetually in a nursery or in Bedlam. There, at least, there is a keeper who keeps the door shut. But when you do your own thing in a Porsche, with several mistresses and a fat bank balance, then you can introduce madness indeed into society.

If the right to happiness turns out to be stealing someone else's wife, or robbing the poor to luxuriate the rich, then the end in sight is merely treachery, tyranny, and the violation of humanity. As C. S. Lewis has pointed out:

*A society in which conjugal infidelity is tolerated must always be in the long run a society adverse to women.*

> *Women, whatever a few male songs and satires may say*
> *to the contrary, are more naturally monogamous than*
> *men; it is a biological necessity. Where promiscuity pre-*
> *vails, they will therefore always be more often the victims*
> *than the culprits. Also, domestic happiness is more ne-*
> *cessary to them than to us. And the quality by which they*
> *most easily hold a man, their beauty, decreases every*
> *year after they come to maturity. Thus in the ruthless*
> *war of promiscuity women are at a double disadvantage.*
> *They play for higher stakes and are more likely to lose.*

We can see that 'the right to happiness' is a dead-end street
by looking at the contemporary assumption that happiness
lies in self-actualization. This is probably the most important contemporary theory of the good life, but on examina-
tion it turns out to be ludicrous. On the one hand, modern
advertising tells us that happiness consists in being liked by
others, and in the things we do, wear, and have. At the same
time, we are also told by how-to-do books that we need to
overcome shyness, remove guilt, deal with depression, and
generally re-tool our personality to become bouncy, a positive thinker, and a popular leader. These two approaches are
incompatible. Advertising cons us that happiness is on the
outside, in the things we possess. But the books tell us that
happiness lies inside, in our psychological conditioning. As
Erich Fromm puts it: 'Happiness is an achievement brought
about by man's inner productiveness, the accompaniment of
all productive activity, in thought, feeling, and action.' Is it
not likely that self-actualization is like happiness itself—it
comes about when we are not feverishly pursuing it?

## Leaving the pleasure garden

What are the characteristics of the happiness that so many
pursue in the modern world? Contemporary happiness is

debased, a shadow of all that true happiness is meant to be. Those who embrace this version of happiness live provisionally, from moment to moment, with little sense of loyalty or fidelity. Life becomes a chancy affair, with either good or bad luck always lurking round the corner. They see themselves as the plaything of forces beyond their control, and gain a deep sense of the meaninglessness of all life.

Gloria, who was quoted earlier, has described her feelings about this:

*Many times I have felt as if I'm trapped on a huge roller-coaster that goes up and down, and round and round. Sometimes I manage to escape and get off the mad ride, but I'm still in the amusement park. Outside the park the world looks exciting, but too risky. I'm not sure that I could survive, so the amusement park remains still the biggest attraction. For everyone is being persuaded to stay inside the gates of the amusement park and to get back on to the roller coaster.*

*Yet I still think of people in the past who have 'gone outside the park'. They are the ones who truly seek God with all their heart, mind, soul and body, and are fully prepared to give it all up. They are the ones who live uncompromising lives, who don't feel the grip of money, the pressure of society, the weakened desire for goodness, the punctured self-discipline, the crushing fear of the future, the horror of death, the threat of injustice, the need of security, the rule of self. They don't struggle for faith, hope and love; they pour out from them, and through them. It is these people who are totally free.*

*But how? I feel the grip of money. It controls so much. I feel the pressure of society. I am not strong enough to stand up for what I believe—partly because I am not sure about what I believe. My desire for goodness is lost in waves of bitterness, deception, and guilt. My discipline is worthless in its inconsistency. I am afraid sometimes of all the things that could happen in the future. Death is frightening and grim. I hate injustice but do not recognize justice. I have little faith. My self inspires every action to satisfy myself. But I am not happy. I wish I could live an uncompromising life outside the amusement park. I wish it, yet I fear it at the same time.*

In her confusion, fear, and possessiveness, Gloria struggles with the desire to leave the amusement park, and yet lacks the courage to leave it. We shall see later how she is helped to turn away and escape.

This is a flight we must all take to gain integrity. In Hermann Hesse's famous novel *Siddharta*, the character Siddharta has a dream. In his dream, his rare songbird, which sings every morning without fail, becomes mute. To his horror he discovers it has died and, like Malcolm Muggeridge's analogy of happiness pursued as a stricken deer that is now 'only a piece of stinking flesh', Siddharta now realizes that all that was good and valued has died with that little bird.

*Awakening from this dream, he was overwhelmed by a feeling of great sadness. It seemed that he had spent his life in a worthless and senseless manner; he retained nothing vital, nothing in any way precious or worthwhile. He stood alone, like a shipwrecked man on the shore.*

*Sadly, Siddharta went to a pleasure garden that belonged to him, closed the gates, sat under a mango tree, and felt horror and death in his heart. He sat and felt himself dying, withering, finishing. Gradually, he collected his thoughts and mentally went through the whole of his life, from the earliest days which he could remember. When had he really been happy? When had he really*

*experienced joy? How many long years had he spent
without any lofty goal, without any thirst, without any
exaltation, content with small pleasures and never really
satisfied! He sat there till night fell. When he looked up
and saw the stars, he thought: I am sitting in my pleasure
garden. He smiled a little. Was it necessary, was it right,
was it not a foolish thing that he should possess a mango
tree and a garden?*

So Hermann Hesse depicts Siddharta shaking his head
sadly, and walking away from his pleasure garden for ever.
'He had finished with that. That also died in him. That
same night Siddharta left his garden and the town and never
returned.'

# 3

# Happiness and Peace of Mind

*Happiness is a matter of getting whatever one wants, and finding it worthwhile when one gets it.*
Theodore Benditt

A cartoon in the *New Yorker* magazine shows a tea time conversation between a husband and wife. He says: 'Of course I'm happy, dear, if you call vaguely discontented happy.' Different people define happiness in different ways. But surely there is an agreed version of what happiness actually is? The problem is that happiness is so deep-rooted in human nature that to dissect its anatomy seems like dissecting humanity itself.

However, this is precisely the game that philosophers have played since the days of ancient Greece—isolating some particular aspect of happiness and saying, this is what happiness means! Philosophers have searched for the meaning of happiness in various ways.

First, they distinguished *eudaemonia*, 'resting from the pursuit of pleasure'. They associated peace of mind with moral goodness, seeking happiness in the virtuous life. Some philosophers like Democritus, 'the laughing philosopher', identified happiness with having a cheerful mind, or what today we would call 'positive thinking'. Aristotle, too, was optimistic. He saw happiness in meaningful action and in enjoying the exercise of his mind. Ancient philosophers believed the mind was superior to the body, and so intellectual happiness was seen as superior to sensual pleasures.

Epicurus was more democratic in recognizing that not everyone has the high intelligence of Aristotle. He associated happiness with peace of mind, or what he called *eudaemonia per ataraxia*—'happiness by peace of mind'. The Greek philosopher Pyrrho, who was in touch with the eastern religions, interpreted happiness as being detached from material things; indifferent to transient affairs. And Varro, the Roman philosopher, interpreted happiness in 288 different ways. The underlying assumption of this mental interpretation of happiness is that if you 'think the right way' you will have happiness.

It is striking that there should be such a long tradition of associating happiness with a rationalized peace of mind. While writing this chapter, a friend came to see me and to share her journal with me. Jane is intelligent, articulate, an English teacher, well versed in literature, and brought up in a devoutly religious home. Yet she begins her journal by this admission:

> *I wish—I wish so much—that I could rise above human incompetence. I am tired of failing. I am sick of my worthlessness. I am disheartened by the fact that I feel like this again. I hate the limitations it puts on my life. Why don't I have the drive to see what has to be done, and do it? Why don't I have the discipline to pursue that which is best? I have so far to go, it is beyond my understanding how God could use this lousy instrument. It bothers me to be defeated and to know that defeat will return again.*

This experience, common to many intellectually capable people, gives the lie to the ancient idea that the achievement of happiness is merely to think positively and achieve peace of mind. Jane has not found that to be the key to happiness.

As Jane and I have talked now many times, it is becoming apparent to us both that she conceptualizes too much. She is in fact more like the ancient philosophers, in their conceptualization of happiness, than she realized before. She distances herself emotionally from all her own world of relationships, as if an inner, hidden Jane stands over the outer, social Jane, rebuking her, telling her what a failure she is, how unhappy she is, and how faithless she remains, in spite of all her best efforts. It is as if, in place of having an emotional life that can be full of joy, spontaneity, affections and love, everything is colourless and gray. She is emotionally colour-blind, translating the world of yellows, greens, reds and blues into shades of grayness everywhere. Many people are like Jane today. They confuse the grammar of the mind with the grammar of the heart, as if the left hemisphere of logic, reason and thought could ever substitute for the right hemisphere of the brain with the need also for intuition, emotions, and relationships.

Why do we do this? Well, the Oxford Dictionary has prescribed all this for us. Happiness is defined there as 'the state of pleasurable content of mind, which results from success or the attainment of what is considered good'. In other words, we are given an excellent classical response! Aristotle himself could not have defined the approach better. Use your mind, not your heart, in the search.

## The pleasures of the mind

For many people, happiness is simply an intellectual pursuit. Perhaps this is because many of them are the 'Observer' type of personality we discussed in the first chapter. There are many concealed assumptions behind thinking like this. College and university life gives some people the idea that intellectual pleasures are the only worthwhile *observable* pursuits. However, it is clear that such an assumption is rooted back in earlier childhood experiences, as we will see later. To people like this, philosophical study is seen as the pinnacle of intellectual happiness, because it satisfies our highest faculty: reason. Heaven itself is presumed to be an exclusive academy for the eggheads! The fear of inner emptiness and loneliness is complemented by populating the inner life with much data, many concepts and much knowledge.

Some people really do believe in 'the goddess of Reason', as the French formally adopted her in 1793. In fact, the genesis of modern culture started with what we still call the 'Age of Enlightenment'. This phrase expresses the joy and the wonder of seeing dawn break over the dark age that went before it. So the 'Age of Enlightenment' is really a conversion phrase, like the 'enlightenment of Buddha'. However, in this case it applies to a whole society, rather than to an individual. Once we were in the grip of our emotions; once we were rationally blind; once we lived in backwardness; but now we see.

Now that the light has come, we experience what one writer has called 'the crisis of consciousness'. In the new vision, science and technology have opened up vast new possibilities for us, in which mystery, miracle, providence, and the whole realm of the supernatural and transcendent are banished as darkness for evermore. We now live in the 'Age of Reason', where logical, analytical and mathematical powers reign supreme.

This error of identifying the highest happiness with the exercise of intellectual skills is based upon a number of assumptions rarely exposed in our culture today. The first of these unspoken assumptions is that all higher happiness is self-motivated, not received through our relationships with others. I am responsible to bring about my own happiness.

As a result, knowledge is the great avenue open to me, to gain happiness by my own skills and know-how.

This belief is reinforced today by the strongly-motivated concern to 'do your own thing', and it extends into many areas of our lives. In health, there is a new trend to gain all the knowledge to 'be your own doctor'; or in the realm of emotions to 'be your own psychologist'; or generally to 'be Mr or Ms Fix-It' about everything else! All happiness is being falsely equated with know-how. Learn to test your own blood pressure, your cholesterol level, your religious faith, your plumbing, your Myers-Briggs temperament classification, your depression rating and mood swings, and you will 'do' just fine. In this way the knowledge of our happiness rating is mistakenly confused with the actual experience of happiness. We learn to know about ourselves, rather than to know ourselves. Life is described rather than lived.

## The battle between thought and feeling

Another basic assumption is that thought is vastly superior to the emotions. Feelings and emotions are messy things, best left alone, severely curtailed, or even repressed. Our emotions are generally unwanted. This is often the case for men. A man is in control when he is not 'too emotional'. As a toddler, he was told, 'boys don't cry'; and as a man he loses touch with his feelings. Instead, he is turned towards the intellectual or technical life, away from the realm of subjective consciousness. What a marvellous instrument the computer can become, as the rational person's best friend! In the Technological Society, techniques and machines become substitutes for all true emotions. It is a blessed relief to escape from all the emotional hassles of other people: the fears, anger, stresses and frustrations. We close the door on all that and escape into the calm realm of the library or into the world of the computer, to enjoy our work, without the messy world of people and emotions.

A third assumption behind the belief in happiness through intellectual pursuit is that I am really better than you are. If only you were reasonable enough to see things from my logical, calmly objective perspective! This reveals the pride that lies so deeply buried in all these assumptions. The more of an intellectual I am, with all my qualifications to back me up, the more readily I am tempted to believe that the intellectual life is really the superior life—the way to handle all of life's difficulties. It is a way of life that is superior to marriage, to family life, even to friendships.

I still remember the day I told my bachelor colleagues in the Senior Common Room at Oxford that I was getting married. A silence came over the room, and the dons glanced at each other. 'Poor Houston,' they probably thought. 'We thought better of you as a scholar, but now you are throwing away your career as a don!' Later, I came to understand how some dons of great intellectual reputation could also behave with childish emotions. Their intellectualism had stunted their normal human growth, and they became unreal people. One philosopher friend put his head into a gas oven, in a mood of utter depression, because no one was close enough to penetrate his scholarly mask, and know how he really felt as a human being.

There are many other assumptions which lie behind the belief that the highest happiness is intellectual rather than emotional. But behind them all there is pride and the lust to control. For the mind is powerfully capable of being in control, and it takes full advantage of doing so. It monitors what is meaningful, selects what it really wants to know, and determines the limits of what it wants to monitor. Control is the dark side of knowledge. The mind that is addicted to control is tyranny. It dictates our lives, all the way from 'taking yourself in charge' to focusing all relationships around one.

Desire is the great enemy of reason. For, while the faculty

of reason is to rule and control, the faculty of desire is out of control when it desires more than reason can supply. To desire too much is to make yourself vulnerable, to open yourself to many uncertainties. Because of this, desire is a powerful escape-route from the tyranny of the intellect. Desire opens us to many creative possibilities—especially to faith and the creativity of trust. When people are strong-willed and dominant, but seek to become gentler and more open to others, to begin to desire great things of God is often the only way that their hearts can change. Desire can soften and tenderize their spirits, making them more sensitive to others and more open to happiness as a relating, friendly experience of life.

## Straightening out our thoughts

A popular application of the mental pursuit of happiness is termed 'cognitive therapy'. It is supposedly based on what is termed 'common sense'. According to cognitive therapy, when we are depressed or anxious we are not really thinking properly, but in a disorderly, negative manner. So with a little effort we can train ourselves to 'think straight'. As we eliminate our painful, unpleasant thoughts, we will become productive and happy again, and respect ourselves more than we did. All this is possible in quite a short time, with little effort. As we start to think in the right way about ourselves, our feelings will automatically follow and, along with them, happiness.

Of course, there is some truth in this approach, but there are also dangers. Cognitive therapy correctly identifies many of the emotional traps into which we fall. These include the following wrong attitudes:

*The perfectionist attitude* of all-or-nothing. It is unrealistic to evaluate life in this way. Such a mentality leads to despair, for no one can ever measure up to such standards.

*The fatalistic attitude*, which believes that because something has gone wrong once, it will always go wrong. Lonely, alienated people can be tempted to think that their life is permanently stuck in 'bad luck' mode. People who feel rejected can deliberately set themselves up for further rejections, simply because they believe that others will always reject them.

*The negative attitude* of seeing life through a tinted filter. We live with an emotional disc within us that was implanted in childhood. As a result, we tend to play the same tune all through our life, constantly repeating the image we had of ourselves in childhood. This attitude makes us think and behave negatively.

*The inferiority complex*, where all compliments are inverted. This negative thinking can be very destructive. All that is praised, appreciated and loved is reversed, as if it were wholly irrelevant to the person to whom it is all directed.

*The dutiful attitude* of personal bondage. An obsession with duty makes people despair of ever being released from the expectations that are thrust upon them. 'I should', 'I must', and 'I have to', are the weary refrains of this kind of person. All of life becomes an unwilling drudgery.

*The neurotic guilt* of always feeling responsible. People who were not given assurance in their childhood often feel like this. They take to heart every area of responsibility they come across. They feel guilty about other people's wrongs, as if they ought to take guilt upon themselves to spare others from blame. This can lead to a crippling distortion of thought.

Cognitive therapy certainly has good things to say to all these conditions—but it can never cure them. There is clearly much value in seeing the importance of clear thinking and common sense in correcting our emotional feelings. But ultimately, cognitive therapy is fatally flawed. It believes in the superiority of reason over the emotions. It implies that the intelligent person should not 'feel' screwed up in these ways.

But that is where we must protest. People of high intelligence can still be afflicted with any of these wrong ideas about themselves and others. Superficially, it might appear that we can fix this simply by reading the right books and applying the right know-how. But this approach only compounds the problem. The attitude that 'I am the master of my fate, the captain of my soul' isolates us from others, increases our personal pride, and consolidates our despair and loneliness. In all these problems, it is much more realistic to respond: 'I need help; I need friends.'

The whole dilemma with a purely thinking approach to life is that it simply does not work! It is like driving a car on only one cylinder, when there are so many other cylinders to be brought to life. We may be honest and rational about our lives, but our feelings will keep bursting into the debate. Life is more than thought. To be fully alive is to experience desire, trust, obedience, love, awe and friendship, as well as thought. To be truly happy, we must exercise our emotions as well as our minds.

## The wild horse and the tame horse

As we have begun to recognize, the rational person is afraid of his or her emotions. They represent what the Greeks feared about the centaurs, half-man, half-horse, that mythologically inhabited the mountains of Thrace, in a state that was half tame, half wild. Plato used a similar image in saying that the soul is 'like a winged charioteer and his team acting together'. One of the two horses of the team, says Plato, is 'good and of noble stock', which is the faculty of reason. But the other, 'is the opposite in every way'. This is emotion. Plato says that the soul will climb to the heavenly realms only if it becomes master of the dark horse which is always trying to drag it downwards. The soul does this by using the whip; in other words, by controlling its feelings. However, this is a difficult task, since Plato recognizes that 'we are reined to the horse, it to us'.

Of these two symbols—the charioteer and his two horses, and the centaur, half-man, half-animal—the latter is probably more realistic in picturing the human condition in its natural state. Our natural emotional condition is truly dark and wild. However, it is this dark, wild realm which we need to explore in our search for true happiness. We need to examine human emotions as seriously, or even more so, than the rational faculty of the mind and its thought. This is because the emotions, working in harmony with all the other parts of our lives, give depth, height and breadth to the experience of being fully alive. This is true happiness.

## Educating our emotions

A trait of our emotional life is that it tends not to have fixed goals, certainly not in the sense that the mind has. That is why we often speak of having 'confused emotions', or even of experiencing 'paralysed feelings'. In place of fixed goals, there is motion, striving and change in the emotions. We sense that our emotional life is the most intimate part of our existence, that which is most 'me'. This is why we so often conceal our feelings, fearing to reveal more of ourselves than we can bear.

Some emotions are deeper than others. We can peel back the more superficial layers of our emotions like the skin of an onion. Some of these layers we call 'moods', but when people are stuck with their moods, we call them 'moody'. This shows that even superficial emotions can become fixed characteristics of our lives. When deeper layers of the emotions are struck, we speak of a 'sulky' person—someone who has become inwardly withdrawn. Negative emotions (which sometimes bear no relation to reality) can also lead to the downward spiralling of depression.

Today, we need to emphasize the importance of educating the emotions as well as the mind. We live in a rationalistic culture, heavily influenced by the exaggerated importance the Age of Enlightenment gave to reason. This means that thinking and knowing are valued at the expense of the emotions. Some speak today of the need to develop a 'post-modern world view'. This means to go beyond the modern world, with its stress on science and technology, and to rediscover what is truly human. The New Age movement is one expression of this post-modern rebellion, although it goes to the opposite extreme by putting its faith in the most bizarre forms of magic and irrationality. Belief in ancient magic and the use of drugs are not responsible ways of responding to the cold rationalism of our age. We need instead to recover the fullness of our humanity, which has been neglected for so long in the modern world.

In order to live with integrity, we need to be put back in touch with ourselves, with our inner lives. We need to be taught how to be real persons, true human beings. We cannot afford to remain heartless brutes if we want happiness and a human environment for ourselves and our children. In order to do this, we have to learn to handle our feelings—especially the feelings which we hardly dare to face.

The good news is that there are signs of hope. The human dimension is being rediscovered in some areas of today's business world. Some companies are beginning to recognize that the morality, integrity, gifts and motives of its employees are more important in the long run than the annual company profits:

*A dynamic personnel force is the most valuable asset of a company. For the purpose of long-term business development, our Company has always paid special attention to this area.*

*Equally, we are of the conviction that morality merits the same priority as ability and experience. Therefore moral education is stressed in our syllabus of lectures and training sessions.*

*It is our wish that every staff member has an amiable character, humble manners, good conduct and leads an upright life which generates desire for knowledge, self-restraint, courtesy, honesty and loyalty in service; initiates self-review to correct all shortcomings; cultivates self-respect and trust among colleagues; shows willingness to help one another in a happy atmosphere of co-existence; and strives to synchronize ability and experience with moral conduct towards the mutual benefit of the Company and himself.*

Such a company seeks integrity and true happiness for its employees and customers. It is not only true to the way humans are, but presumably also makes good business sense!

The modern world worships the machine and seeks machine-like efficiency. This technocratic spirit is the enemy of our true feelings. To the technician, emotions are merely 'subjective' and get in the way of the efficient running of the machine. The dominant theme of technology is to control and overcome nature. We lust for mastery over nature. This extends even to the idea that we can overcome death, by remaking ourselves. With surgical skills we can replace the worn-out parts of the body. However, this is dangerous thinking, for it tends to see us only as efficient technicians, managing our bodies well, but neglecting our souls in the process. This tendency to see everything in only one dimension—the technical—can lead to only one result: the death of our humanity.

One way in which this happens is that we begin to rely on technical 'experts', turning a deaf ear to our inner feelings, convictions and conscience. We start to rely on reading the authoritative manuals, or visiting our analyst, seeking 'professional' advice. We end up depending more on 'how to' books than on our own souls before God. Many people now distrust their own feelings, and turn for guidance to self-tests or courses of therapy. When such testing, applied by a stranger to us, appears more reliable than our own inner convictions, it is a sign that we are becoming increasingly directed from outside ourselves.

Either we trust in 'life', or else in a personal God; either in 'ideals' or in friendship with God. Trust in our own feelings should lead us either to trust in the unconscious welling up from within ourselves, as Freud and Jung have described; or to trust in the presence of God within us, as his Holy Spirit lives in us. This is why our rationalistic age is afraid of allowing us to be ourselves. If we follow our feelings, we will eventually come to faith of one sort or another. Our age, so good at making machines, cannot cope with faith. It can invent no 'faith-machines'.

You cannot produce real personal faith by the marketing technology approach, any more than you can produce real friendship. The junk-mail firms try to synthesize friendship, with personal names littering their word-processor letters. But it fools no one. The truly personal element just is not amenable to this kind of approach, and faith is essentially a personal thing.

And so there are two fundamentally different types of consciousness today. The first leaves us alone with our own hearts: alone, even though we may live perhaps more instinctually by compulsions that are addictive, or deluded that we have power to control our own destiny and indeed choose to create our own faith. Any such faith is one where we have self-knowledge, we enjoy the 'life-force', we have 'enlightenment', without any reference to the reality of God's grace and love. So the second type of consciousness is where God is communicating his personal love, as evidenced in the gift of his Son, dying and rising on our behalf, and giving us his Spirit so that we can live in him and for him.

This is where we left Jane struggling, trying to accept that need to trust God which cannot merely be described and rationalized about, but has to be received and responded to in faith, hope and love.

## Waking up our emotions

Fear of our emotions is real for many of us. For many, happiness can only be defined negatively, that is, as freedom from negative emotions. We need only exist to discover how soon we are beset by unhappiness—miseries of body or of spirit; miseries in our relationships with others. In compensation many concentrate on bodily well-being. At least we can keep ourselves in good shape and fitness. Like exercise of the mind, exercise of the body keeps us in control. We control our bodies through diet, exercise, and knowing the causes of our aches and pains. But when the aches and pains come from deeper in, from our spirits, we turn against ourselves. Instead of listening to our inner pains, we repress what we do not like to know about ourselves.

We are afraid of experiencing our hearts and knowing what the desires of the heart might be. We fear that this would make us too vulnerable, too honest with ourselves. And as for being honest about ourselves with other people, our divorcing culture shows us how we fear self-exposure in relationships too. We should not be surprised at the phenomenon of runaway children in our society today, when parents have also run away in the search for new relationships. Some 1.5 million children in North America run away from home each year. This is why it is so easy to think of happiness simply as the negative relief of moving away from misery. For 'sickness of heart' is such a common feature of our adulterous generation.

Misery with one's self is one type of unhappiness. Those who open themselves in love to others become vulnerable to a deeper form of unhappiness, as they see those they love falling into evil. This is the cry of a mother for her lost child, or the agony of a spouse for an unfaithful marriage partner. In Shakespeare's play, Othello describes the combined feelings of his own grief at being cuckolded by Desdemona, and the hurt of seeing his beloved in moral evil:

> *But there, where I have garner'd up my heart,*
> *Where either I must live or bear no life,*
> *The fountain from which my current runs*
> *Or else dries up; to be discarded thence!*
> *Or keep it as a cistern for foul toads*
> *To knot and gender in!*

A heart open to others, especially to one's beloved, keeps the fountain of love flowing. To close it is to 'bear no life' or, as the Bible describes it, to have a 'hardened heart'. Then it is useless, indeed 'discarded'. If, on the other hand, love is allowed to flow, but that love is abused by treachery or deceit, then it is like the pool in which 'foul toads', indeed false lovers, take advantage to mate and bring forth their own breed. No wonder, in our own adulterous society, so many people are cynical of exposing themselves emotionally.

## A matter also of the affections

In the mid eighteenth century, as thinkers such as John Locke were contributing to the rise of intellectual modernism in the Enlightenment, perhaps the most brilliant mind in America at that time, Jonathan Edwards, was refusing to accept a division between mind and heart, or of the separation of thought from emotion. He did not separate the two realms of cognition and emotions (the affective), because he saw the vital role played by a third realm that we may call 'the conative'. The cognitive has to do with 'knowledge' and is usually taken to comprise all the kinds of perception concerned with thinking and reasoning, as well as with memory and the imagination. The affective has to do with the emotions and the feelings we have. But conation has to do with impulses, desires and the will. Indeed, it is the will that so often controls the ways we want to see things, the mind-set we want to have in our thinking. So the conative is pivotal to the ways we integrate the mind and the emotions. We really do not have an option to separate the mind from the emotions, for in fact our will and desires are very much part of such attitudes we have as being more cognitive or more emotional.

When Jonathan Edwards wrote his *Treatise on the Religious Affections* (1746), there was much confused and misguided emotionalism rampant in the churches in New England. So he saw that truth could neither be 'coldly logical' nor could it be swamped in unwise 'enthusiasm'. The religious wars of the previous century had made it plain that it was more civilized to drown in ink, by written polemics, than spill the blood of many thousands of innocent people. So religious 'enthusiasm' became highly suspect, in the reaction to so much warfare. Yet truth was not naked of the true affections of genuine desires, and the truly directed will. In other words, cognition cannot operate without conation. So in a famous passage Edwards observes:

> *Take away all love and hatred, all hope and fear, all anger, zeal and affectionate desire, and the world would be, in a great measure, motionless and dead; there would be no such thing as activity amongst mankind, or any earnest pursuit whatsoever...so in religious matters the spring of their actions is very much religious affection: he that has doctrinal knowledge and speculation only, without affection, never is engaged in the business of religion.*

Why then are modern people not sufficiently aware of the conative, while we are fully aware of the cognitive and emotive faculties we use daily? Because the wilful do not wish to be reminded, perhaps, of how wilful they are. The rational intellectual wants to pose as an objective observer of life, who is not wilful but reasonable. Yet it is the deliberate rejection of God that clearly demonstrates wilfulness, if in fact it is a struggle between wanting one's own independence and any possible threat that God may rule over our hearts and lives. So we are probably all more dominated by our desires and wills than we usually acknowledge. After all, we have already seen in the first chapter how we all have personality traits characterized by one dominant evasion or other that help explain how addictively we behave.

In the light of this, Edwards saw too that, since we are naturally wilful against the authority of God in our lives, we need new hearts, or 'gracious affections' that can be given us by God, so that we can now have new attitudes, new desires, a new mind and will for God. The defences, avoidances, repressions and reactions we described in the first chapter are closely identified with overcoming a sense of shame, or inferiority or isolation, as well as overcoming mistrust, guilt, confusion and despair. All of these are more or less according to our personal history, but summarized in what the Old Testament prophets called the need for a 'new heart', a heart that is open and submissive to God, so that he in turn can give us new affections of will and desire for himself. It is the bonding of self-knowledge with the growing knowledge of God himself that relates to 'gracious affections', for God too takes initiative in reaching out to us, and even giving us by his Spirit the desires to reach out to him and seek him with all our heart. This is truly amazing and even miraculous to us when we reflect how addictive our natural behaviour really is, in the ways we naturally determine the means by which we think we can be happy and have our own well-being, self-concealing as they always are! Since God is now the inclination and desire of our life, they are God-shaped, that is to say they are infinite, limitless, holy, and loving affections.

Edwards sees clearly that these new affections for God are not natural to us. They do not reflect the addictions and bondage of our natural personalities. For they are not self-willed, but rather more like the experience of 'falling in love', that is to say literally feeling that we are going outside ourselves, as we do with someone with whom we want to share all our life. Such affections, then, are never self-directed but directed towards God alone.

A merely notional view of God leaves us only with ideas about God. It is wholly inadequate, for it leaves the spectator outside, without the experience of God within one's own heart. Many people watch Christianity from the outside, longing to get inside. But the heart must be transformed, if our whole lives are to be changed with transforming happiness. So this is what happens when we are given by God's Spirit a new 'sensing' towards God, as we cultivate the life of prayer, as a gradual process of conversion of our whole life takes place. We are given a 'taste' for new things, new attitudes, including new insights about our natural personalities, that we see are wrong and sinful.

These changes, in turn, give us more 'spiritual understanding' to appreciate the ways and character of God. Knowing ourselves better, we want to know God better, and the two desires keep step together. God's love for us begins to be appreciated much more richly and deeply, whereas before we paid scant attention to him, and assumed he did the same with us. The whole of one's life now begins to be orientated around God, relating the details of our life, our emotions as well as our thoughts, in longing for his presence with us everywhere, all the time.

We will now begin to be profoundly convinced that humility is vital for such affections towards God. We certainly cannot pray authentically if we are proud. We cannot know ourselves if we are not humbled to allow insight into our deficiencies and addictions. We cannot know God with a proud heart. So then, awed more and more by God in holiness and seeking more and more consonance with God's desires, we seek to live in increasing humility before God. It is in fact morally realistic to do so. It is the path of wisdom and of right relationships. It is the way our deceit and defensiveness are broken down. So real changes become apparent in our natural temperaments and personalities, with healing of the wounds from our childhood experiences.

A further quality of the affections given us for God and his love is the new gentleness we receive towards ourselves and towards others. The rough edges of our personalities are smoothed and the hardness within our hearts begins to dissolve. We become more understanding of other people, and we gain and enjoy more inner freedom. The desire for more personal candour and honesty grows, as we can begin to replace self-knowledge with more sense of God's presence within our lives. Where we have self-hate God's love takes its place. Where we have fear or loneliness, or indeed inadequate handling of our inner emotions, we now seek God's help. So the tendencies to be a 'Perfectionist', or a 'Giver', or 'Performer', or a 'Romantic', or an 'Observer', or 'the Responsible One', or 'the Fun-Lover', or 'the Strong Boss', or 'the Mediator', or overall 'the Avoider' begin to recede in a change of heart. In fact, we grow in a new tenderness, like that of a little child, with a new simplicity, a new depth of trust. We now find we need to exercise much less perspiration, because of a new depth of inspiration!

Thus there is the growing sense of a new balance of character, gradually developed within us. We are less lopsided in our traits of personality, cultivating new strengths where before we were weak, and less interested in old strengths that now take a more balanced role in our make-up. Symmetry, serenity and symphony now mark our lives, in place of imbalance, restlessness and discord. The cultivation of an aesthetic life is now not just in being 'arty' but in enjoying the beauty and glory of God in life all around us and within our souls. For our hearts are joyous and celebrant. Yet the insatiable hunger and desire for God grows and deepens within us and beyond us. For joy leads to greater joy, and as God become more and more important in our life so the greatness and beauty of his holiness induces us to have infinite desires for him and from him.

Does all this seem too far-fetched and idealistic? How can we really know that these changes within us are genuine, and not wishful thinking romanticism? Only because they really produce very practical consequences. They are not what is commonly said of those who are so heavenly-minded that they're no earthly use! Rather the reverse. They are so heavenly-minded that they have become the most practically useful people on earth. They are just not the same people as they once were. All the energies once devoted to bolstering their defences are now more outward flowing in real love and concern for others. Egocentricity is replaced by more authenticity, self-protection by more self-awareness, though of course the task of discovering the truth about ourselves is never finished. But we become freer to discover the real contributions we are able to make to the welfare of society and to individuals, and we sincerely try to meet them. Evidence then of living more practical lives is that we are gaining in moral realism, and not hiding behind generalities, ideologies, or romantic notions of an unreal world. Blandness of person, sentimentalism of religion or impersonal postures are being replaced by being more awed by God and more loving in our personal life.

In such ways then, we begin to be more fully convinced we can never isolate our minds from our emotions, nor indeed from our desires and our will. A philosophy of 'peace of mind' is just not enough. Notions are not sufficiently transforming. Even our own ideas of happiness need transforming. That is why some of the great hymns of worship tell us to lift our hearts to desire God for his own sake.

*Spirit of God, descend upon my heart:*
*Wean it from earth, thro' all its pulses move.*
*Stoop to my weakness, mighty as Thou art*
*And make me love thee as I ought to love.*

*Hast thou not bid us love thee, God and King?*
*All, all thine own—soul, heart and strength and*
*mind.*
*I see Thy cross—there teach my heart to cling;*
*O let me seek thee, and O let me find.*

We are afraid of desire because we fear to expose ourselves to further vulnerability. Desire also loosens our grip on the controls of our life. But it is only through desire for God that our hearts will widen and grow in love. Augustine, one of the great minds of the early church, discovered that knowing God is the key to happiness. In this passage from his *Confessions*, Augustine contrasted the great knowledge he had gained with the joy of knowing God:

*Tell me, Lord God of Truth, is he who knows these things thus pleasing to you? Unhappy is the man who knows all such things, but does not know you. But happy is he who knows you, even if he does not know such things. Truly he who knows both you and them is not happy because of them, but because of you is he happy, if in knowing you he glorifies you and gives thanks and does not grow vain in his thoughts.*

Or in the well-known words near the beginning of the *Confessions*:

*Great art thou, O Lord, and greatly to be praised...And man desires to praise thee, for he is part of thy creation— man, who bears about with him his mortality, the witness of his sin...Thou hast made us for thyself, and restless is*

*our heart until it come to rest in thee...I call upon thee, O
Lord, in my faith, which thou has given me, which thou
hast inspired in me through the humanity of thy Son.*

Ten years earlier than the *Confessions*, shortly after his conversion to the Christian faith, Augustine, his mother Monica and some friends were discussing together the meaning
and reality of the happy life. They agreed that personal
knowledge of God was the basis for such happiness. 'He
who possesses God is happy,' as Augustine later wrote. But
who possesses God? they asked. Some argued that it was
those who did the will of God. Others said it was those who
lived well before God. Others argued that it was being pure
in heart before God. Augustine concluded, as we may now
conclude this discussion:

> *This, therefore, is the complete satisfaction of souls, that
> is, the happy life: to know precisely and perfectly Him
> through whom you are led into the truth, the nature of
> the truth you enjoy, and the bond that connects you with
> the Supreme Measure!*

Monica, who had long prayed for her son to enter into this
realization, responded in prayer:

> *Assist, O Trinity, those who pray...This is indeed the
> happy life, a life which is perfect, towards which it must
> be presumed that, hastening, we can be led by a well-
> founded faith, joyful hope, and ardent love.*

# 4

# Happiness, Imagination and Childhood

*Perfect happiness, the oceanic feeling of complete harmony between inner and outer worlds, is only transiently possible. Man is constantly in search of happiness but, by his very nature, is precluded from finally or permanently achieving it either in inter-personal relationships or in creative endeavour.*

Anthony Storr

In the last two chapters, we explored happiness-in-pleasure and happiness-in-peace-of-mind. Neither of these choices lead to true happiness, so what other options are open to us? Did we ever, as a child, have other forms of happiness? Perhaps we have vivid memories of the special hiding place which was ours, perhaps a tree whose leafy foliage hid a child like William Golding, or a special nook in the garden of Alice, or a secret waterfall which no one had discovered before. It might be the attic room, never visited by adults, like the one in which C. S. Lewis hid with his brother; or even the exploration of a wardrobe as in the fantasy of

Narnia. Such places of secrecy are hiding places of delight, without fear, where all we wish for is ours.

Brueghel, in one of his paintings, has people lying around with food literally flying straight into their mouths, alongside rivers of wine, with no need to work or fear death. How graphically some of us remember placing a pillow at the foot of our bedroom door, allowing us to read long into the night without adult intervention. This happiness, found in the privacy of our own imagination, is another sphere we need to explore.

The Duke of Athens, in Shakespeare's A Midsummer-Night's Dream, is well aware of the power of the imagination:

> The poet's eye, in a fine frenzy rolling,
> Doth glance from heaven to earth, from earth to
>     heaven;
> And, as imagination bodies forth
> The forms of things unknown, the poet's pen
> Turns them to shapes, and gives to airy nothing
> A local habitation and a name.
> Such tricks hath strong imagination
> That, if it would but apprehend some joy,
> It comprehends some bringer of that joy;
> How in the night, imagining some fear,
> How easy is a bush suppos'd a bear?

The impulses to use imagination are varied and diverse. Shakespeare reflects upon the range of this whole spectrum, from the madman and the poet to the lover:

> Lovers and madmen have such seething brains,
> Such shaping fantasies, that apprehend
> More than cool reason ever comprehends.
> The lunatic, the lover, and the poet,
> Are of imagination all compact.

Just the same, while imagination can run riot in excessiveness, reason can also be too cool and over-confident of its powers, as we have seen in the last chapter. Shakespeare knew this too:

> *There are more things in heaven and earth, Horatio,*
> *Than are dreamt of in your philosophy.*

## Happiness in Utopia

A significant impulse to achieve happiness by imagination is in the construction of Utopia. This dream world where all fears, death and evil are eliminated, has been imagined and hoped for since the beginning of written records. A tablet from the temple of Nippur describes 'the land of Dilmun' in the third millennium BC:

> *The land of Dilmun is pure, the land of Dilmun is*
>    *clean*
> *It is a clean place, it is a place most bright*
> *In Dilmun the raven utters no cry,*
> *The kite utters not the cry of the kite,*
> *The lion kills not,*
> *The wolf eats not the lamb,*
> *Unknown is the kid-killing dog,*
> *Unknown is the grain-devouring boar*
> *The sick-eyed man says not, 'I am sick-eyed',*
> *The old woman says not, 'I am old'.*

Dilmun is the land of unqualified, unlimited life, without disease, danger and death. Wild animals do not deprive people of their food, nor destroy each other. And at a deeper level, it is a sphere of purity, cleanliness and brightness. This tradition was passed on later to the Epic of Gilgamesh, in which Gilgamesh (the hero) journeys to Dilmun.

However, Gilgamesh becomes caught up in the futility of his own mortality.

In terms of language, the Old Testament prophet Isaiah has a similar vision of the future age:

> *The wolf will live with the lamb,*
> *the leopard will lie down with the goat,*
> *the calf and the lion and the yearling together;*
> *and a little child will lead them*
> *The infant will play near the hole of the cobra,*
> *and the young child put his hand into the viper's nest.*

However, there is a vast difference between Utopia and God's promised future. Utopia is a fantasy which enables us to plan for our own well-being, while the prophecy of Isaiah, and others like it in the Bible, calls us to depend upon our creator to fulfil his plans for the future.

The Epic of Gilgamesh is about human effort pitted against the malign power of the gods. In contrast, the Old Testament prophets show us a realm where God is sovereign; where people will be free to live in happiness and harmony under God's rule.

## Weightless Utopias

The concept of Utopia arose because of the misery and unhappiness of the world. Utopian writers sought to put right the evils of the world through imaginative fantasy. In his *Republic*, Plato envisaged an idealized city state which adhered to his philosophy. A political product of the wishful imagination was Thomas More's *Utopia*, written in 1516, which launched a whole series of utopian plans for cities and republics. These blueprints reflect a number of assumptions: human nature is inherently moral and good; human effort can bring about Utopia without God's assistance; and the utopian planners know exactly what is needed to redress human wrongs.

Many of these blueprints were used as political manifestos to influence the rulers of the day. Campanella wrote his *Civitas Solis* in 1623; Francis Bacon his *New Atlantis* in 1629; and James Harrington his *Oceana* in 1656. A whole spate of utopian schemes for social engineering followed, especially in France after the French Revolution. With the birth of sociology and socialism in the nineteenth century, a new movement of utopian planning sprang up: Marx's *Communist Manifesto* (1848); Samuel Butler's *Erewhon* (1872); William Morris' *News from Nowhere* (1872); and Edward Bellamy's *Looking Backward* (1888).

With the fiction of H. G. Wells, science was used to give the idea of Utopia a new twist. Utopia now became ambiguous, as the increasing power of technology allowed humanity to recast the world closer to his own desires than ever before. The decline and fall of Utopia was the result—brought about by the fear of our destructive, 'Frankenstein' capabilities. By the time of Aldous Huxley's *Brave New World* (1932), and George Orwell's *1984* (1948) Utopia had given way to its opposite: Dystopia. The celebrations of technology were proving more fateful and sinister than the political ideals of the past Utopias.

There is a weightlessness, however, about all such Utopias. They have an atmosphere of unreality, peopled as they are with non-spiritual beings who inhabit a world of light pastel shades. All problems are dealt with as social problems, for there is no recognition of personal uniqueness. There is a bland homogeneity about people in the mass, except for the totalitarian powers of the ruler or the state. Humankind is viewed wholly in naturalistic terms, without a spiritual dimension. This allows bureaucracy to prevail, as it always does in Utopia. Pride and original sin are absent, so there are no human perversities and no choices allowed.

Most Utopias since Thomas More's *Utopia* have been

political dreams, with a weakness for human inventiveness and a shallow optimism about what science and technology can do. Such Utopias lack political and personal power because they deal in abstractions of the mind rather than with real situations. The very pun on the Greek u-topia, which literally means 'no place' and eu-topia, meaning 'pleasant place', suggests that the dreamland will never actually appear on a map. Like romantic love, utopianism titillates us, but cannot direct or transform the human condition.

## Christian visions of the future

'Eschatology', the study of end-times in the Bible, is very different to Utopia. It begins with God rather than with human beings. Biblical hope is in God's intervention in human affairs rather than in human dreams for a better future. This hope for the future is therefore a statement of faith. It breaks through a purely secular way of thinking, destroying the possible achievements of humanity with a vision of God in action. Because of this, eschatology is intensely critical of our confusion and moral bankruptcy, in spite of our best efforts. While Utopia is an appeal to human action on the basis of human reason, eschatology steps in after our total failure to bring about what we have dreamed of achieving.

Eschatology also points to the importance of divine-human relations, rather than human-focused achievements. The prior achievements of God, as creator, redeemer and judge, eclipse any human ideology of achievement. In fact, humans are not seen in terms of their achievements, but in terms of relationships: with God, others and ourselves. Finally, eschatology does not set an agenda for the rest of history. It is wholly in God's hands, outside the limits of time and history.

Biblical eschatology has been illustrated by another

literary genre: pilgrimage. Books focused around the idea of pilgrimage give us an allegorical representation of time and eternity. The most famous of these books include Augustine's *City of God*, Dante's *Divine Comedy*, William Langland's *Piers Plowman*, Herbert Spenser's *Faerie Queene*, John Comenius's *The Labyrinth of the World and the Heart of Paradise*, and John Bunyan's *Pilgrim's Progress*. Comenius describes his work in his book's subtitle:

> *A bright portrayal showing that in this world, in its works, there is nothing but confusion and staggering, floundering and drudgery, deceit and fraud, misery and sorrow, and finally weariness and despair with all: but he who remains alone with the Lord God, comes to the full and complete peace of mind and of joy.*

Love of God and love of others sum up the essence of such a way of life for Comenius—and this is true of the Bible generally. Comenius's concluding chapters find his pilgrim in the company of those whose 'hearts are devoted to God'; finding 'all things light and easy'; possessing 'an abundance of all things'; secure in their commitment to God; enjoying 'complete peace', 'constant joy in their hearts', and in beholding 'the glory of God'. These allegorical works are intended to sharpen the reader's focus upon real enjoyment, happiness and blessedness. Their purpose is not to dream of happiness in the future, but to possess it now in this present life.

So there is a tension between these two interpretations of happiness within the imagination. There is utopian happiness, described by the Bible as 'the imagination of men's hearts'. This happiness uses the imagination to worship ideas and achievements rather than God the creator. Eschatological imagination is in sharp contrast. It focuses on God in worship and trust. It moves from what is already good to what is better, and ultimately to what is best, for it lies in being with God alone. In looking at the happiness of child-hood and imagination, we will be exploring the tension be-tween these two interpretations of happiness.


## The happiness of the secure child

Thomas More, unlike most of his followers, wrote his Uto-pia with his tongue firmly in his cheek. His Utopia was an is-land, but its coordinates had been lost. Because it was really 'no place', it could never be realized in an earthly setting. The narrator has a Greek name meaning 'the Babbler', sug-gesting that his description is no more than useless chatter. More himself is made to appear as a sceptical listener whose stance is one of irony. The whole book is all a take-off on so-ciety, a form of political recreation that has no serious pre-scription for the human condition.

However, if we seriously attempt to search for the basis and experience of happiness, then our imagination must focus upon our true condition. So the stories of Kevin, Jane and the many others that are told below help to mirror our own thoughts and experiences.

Within each one of us there is a child—the child we once were—as well as the adult we have now become. The un-healed child within plays an emotional disc which we will re-play many times over in our life, unless our wounded personality is healed and transformed. Listening to 'the child within' is realistic, and ultimately essential, if we are to make progress in personal integrity. Without its healing, our personal relationships will continue to be profoundly influ-enced by it, affecting those with whom we come into con-tact. Our happiness or unhappiness depends on the response we make to the inner child.

This series of wise observations expresses the importance of our child:

*Children learn what they observe.*
*If children live with criticism, they learn to condemn*
*    and be judgemental.*
*If children live with hostility, they learn to be angry*
*    and fight.*
*If children live with ridicule, they learn to be shy and*
*    withdrawn.*
*If children live with shame, they learn to feel guilty.*
*If children live with tolerance, they learn to be*
*    patient.*
*If children live with encouragement, they learn*
*    confidence.*
*If children live with praise, they learn to appreciate.*
*If children live with fairness, they learn justice.*
*If children live with security, they learn to have*
*    faith.*
*If children live with approval, they learn to like*
*    themselves.*
*If children live with acceptance and friendship, they*
*    learn to find love in the world.*

The child is where the quest for integrity must begin. We can see the wisdom of Jesus, when he said, 'Anyone who will not receive the kingdom of God like a little child will never enter it.' Life ends as life was lived, unless there comes the intervening grace of God to heal, restore and redeem the negatives of childhood. The following stories illustrate our own needs in our personal search for happiness.

## The introverted child

Andrew is very slow in developing relationships. Since the age of ten, when his family first installed their TV, he spent about four or five hours each day watching 'the tube'. His parents, who both worked as teachers, were distant and never showed tenderness or close affection. For Andrew, TV was an escape, and he has still not broken his addiction to the tube as a means of relaxation. From its programmes he learnt about relationships, sex, and the outside world.

The utopian world of television made Andrew very selfish. He did not have to live for others, but could simply be a spectator of others' affairs. He also felt that he could control others, merely by turning the switch to other channels. The choice was entirely his own, according to his whim.

Shutting the rest of the world out, while under the illusion of letting the whole world into his room, gave Andrew a distorted view of reality. Boredom played a large role in suppressing his imagination; instead of being creative, his mind came to expect to be entertained. It has filled him with an excitement for fantasy rather than reality. He is excited about 'going places', travelling the world in flight from the 'ordinary'.

As a result, avoidance has become Andrew's besetting sin. He avoids responsibility and hard work. He avoids making personal decisions because he fears that others will reject him. He avoids taking any emotional initiatives with other people, even those close to him. Instead, he wants the attention and acceptance that the TV celebrities receive.

Andrew has now become a Christian. The transformation of his character has focused around forming true and deep personal relationships. As he now admits: 'Relationships make a lot more sense in God's plans, than in my own hands.' As he seeks happiness in a change of living this is his own prayer:

*Lord, I don't know how to meet even everyday issues without you. I often deal with them only by avoiding them. Help me to meet the problems that arise, and not avoid them.*

*Lord, help me to let people be real people. I must not turn to them for my entertainment, nor for my scheduling. Help me to love them as unique persons. Help me to be kind to them, and to see people as different and independent from my own desires.*

*Lord, help me to accept life with its 'everydayness'. Life is not, and does not have to be, exciting and full of glitter. Help me to face and to participate in the real world, which means having you as my dearest friend.*

## The dream child

Stephanie was only eight years old when her father, then only thirty-six, died suddenly. She had been a day-dreamer before, but her father's death made her more reflective, and she withdrew within herself. For the following three years she believed that somehow it was all just a dream, and that one day she would wake up and find her father alive after all. She wondered when she was ever going to wake up:

*At that time, I also felt that I could look inside other people, and see the world through their eyes. I found that my dreams at night were so lifelike that I had difficulty in distinguishing them from memories. I would go for days before discovering that some particular event in a dream hadn't actually happened.*

*Even today, I must be very careful about what books I read or what films I see. My imagination is so strong that the characters' attitudes, reactions, pains and griefs spill over into my own emotions.*

*Growing up without my father, in an all-female household, I never thought of myself as a girl, nor did I come to terms with my femininity until I became a Christian at the age of twenty.*

Since becoming a Christian, Stephanie has found that the biggest change in her life has had to do with perspective. She looks on the physical world and sees things in terms of their deeper spiritual realities. She unexpectedly found that her childhood inclination to dream fuelled her Christian experience as a visionary.

'Some people say that I am a bit 'other-worldly', she admits, 'or that there is an ethereal quality about me. Well, if this is what God has done with my childhood traumas, granting me a heightened sense of vision for the spiritual realm, then I am pleased. It is in our weaknesses and infirmities that God touches us with his healing power, using those very weaknesses as points of healing for others.'

## The shadow child

As a small child, Stephen loved his father very much, and was inseparable from him. However, he saw himself as his father's shadow, with no life of his own. He wanted desperately to please him, but he seldom did so, and seldom received any credit for his role as a shadow. His father was a man of the world, who made his way in it by lying, cheating, womanizing and so on. He had little time for Stephen.

At the opposite pole, his mother showed honesty, integrity, faithfulness and love. Her life had been transformed by God. Stephen also wanted to please her, and the tension between trying to please both parents led to an extreme state of confusion:

> I wanted to please my mother desperately, and she was
> pleased when I acted in a Christian way. But how could
> I be both the child of God and the shadow of my father at
> the same time? So I lived in intense confusion and guilt.

As a result, Stephen's teenage years were filled with terror, not knowing who to trust. At the same time, he longed to live his own life—but what could he call his own? He developed a compromise lifestyle that reflected the contrasting values of both parents. He became a clone of Elvis Presley, in black leather jacket and dark glasses, listening to a constant diet of rock'n'roll. But at the same time he went to church regularly with his mother.

One day, the three images of shadow, child of God and loner came together in confrontation with God's image of himself. Stephen realized for the first time that God was his Father and Mother, and in him there could now be a resolution of the lifelong conflict over who he really was. This was an important stage in the struggle to become himself.

At art college, Stephen had to live in a militantly antichristian atmosphere, which helped him to realize that he could no longer go through life trying to please everybody. The only person he could truly please was God. This reshaping of his person was incredibly hard, but he slowly developed backbone and learned to stand up for what he truly believed in. He was still angry about his former shadow life. But as he committed himself to Jesus Christ, he grew in his own identity and became more and more a real person.


## The cheated child

Valerie grew up in a home where her parents appeared to love each other dearly. But early on she noticed that her mother had to set all the rules for the family of a brother and three sisters. Her father, who took no initiative in making any of the rules, would often break them himself. Her mother was gullible about her father; he could always spin a yarn and get away with it.

Slowly, Valerie began to recognize that life was not as beautiful as she thought. In quieter moments she would discover her mother crying by herself, and Valerie could not understand her tears. There were times when her mother told the children to go and play and leave Father to rest by himself. These were the times when she began to smell alcohol on his breath. As her father drank with increasing regularity, the family's debts mounted. The meals became more frugal and there was less money for clothes and toys. Money-collectors began to visit the house, and Valerie's father began to absent himself more and more from work.

When she was fourteen, Valerie realized the full horror of the situation. 'How I longed for a father of whom I could be proud. Our mother taught us to be bold and face the world, but that did not fill the gap or stop the questioning about our father.' In her sorrow Valerie could never ask her friends to the house, and many were the dreams that could never materialize because of the family's poverty. Unexpectedly, in this crisis Valerie experienced God:

*The Lord came to me and spoke to me of love. My joy knew no bounds. I transferred all my longing for a father to God. I was like a little sponge soaking up all God's love for me, and learning the differences between God and my own Dad. But I still thought of God as a kindly benefactor and I did not take kindly to the reality that God is much more than that!*

*I had to travel over half the world; in growing up, meeting friends I learnt to trust and love, before the shadow of my father was displaced from my confused understanding about God.*

These words of Jesus brought home to Valerie the deep reality of God's care and concern for her:

*Come to me, all you who are weary and burdened, and I will give you rest. Take my yoke upon you and learn from me, for I am gentle and humble in heart, and you*

*will find rest for your souls. For my yoke is easy and my
burden is light.*

For the first time, Valerie could face her father's drunken-
ness and not feel embarrassed. For now she truly knew that
God was her Father, and would always be with her.


## The abused child

Winifred's father was a violent man who was frequently
drunk. She remembers vividly one day that he came home
the worse for drink. She began to cry with the dark fear that
terrorized her childhood. In a rage he stripped off his
trouser belt with a large brass buckle, and threatened the
little child that he would belt her unless she stopped crying.
Terrified, she really believed that her angry father was
about to kill her. She always shrank from him, afraid to be
near him.

On one occasion, an uncle whom she trusted abused her
sexually, and this intensified her fear of all males. As she had
no brother to relate to, her fear of men intensified. The only
safe world was the world of women, where she gave and received love, but also entered lesbian relationships. She still
struggles to believe that one day she could ever really love a
man deeply enough to commit her life to him. She is slowly
being freed from her painful past, and her emotional life is
being healed by a growing insight. She has started to pray
the words of Paul the apostle:

*For this reason I kneel before the Father, from whom the
whole family of believers in heaven and on earth derives
its name. I pray that out of his glorious riches he may
strengthen you with power through his Spirit in your
inner being, so that Christ may dwell in your hearts
through faith. And I pray that you, being rooted and*

*established in love, may have power, together with all the*
*saints, to grasp how wide and long and high and deep is*
*the love of Christ, and to know this love that surpasses*
*knowledge—that you may be filled to the full measure of*
*all the fullness of God.*

As Winifred gradually learns to pray this, the reality of
Christ's love enters deep within her wounded psyche. The
new excitement for her is that she can now become 'rooted
in love', no longer rooted in terror. In the outcome, fear and
dread, anger and resentment are being expelled. Her old life
is being demolished like an unsafe house with false foundations, so that a new inner home, in which Christ lives with
her, can be built. This home is 'established in love'.

Winifred is now a counsellor, with the gifts of great sensitivity and love for other people. These gifts reflect her
healing from the violence of the past.

## The symbol of childhood

How many more children there are: the spoilt child; the unrecognized child; the lonely child; the strong-willed child;
the judgmental child; the child with an inferiority complex;
the 'good' child. For each one of us, our uniqueness reflects
the inner image we have of our childhood, which is more personal to us than our fingerprints. Consequently, if we seek to
become whole, integrated people, we dare not ignore our
childhood. It is the acorn from which an oak tree has grown.

Significantly, every romantic movement that has tried to
revive the human ideals which have been flattened by a
rationalistic culture has returned in some way or other to
childhood. This explains how some children's stories are so
adult: *Alice in Wonderland, The Wind in the Willows*, the
Narnia tales. Looking at the child, we are able to see through

all the layers of subterfuge and hypocrisy which adults use to camouflage themselves.

The potential of the child develops with the growing years, but the woundedness of childhood also tends to remain. This makes it essential for us to return to our childhood to redeem the past. Once the emotional fractures of childhood have been finally dealt with, we can learn to live more fully human lives.

Jesus understood children, and he saw the symbolic value of them for adult life. He once said:

> *Let the little children come to me, and do not hinder them—for the kingdom of heaven belongs to such as these.*

Jesus takes the symbol of the child to show that childlike trust and simplicity are the marks of those who belong to his kingdom. To lead our own children to a trusting relationship with Jesus is the greatest privilege we can have, because it will shape the character of the child for the rest of life. That is where personal integrity first begins.

## Cultivating inner space

As we have seen, the child within us keeps a recording of the memories of childhood that either allow or prevent our personal growth and our relationships with others. The inability of some women to relate to men, or men to women, can be traced through their childhood stories, as we have seen in the story of Winifred. There are emotional tales to tell behind all of our relationships with others.

This is where we face the crucial question. How can our inner space be cultivated, like a secret garden, to bear positive, spiritual fruits in our maturity? How can our inner lives bring peace and joy to the lives of others? We can begin by understanding those who are reconciled to their own child-hood; whose map of the road ahead can guide our journey.

For me, the experience of the novelist William Golding—perhaps best known for *Lord of the Flies*—shows a glimpse of this journey.

Golding's father was a science teacher who could only be-lieve in the logic of a scientific world-view. Young William escaped from his father's cold, all-knowing beliefs into the leafy hiding place of a large tree, overlooking the church cem-etery next door. Here William found solitude, and could also listen to the whispers of love from a couple huddling below him in lovers' lane outside the walls of the garden. Later, William used his solitude to visit the British Museum. In the gallery of Egyptian mummies, he was spellbound by the ancient symbols of death, and used this to reflect on the es-sential mysteriousness of life.

By using his inner space in solitude, Golding has given us in his books many deeply rewarding perspectives into the labyrinth of human personality. His awareness of the child within him has been keenly developed.

If some children have sought solitude, others have had solitude thrust upon them. For the Christian writer C. S. Lewis, the attic was the castle which he and his brother War-nie could enter on rainy days to tell stories to each other. In Lewis's famous book, *The Lion, the Witch and the Wardrobe*, it was through the old wardrobe in a forgotten upstairs room that Lucy and her brothers and sister entered Narnia. Others, through deafness or blindness, are forced in on their own solitude and discover there a whole creative world. Beet-hoven was only twenty-six when he began to lose his hear-ing—deep agony for a child musician. In a testament left after his death to his brother, he confesses:

*What a humiliation for me when someone standing next to me heard a flute in the distance and I heard nothing, or someone heard a shepherd singing and again I heard*

*nothing. Such incidents almost drove me to despair; a*
*little more of that and I would have ended my life—it*
*was only my art that held me back.*

Another great artist, Goya, became deaf after an illness in
middle age. His temperament had always been to please
others, and this had found expression in his portraits of the
aristocrats at the Spanish court. With his deafness, he was
forced to turn inwardly upon himself, leaving behind his
rather superficial way of life. This was not easy. As a result,
Goya developed the horrific ability to imagine black fantasies. He filled his home with his shocking paintings depict-
ing the impact of bloody cruelty during the Napoleonic
Wars. His biographer Andre Malraux sums up what happened to Goya:

> *To allow his genius to become apparent to himself it was*
> *necessary that he should dare to give up aiming to please.*
> *Cut off from everyone by deafness he discovered the vul-*
> *nerability of the spectator, he realized that the painter*
> *has only to struggle with himself and he will become,*
> *sooner or later, the conqueror of all.*

The enforced imprisonment of some people can be highly
creative. Alexander Solzhenitsyn, the Russian writer, wrote
powerfully about his prison experiences, and John Bunyan
wrote his *Pilgrim's Progress* while in prison. But not everyone is able to emerge from prison with their faith or their
sanity intact. A long-term prisoner in Durham prison in
England describes the destructive impact of prison:

> *Can you imagine what it is like being a prisoner for life?*
> *Your dreams turn into nightmares and your castles to*
> *ashes. All you think about is fantasy and in the end you*
> *turn your back on reality and live in a contorted world of*
> *make-believe.*

The alternative, redemptive use of such solitude has been deeply communicated by Solzhenitsyn from a Russian Gulag:

> It was granted me to carry away from my prison years on my bent back, which nearly broke beneath its load, the essential experience: how a human being becomes evil and how good. In the intoxication of my youthful successes I had felt myself to be infallible, and I was therefore cruel. In the surfeit of power I was a murderer, and an oppressor. In my most evil moments I was convinced that I was doing good, and I was well supplied with systematic arguments. And it was only when, in the Gulag Archipelago, on rotting prison straw that I sensed within myself the first stirrings of good. Gradually it was disclosed to me that the line separating good and evil passes, not through states, nor between classes, nor between political parties either—but right through every human heart and through all human hearts. And that is why I turn back to the years of my imprisonment and say, sometimes to the astonishment of those about me: 'Bless you, prison!'

However, many others in solitude have fallen into madness. The Marquis de Sade became infatuated by power, ending his days in an asylum after writing some of the most perverse literature of all times. Nietzsche, also consumed with lust for power, eventually lost his sanity. Hitler used his imprisonment to write the evil *Mein Kampf*, which played a part in the holocaust that scarred our century.

The awesome choice of the use of solitude affects not only our childhood, but faces us throughout life, whether we like it or not. How trivial then are the utopian uses of our imagination, compared with the realities of our lives. Tragically, Thomas More is best known for his *Utopia* and not at all for another of his books. His *Dialogue of Comfort against Tribulation* is a masterpiece of wisdom, written during his imprisonment in the Tower, shortly before his execution in 1535. The world prefers to play with Utopia than face the suffering of real life.

## Happiness as relating beyond ourselves

Happiness lies in achieving a balance between creative solitude and the giving and receiving of friendship. Highly-creative people do not find complete happiness through their achievements alone. If our childhood solitude is not healed in personal relationships, we remain unbalanced and inward-looking. No matter how brilliant or successful we are, we will ultimately come unstuck if we fail to make true contact with those around us.

This, of course, is the theme of the unknown author of the Bible's Book of Ecclesiastes. This book was written at about the same time as the Greek philosophers we looked at in chapter three were expressing their ideas. The writer examines the whole spectrum of human activity: creativity, business, love, and religious feeling. He admits that there is a time for it all. There is a place for all it means to be human. But he adds:

> *I have seen the burden God has laid on men. He has made everything beautiful in its time. He has also set eternity in the hearts of men; yet they cannot fathom what God has done from beginning to end. I know that there is nothing better for men than to be happy and do good while they live. That every man may eat and drink, and find satisfaction in all his toil—this is the gift of God.*

The writer concludes that the 'bottom line' is in terms of righteousness or right relationships, primarily with God himself. So he adds: 'I know that everything God does will endure for ever.' Our foolishness is that we so often become mesmerized by creaturely things, worshipping them instead of the creator who made them.

Shy and lonely people do this frequently with music. As the writer Alex Aronson has observed:

> *In our novels, it is music, among all the arts, that isolates the individual from the society of his contemporaries, makes him aware of his separateness and, finally, provides a personal significance to his life regardless of his social or even personal loyalties. It is the one measure of survival which never fails.*

Great though music is, it is still only what Martin Buber saw as the lowest level of relationships: the I–It relationship. The same is true of our relationship with nature. A friend of mine from Papua New Guinea remembers joining his father on fishing expeditions as a young boy. The sweep of the ocean before them gave him a deep mystical urge to be identified with its immensity, and with all the glorious beauty of the sunrise and sunset over its horizon. Despite these powerful feelings, identification with nature is not enough. At Tintern Abbey, William Wordsworth stood with his sister Dorothy, realizing as he stood on the banks of the river Wye:

> *Wilt thou then forget*
> *That on the banks of this delightful stream*
> *We stood together; and that I, so long*
> *A worshipper of Nature, hither came*
> *Unwearied in that service: rather say*
> *With warmer love—oh with far deeper zeal*
> *Of holier love.*

For Wordsworth, as for most people who live lonely, inner lives that fear to reach out in inter-personal relationships, pantheism is more appealing and 'natural' than the intense self-exposure and vulnerability to love that Christian faith requires. Perhaps it was his sister's love that awoke him from the I–It relationship with objects and things to the I–Thou relationship of God's infinite personalness and love, that prompts 'far deeper zeal of holier love'. It remained a tortuous journey for Wordsworth to grow from love of nature, to love of friend, to love of God. Yet the conclusion is in the dedication of the poem, 'Thou my dearest Friend, my dear, dear Friend' is still only to his sister, not to his God. There is still the journey ahead from love of neighbour to love of God, from human brotherly love for his sister, to love of God. So the poet also confesses:

> My whole life I have lived in pleasant thought,
> As if life's business were a summer mood;
> As if all needful things would come unsought
> To genial faith, still rich in genial good;
> But how can He expect that others should
> Build for him, sow for him, and at his call
> Love him, who for himself will take no heed at all?

Wordsworth is still not there! He sees God as still indifferent to our human existence and personal needs. So Wordsworth is simply showing to us that we need to seek a love that is more than the love of nature, or even the love of others. What is needed is more of what Jonathan Edwards has given us in the previous chapter.

We have seen the illusion of even cognitive therapy, as if the mind matters more than the depths of our emotions. Now we have seen in this chapter that we have to cope with our imaginations as well. As John MacMurray said so wisely four decades ago:

> The intellect, because it is instrumental, can only deal
> with life piecemeal. It must divide and it must abstract.

*It is in the emotional life that the unity of personality,*
*both its individual and its social unity, is realized and*
*maintained. Emotion is the unifying factor in life.*

But religion takes us further still. It opens us up to a relationship with God beyond our experience and understanding, and it transforms our friendships with those who are close to us. Friendship, as a living experience of life, is fundamental to religion. This is why the great enemy of religion is individualism—an egocentricity that we will be exploring later in this book.

The happiest lives are not those dedicated to the pursuit of 'success'. This only fragments our humanity. The 'achieving' type of society will only intensify alienation. In place of achievement, we need to seek for wholeness of body, mind and spirit. Wordsworth in his *Prelude* recognized this, saying:

> *When from our better selves we have too long*
> *Been parted by the hurrying world and droop,*
> *Sick of its business, of its pleasures tired,*
> *How gracious, how benign, is Solitude.*

This is true. But, as our stories have reflected, solitude must also work in partnership with our relationships if it is to be creative rather than destructive. This does not simply apply to our human relationships, but in the awareness of what Solzhenitsyn and others have found—God himself—even within prison walls.

# 5

# The Politics of Happiness

*Of course, no honest person claims that happiness
is now a normal condition among human beings;
but perhaps it could be made normal, and it is upon
this question that all serious political controversy
really turns.*

George Orwell

Alongside the different prescriptions for happiness de
scribed so far, we have what we may call the politics of happiness: a whole new professional industry of supply and
demand for happiness in the health and behavioural sciences. These penetrate the contemporary soul more deeply
than the intellectual pursuit of the classical philosophers for
peace of mind, or of the social planners for utopia. For a new
secular religion of happiness is being offered in the name of
'science', with a resultant respect for its rational authority
and professional reputation.

Thus the pursuit of happiness is no longer an individual
quest as in *Pilgrim's Progress*, but more like being sub-
merged among the thousands in California's Crystal Cathed-
ral, whose pastors have become entrepreneurs of high
efficiency. The search for happiness is over, for the advertising experts assure us that to acquire their goods is to see this

alchemy take place before our eyes. That is why we can now speak of 'the politics of happiness'. Wear the right deodorant, choose the right car, live in the 'right area', and of course make sure of the successful career, and you're made!

Perhaps another cause for the politics of happiness intensifying our quest today is that we no longer need to be preoccupied about the weather for our future well-being, at least not for the vast majority of our urbanized populations. Where previous generations of humankind were subject to the vagaries of nature, of famine, flood and the dangers of travel, we are now becoming more afraid of what we are doing to nature in environmental deterioration.

Modern affluence has therefore turned our fears and preoccupations from nature towards ourselves, our personal relationships, our own inner hang-ups. Peasant or even more primitive societies don't have the luxury of being psychoanalysed, because survival is a more pressing immediate concern than wondering about one's popularity rating. It is perhaps evidence of our affluent boredom that we spend our time looking at soap operas on the television to then apply their scenarios to others and to ourselves. Now in addition to the frequent attention from the dentist, doctor and pharmacist, we have added the regular visit to the professional counsellor or psychologist.

## On Dr Freud's couch

Psychiatry and psychology are relative newcomers in human history. They did not arrive on the scene until the end of the nineteenth century. Before the First World War, they had little popular application, yet today they have enormous appeal and significance. Their focus is not so much on giving us prescriptions for happiness as dealing with the causes of our unhappiness. Psychiatry is concerned with the alleviation of depression, anxiety, and diseases such as schizophrenia and paranoia. The ultimate cause of distress is death itself but, while Freud saw its importance for our emotional life, few psychiatrists deal with this central problem.

Psychiatry, like medicine, assumes that healing comes about only through natural means—even when dealing with the emotional and spiritual realms of human life. It excludes any reference to the religious or supernatural dimensions of life. This has led to a growing emphasis on the use of sedatives, tranquillizers, antidepressants, and anti-repressive or mind-releasing drugs in dealing with emotional problems. Is it coincidental that such legalized use of drugs, which neglect the personal and spiritual needs of patients, is occurring at a time when drug addiction has become such a problem in our culture? Could it be that psychiatrists, who are experts at dealing with emotional repression, are themselves repressing the other ways of approaching emotional problems?

Because of its naturalistic bias, psychiatry has a strong physiological tradition. Its use of treatments such as electro-convulsive therapy, insulin treatment, and neuro-surgery all follow the biological approach to dealing with unhappiness. Another branch of psychiatry is psychotherapy, which takes a verbal approach to alleviating anxiety and stress. Psychotherapy is based on the assumption that none of our feelings should be suppressed, but that instead the underlying causes of unconscious conflicts must be dealt with. These unconscious conflicts come to the surface as the therapist enables the patient to talk about them.

This is where the great breakthrough came in psychiatry. It began to deal with humans in both their physical and spiritual dimensions, an approach that no other science takes. Sigmund Freud, the 'father of psychotherapy', has had an enormous influence on our culture. He was a revolutionary figure, in the same league as Copernicus or Newton. He began as a physiologist of the nervous system, experimenting with the use of hypnosis to treat hysteria. As patients began to discuss their emotional problems, he gave up treatment by hypnosis, and instead encouraged his patients to relax on his famous couch. He encouraged them to communicate whatever was there to say, however obscene, absurd or unpleasant it might seem to be

Collecting case studies, Freud began to develop theories of unconscious motivation, repression (the process of making an experience unconscious), resistance (the way it is kept unconscious), transference (the emotional relationship between analyst and patient) and the causes of the neuroses ensuing from these processes.

The theories of Freud focused almost exclusively on the sexual drive. As a result, one of his colleagues, Alfred Adler, broke away from Freud's circle of psychoanalysts. Adler argued that the struggle for power which characterizes all human beings was not simply to deal, as Freud maintained, with sexual gratification, but with inferiority feelings as well. Three years later, another collaborator with Freud, Carl Gustav Jung, also broke away to create a very different school of thought. Jung was concerned with symbolism and religion.

Meanwhile, the impact of the First World War, with its war-stressed soldiers, gave Freud much more to think about than sexual repression. If the 'life instinct' or 'libido' was largely focused on the sexual drives for pleasure gratification and reproduction, what of the 'death instinct'? This question was thrust upon Freud because of the terrors which trench warfare had brought to Europe. Is there an innate tendency in human beings to be aggressive and self-destructive? Could suicide merely be the failure of the individual to deal with these aggressive drives?

In exploring these areas, Freud first tried to deal with what was unconscious and make it conscious. Then he saw the need of sublimation, to divert aggressive drives into more creative channels: a pyromaniac might be recruited into the fire service, or a criminal could become a policeman. Finally, Freud began to explore the relationship between the analyst and the patient in handling inter-personal relationships.

Freud eventually came to believe that civilizations are the product of humanity's aggressive drives, sublimated in one way or another. His examples are taken largely from the classical world, especially the myths of Oedipus and Electra. For Freud, religion is the attempt to externalize our inner drives. As a result, he dismissed religion as 'the universal obsessional neurosis of humanity', in which inhibiting forces continue to perpetuate more neurosis. The same is true, he argued, about civilization. The more civilized the society, the more suppression, discontent and neurosis it will have. Less civilized societies have less suppression and neurosis.

However, Freud recognized that less civilization does not lead to greater happiness. Once the inhibiting forces of civilization are removed, we see human nature in its true light. Freud described those with unleashed human feelings as 'savage beasts to whom the thought of sparing their own kind is alien'. Freud is no prophet of human happiness. He is a prophet of gloom and doom. Human nature is apparently fixed in its destructiveness.

## The power of psychoanalysis

If politics is the exercise of power, then psychoanalysis has sustained its power base today for the following reasons. First, it is a very good theory which takes human nature very seriously. If, as we have seen in our first chapter, our personality types are expressive of various forms of avoidance and deceit, then psychoanalysis is here to stay! It explains an immense amount of data about ourselves, at varying levels of interpretation, with a minimum of assumptions and in an economical way. If you have to be a secularist, rejecting any other dimension of thought than the 'natural' and the 'scientific', then it may work quite convincingly, within such a 'closed-system' of thought. Second, it operates best when it focuses upon the psychosomatic than upon the soul. That is why the efficacy of administering appropriate drugs is clearly recognized, and why some psychiatrists get impatient with the slowness of personal therapy and the speed with which wonder drugs can bring about changes. Third, the sexual emphasis of Freudian psychoanalysis was likewise focused upon the psychosomatic, since sex is expressive of both the body and the psyche. But other psychiatrists such as Jung reacted against the over-emphasis of Freud on sexual interpretations, powerful as such drives are. Fourth, the politics of psychoanalysis is very weak in the area of morality. Psychiatrists have been frequent witnesses in criminal court trials, and affirming mental sickness to such a wide coverage of criminal delinquency has come to be an abuse of individual moral choice and freedom. As one critic has put it:

> The employer may be very sorry to hear that his factory manager suffers from an anxiety neurosis, but what he really wants to know is why it should be that this man's symptoms demand rest at home specifically at times when important problems are cropping up. The magistrate or judge may understand perfectly when he is told by a psychiatrist that the men arrested for importuning have always been practising homosexuals, that the respectable lady found stealing pencils was symbolically stealing love (or even something more concrete if the psychiatrist has strong Freudian leanings), that the man who attacked the policeman was in effect attacking the drunken father who beat his mother every Saturday evening. But he is unlikely to see what all this has to do with breaking the law, because in the eyes of most people explaining is not the same as condoning.

Useful as psychoanalysis may be against self-deception it can also be naive if it is so prejudiced against the religious life that it interprets all religion from the viewpoint of a person's childish needs and wishes. Paul Vitz has effectively used psychoanalysis to explain Freud's antireligious beliefs as expressive of his own unconscious needs and traumatic childhood experiences. For one thing, Freud lacked experience in dealing with religious patients. He suffered deep neurosis in the early loss of a religious nanny, who later appeared to him as an 'unfaithful religious nanny-mother figure' who had let him down. He rejected his own Jewishness—a rejection also of his father. God too was rejected as a 'father figure'. All of this and more merely indicates that psychoanalytical explanations can cut both ways, against religious beliefs that are neurotic, but also even more deeply against atheism. Indeed, as Vitz has shown, the theoretical structure of psychoanalysis is much more firmly attached to atheism than it is to religious belief. For atheism illustrates much more clearly such Freudian concepts as repression, projection and fixation than trust and belief in healthy, loving relationships. Communism too has completely failed to demolish religion and replace it with atheism, so that worldwide more people believe in God and less people proportionately accept atheism today than after the beginning of the Marxist revolution. A more honest approach in psychiatry and psychology is required in future to the question of the reality of God in people's lives.

## The politics of psychology

Perhaps the fogginess of the uncertain realm of human behaviour is worsened in psychology, because it is more of a descriptive and observational discipline than psychiatry, which as a medical profession is committed to healing, if largely by drugs. After all, psychiatry did originate in physiology. But psychology originated in philosophy, so it has remained more descriptive and analytical, less concerned or preoccupied with the health of its subjects. Of course it could be argued that clinical psychologists and counsellors are very preoccupied with the emotional health of their patients and often are more relational than many psychiatrists. So there appear two divergent tracks in psychology, one more academic and observational, the other more clinical and involved with people's lives.

The amoral posture of many psychologists, in line with the atheism of the Freudian tradition, does make psychology as a pseudo-science of the heart particularly vulnerable to popular culture, as well as contributing to cultural attitudes. The personality type of 'the Fun-Lover', that we think of as being typically 'Californian', or 'Australian', if 'bums, beer, beach' express a way of life, is a great market for the politics of happiness. There the psychological role is how to keep happy with enough counselling, to avoid guilt in sexual licence, avoid being sinful before God, and avoid moral responsibilities in family break-down and other causes of personal failure. It all gets deeply narcissistic. There is now a huge 'happiness industry' geared to the modern fashion of being 'Psychological Man', smart in self-analysis, but often madly foolish in morality.

This may be unfair to good family counselling and marriage therapy. No doubt many lives are saved from mental breakdown and suicide because of the genuine love and care of their therapists. But the general tendency surely is towards 'the customer is always right', and such a paid form of friendship is under great pressures against speaking the moral truth and challenging patients to see their own sinfulness as well as their emotional sickness. If self deception is so innate to us all, exposure in love is more necessary than being lulled into a cultural sleep of what is fashionable for a fun-loving generation. The 'right to happiness' as spelled out in the American Constitution is having disastrous consequences in our society when amoral psychology is compounded by a drug-fixated culture.

Further indictments can be made against the psychological prescriptions of our culture today. In *The Sorcerer's Apprentice*, Mary Stewart van Leewen makes evident that psychology should be viewed firstly as a humane discipline. So even a physicist, Robert Oppenheimer, in 1955 at an annual assembly of psychologists, responded that psychology should never have modelled itself exclusively upon the natural sciences in the first place. For human beings are more than material substances and psychology, of all sciences, should realize that most of all. Few heard him, though some are beginning to do so now.

It has been excusable for psychiatry to link with science stemming out of the science of physiology, but it is inexcusable for a discipline of philosophy to do this. It did so, because pioneers like Wilhelm Wundt in Germany (he established the first scientific laboratory of psychology in 1879), and William James in America were both physiologists by training. Their emphasis on the experimental method led them to use such means to explain all psychological events.

Secularism and prejudice against religion added momentum to the 'scientific' character of psychology. In America especially, many leading members of the psychological profession started as seminarians who had either lost their faith in training or never had one to begin with and decided that the pastoral profession was not their milieu after all. Reaction against religion makes the natural sciences seem all the more attractive, in a manner that never would have motivated natural scientists themselves.

A second indictment that is now also being made is that psychology is becoming a religion anyway, in its cult of self-worship. The theorists of psychology, writers such as Fromm, Rogers, Maslow and May, have also become popularizers, and their followers are putting into practice what these writers only theorized about. Encounter groups, partner-swapping, sexual experimentation, the social acceptance of homosexuality, and much else are now being legitimized within the approach that human impulses are 'natural', 'good' and that only inhibitions are 'wrong'. The central moral issue for many psychologists today is that of their client's well-being. This is understandable, for after all the client is always 'right' in the business of making money. The travesty of such a perspective is compounded by the defence that selfism is both 'scientific' and 'morally right'. What more could anyone want today than to gain the respect of the two gods of our culture, Scientism and Me?

No wonder that the 1980s have been labelled a 'narcissistic culture', a 'Me-generation'. As a creed for our youth, it leads us to exclaim, 'hell is living with teenagers'. Indeed, it leads some to reflect upon the childishness of our wholly irresponsible culture. As professional psychologist Paul C. Vitz has written:

> *Humanistic selfism is not a science but a popular substitute religion, which has nourished and spread today's widespread cult of self-worship.*

In fairness to the emotional health professions, it needs to be pointed out that there have been significant shifts of emphasis, especially in Europe, in psychiatric and psychological perspectives. During Freud's lifetime, there was the wide assumption that if a person was happy then he or she must be enjoying a satisfying sexual life, and a neurotically unhappy person must be disturbed in sexuality. Sex was the touchstone by which to evaluate all sense of well-being. Popularly, that is still the impression, certainly in North America.

However, with the wartime researches of a new breed of psychiatrist, such as John Bowlby, has come a new interest in the dependency of infants, and of bonding, as affecting later emotional growth and personal relationships. Psychoanalysis has often been criticized for being too individualistic, purely a relationship between patient and doctor. But now the wider implications are being seen of personal relationships, and of the generational influences working through family histories.

This is a healthier, more realistic appraisal of the human condition. Meanwhile, however, all the impact of previous self-indulgent therapy is still passing through our culture in a veritable flood of self-love. There is a race on between the breakdown of the family in our society and the recovery of a more social sense of relationships as providing the key to the future emotional and spiritual well-being of our grandchildren.

The deepest wounds of all are caused when our unique personhood is not recognized. No human science of behaviour can satisfy that hunger and desire for the well-being of our unique soul, for science can only generalize and describe, not specify and personally relate. Only love can meet our uniqueness, and therefore ultimately only God's love can adequately meet and uphold the needs and mystery of our individual identity. Without a living, growing contact between our person and the person of God, we will not achieve or maintain any substantial degree of maturity in our personality. Without a strong faith in God we will remain imprisoned in some form of addictive behaviour, because God is the source of all true personhood.

## The Me-Generation: giving narcissism a bad name

In previous generations, it was relatively simple to decide what we thought of selfishness. It was plainly wrong! Today, our lack of morality makes it a matter of dispute. We no longer decide between right or wrong. Instead, we choose right or left. The popular assumption is that if you talk about morality you are 'old-fashioned'. Those who care about morality are seen to be conserving traditional values, which makes them conservative, and therefore on the 'right'. To be

on the 'left', you must be a 'radical' morally as well as politically.

Pop-psychology has to bear a great deal of responsibility
for creating this climate. It has diverted our hunger for personal salvation towards trivial pursuits: the momentary feeling,
the illusion of personal well-being, bodily health, and psychological security. As individuals in a constant state of flux
with fashion and fads, adjusting to them all in varying 'life-
styles', we live in a great biological stream of novelties. 'I
feel good' is the reflex action of living in constant change—
of relationships, jobs, pleasures, and environments. An ad-
vertisement for hair dye declares: 'If I've only one life, let
me live it as a blonde!' There is also the illusion of self-
power: I can do what I like! This illusion melts away as we
feel the waves of peer pressure and our dependence upon
others to prop up our self-esteem. The decline of institutio-
nalized authority in this permissive and indulgent society
leads to further intensification of illusion and unreality.

We are in the midst of a cultural revolution. The revolution began in the sixties, and now in the nineties we have statistical proof of change. Daniel Yankelovich, author of the
book *New Rules*, charts significant changes in our society
across twenty social norms, including sexuality, marriage
breakdown, family values, the intensification of selfishness,
the absence of personal sacrifice, and much else. The failure
of community interests, an increase in loneliness, the uncertain role of the sexes, the rise of militant feminism, an increase in political corruption, heightened militancy in
business, the loss of morale in education—all these suggest
that we are not living in happy times.

The breadth of these changes encompasses the full sweep
of modern life, from the private space of our inner lives and
the semi-public space of our family and community lives,
through to the public space of national and international cit-
izenship. All these areas have been invaded and have seen
their traditional institutions undermined. The stakes are

high. It is an incredible act of faith to set aside the traditional sources of personal well-being and happiness in one's job, family or religion, and live according to the prescribed therapies of the moment.

Our culture is adolescent. To see the meaning of life in gratifying our personal needs is childishness. An addiction to material satisfaction is a sign of immaturity, whether in the infant or in the grown-up. At the end of it all, our self-focused fantasies can only lead to disillusionment. The Me-Generation is ultimately stranded on a desert island of diminishing expectations. The trivialization of life is the end of this sequence of consequences.

## The impact of capitalism

If ninety per cent or more of western populations are heading towards life in the city, then the anonymity of bigness in every area of our lives dwarfs the human scale to triviality. We are cut down to size by the skyscrapers, institutions and bureaucracy of capitalism. John Naisbitt, in his book *Megatrends*, says that our natural reaction is to abandon hope of finding much help outside ourselves. In the 1970s, Naisbitt argues, people began to turn their backs on the entire range of external institutions and to look within themselves.

For example, instead of believing the local doctor about their own health, they began to jog, diet and eat healthier food. Parents began to investigate more critically their children's schooling. Others began to check on the variety of holiday packages tourist agencies could offer, and much else. There has been an entrepreneurial explosion of small businesses, as well as a do-it-yourself mentality for home care, car maintenance, religion and much else. The ecological issues may be too big for most people to think about, but at least their gardens have never looked better!

At the same time, multiple options have replaced the formerly more restricted choice of either–or. Either we got married or else we remained a bachelor or spinster. Now there is a whole spectrum of sexual options, including promiscuity, live-in arrangements, chastity and marriage. Either we worked nine to five or we were unemployed. Now we can opt for part-time employment, take sabbaticals between jobs, or create other opportunities. Once it was either vanilla or chocolate ice-cream. Now there are many varieties to choose from.

The multiple-choice society has become a new game where advertisers help to define and manipulate the fears and insecurities of society. Much of the multiple-choice nature of society leads to greater and greater opportunities for self-expression, whether it is in education, the arts, religion, politics or leisure. It implies that there can be a market for just about anything, provided enough people follow the whim.

In such a society, advertising becomes increasingly pervasive and it penetrates our privacy as never before. We have come a long way from the street crier who used to shout out the list of commodities available. However, advertising has been with us for some time. In 1758, Samuel Johnson could complain: 'Advertisements are now so numerous that they are very negligently perused, and it is therefore become necessary to gain attention by magnificence of promise and by eloquence sometimes sublime and sometimes pathetick.'

Today, creative strategy depends upon the principles of 'reach' and 'frequency'. New products need to penetrate the market, while products with a track record need to be seen frequently. The timing of ad campaigns is calculated even to the times of the day and the seasons of the year. While the claims made for many products appear ridiculous, their subliminal messages are expert at catching the unwary, generating greed for more or for new products, whose benefits create utopias in themselves.

The sex appeal of owning the right car and the right jeans, going out with the right companion for the evening, eating foods that virtually guarantee a long life—all suggest an illusory world of happiness for ever after. Commercial television and radio are financed by this industry of advertising, while the newspaper world could not exist without it. Malcolm Muggeridge, himself a product of the mass media, has said:

> *The media in general and TV in particular are incomparably the greatest single influence in our society today. This influence is, in my opinion, largely exerted irresponsibly, arbitrarily and without reference to any moral or intellectual still less spiritual guidelines whatsoever.*

Of course, the multiple-choice society gives us all more opportunity for personal enhancement and family well-being. We can choose more appropriate styles of living to suit our own moral and personal well-being. We can express our convictions of faith by more time spent in sabbaticals, in reflection, on retreats, in building up friendships, in prayer, in leisure as well as work roles. These opportunities merely intensify the ambiguities of the choice we have to grow spiritually and emotionally, or to destroy ourselves. So if we really do delight in God then Sunday as a day set apart for him will take on a new meaning. If we really do value friendships, more holidays can be devoted to being with friends. If we really want to take other people seriously in our lives, we can choose how much time we spend with them, and not be addicted to workaholic roles.

Nevertheless, left to the advertising industry, happiness is a shopping list. Left to the social scientists, happiness is also a shopping list, stripped of some of its commercialism. Books on happiness tend simply to list the types of happiness people pursue. For example, Michael Argyle, in his *Psychology of Happiness*, lists the statistical evidence for happiness within the nine spheres of human life: social relationships; work and unemployment; leisure; money, class and culture; personality; joy; satisfaction with life; age and sex; health; and enhancement, which is the sum total of these spheres of living. The conclusion of the book, which is typical of many like it, is that by 'going the right way it is possible to increase the happiness of oneself or others'. However, we are not told what that 'right way' may be. The uncertainty about the ingredients of happiness makes us very vulnerable to the capitalism of happiness: an industry geared to leave us with our illusions and our idols.

In sum, then, we are seeing that the politics of happiness do not leave us happy enough! For they are too caught up with power-seeking and not clearly and personally enough with love-seeking. Control is what we naturally want, not genuine relationships. Psychoanalysis and atheism are thus counter-productive, recognizing and denying at the same time. We cannot be authentic if we see the need to know ourselves and yet refuse to admit the possibility of also knowing God. Perhaps we are being driven to the conclusion that the knowledge of the self needs also the knowledge of God. That the one is impossible without the other.

Psychoanalysis is like looking at the landscape through the window, but instead of seeing the view we only see the window itself. So we end up seeing nothing.

A foreground needs a background. The background of all our lives must be bigger than ourselves; it must be God himself. Granted you recognize your personality type. Granted you have even had psychoanalysis. So what? Have you yet accepted yourself as a unique person? Have you stopped blaming your circumstances and seen that the buck stops with you? Indeed, does God frame your life with assurance, acceptance, forgiveness, and the profound sense of being loved by him? Looking *at* God, *through* the insights of our own person, gives us a place to stand, a reference point for our future, a healthy context in which to sustain the dignity of our own unique being.

Certainly we do not want to be unfair to all the human effort of health care and family or personal therapy so much needed in our neurotic world. But it is presumptuous to think a professional 'science' can save the unique souls of mankind without any reference to God or any awareness of whence this mysterious quality of humanity or personhood comes. In many ways our society has more abnormality than normality about it. If, as we have argued in this chapter, science simply does not have the means to create deep relationships or to rescue our authenticity, then are other values and interpretations of happiness also out of step with reality? This is what we must question further.

# 6

# Happiness in the Post-modern World

*Man is the only organism in nature fated to puzzle out what it actually means to feel 'right'.*

Ernest Becker

*'Sir', I said to the universe, 'I exist.' 'However,' replied the universe, 'that fact has not created in me a sense of obligation.'*

Stephen Crane

So far we have explored various movements, past and present, in our culture. Each has sought and given expression to the desire for human fulfilment in various ways. Now we turn to the post-modern world. The phrase 'post-modern' was first applied to a trend in art, a reaction against the technocratic spirit and rationality of our times, just as the Romantic Movement in the nineteenth century reacted against the rationalism of the Enlightenment. The 'post-modern' wants to do away with the rational faculty in modern people, to focus more upon feeling and intuition rather than on logic and reason. This heralds a more 'holistic' age, focussing on envionmental concerns for the planet, medicine for the whole person, and on humanity's spiritual as well as material needs.

The phrase 'post-modern' also implies that all the movements we have looked at have been weighed in the balance and found wanting. According to 'post-modernity' the past is bankrupt, and the pursuits of the present are futile. In contemporary society, we are therefore left with a haunting question: now what? That is our dilemma today.

Modernity is another name for spiritual poverty in the midst of affluence, surrounded as we are by the rational, material, and technical gadgetry of our age. Surrounded even, we may add, by religious gadgetry, too. We live in what one writer calls 'the civilization of always more'. Despite having more money, more sexual freedom, more novelty and thrills and more religious experiences, post-modern people are still unsatisfied and unhappy. The acquisitive society simply creates an itch for more. If gluttony was one of the deadly sins of the past, it has now been reinterpreted in our own age as the gluttony for ever new varieties of novelty.

## Unhappiness with the 'normal'

After the Second World War, psychologists and other health therapists began to see a new type of client or patient: 'the successful malcontented'. It has always been a belief of our society that if we are 'normal' then we will automatically be happy. Now, however, therapists are inundated by the demands of people who are 'successful' in terms of the canons of our society. They hold good jobs, enjoy high salaries, have many acquaintances (if not real friendships), and yet they are unhappy with normal daily life. They ask new, awkward questions: 'Isn't there more to life than money, sex, career, or a good social life?' 'Where is the meaning in all that I have or do?' In answer to these questions, conventional therapy has little meaning or value. Instead, the 'successful malcontented' has to dig deeper, and explore beyond what affluent suburbia has given him or her. This is where the drug culture holds a dangerous fascination for those beset by this craving for the meaning of being alive.

In the face of this, the narcotic many people turn to is busyness. Busyness has become a welcome distraction to the ordinariness of everyday life. One of the seventeenth-century English poets, George Herbert, challenges us on this issue:

> *Must business thee from hence remove?*
> *O, that's the worst disease of love.*
> *The poor, the foul, the false, love can*
> *Admit, but not the busied man.*

Business or busyness is the greatest distraction from all the areas of our lives: from the cultivation of friendships, from family life, from the matters of the heart. It is indeed 'the worst disease of love'. Clearly, ambitious people cannot live wholesome lives, because they are in love with themselves more than they are in love with others, God included. So, then, it is really self-aggrandizement that is the great enemy of contentment with being an ordinary person, living with genuine humanity. The busy life is a hollow shell, and living inside it is the lust to achieve selfishly, with all its overwork, professionalism, organization and activism. Only 'burn-out' may eventually reveal how false such a way of life has become. Busyness does not give much real happiness to its addicts.

Many today feel let down by our professions or institutions. They are given no guidance on how to live as ordinary, happy human beings. As a result, the modern tendency is for each person to do his or her own thing. All of life, including religion, has become a la carte. In the ever-expanding opportunities of choice, we can see everything, even religion, from a consumer's point of view. People's religious ideas are also consumer items that either fit or do not fit into the lifestyle that is wanted. Obedience, commitment, faithfulness, righteousness and truth are not the buzz words of those who talk about 'shopping around'. Increasingly, we can expect individuals to move around, experiment, and make up their own doctrinal expressions of what they hope will give them peace of mind and happiness of heart.

The problem is that modern society is not merely failing to cope with our problems; it is partly responsible for them. This can be seen in all the symptoms of modern social problems: vandalism, crime, disruption of family life, divorce, child abuse, addiction, loneliness, gambling and suicide. All these gloomily point forward to the actual breakdown of society. Without common standards of civic responsibility, without a common voice in religious persuasion or personal integrity in morals, the future of western society is itself in jeopardy. We have lived too long on the borrowed capital of our past traditions. As a result, many people, both those from inside organized religion and those who would see themselves as unreligious, are hungry today for spirituality. They long for something that will give their lives the meaning they were meant to have.

## The hunger for spirituality today

The search for true spirituality has surfaced at many times over the centuries. In the fourth century AD, when the church was steadily becoming more bureaucratic, a group of Christians went out into the desert to seek a faith free from all the trappings of worldliness. This led to a new movement in the church, later known as monasticism. In the decline of faith that characterized the Middle Ages, others devoted themselves to the exploration of mysticism. It seems as if it has been at turning points of history, in periods of rapid change, that spirituality has become a prominent concern for many people. This is also true for our age. However, today's search is less a pursuit of asceticism, and more the desire for personal experience and integrity.

Carl Jung, the psychiatrist, has become the voice for many seeking contemporary spiritual values. Jung's father was a Lutheran pastor with a rigidly conventional faith. He wanted his son to remain conventional like himself. However, Jung had a profound need for spiritual reality, which he expresses in his autobiography:

> *The best cannot be told and the second best does not strike home. One must be able to let things happen. I have learned from the East what is meant by the phrase wu wei: namely, 'not doing, letting be' which is quite different from doing nothing. Some Occidentals, also, have known what this not-doing means; for instance, Meister Eckhart, who speaks of sich lassen, 'to let oneself be'. The region of darkness into which one falls is not empty; it is the 'lavishing mother' of Lao-tzu, the 'images' and the 'seed'. When the surface has been cleared, things can grow out of the depths. People always suppose they have lost their way when they come up against the depths of experience. But if they do not know how to go on, the only answer, the only advice that makes any sense is 'Wait for what the unconscious has to say about the situation'. A way is only the way when one finds it and follows it oneself. There is no general prescription for 'how one should do it'.*

Since the end of the last century, there has been an increased emphasis on knowing who we really are. Starting with the deep psychology of the novels of Dostoevsky and Tolstoy, and followed by the systematic exploration of the unconscious by Freud, we are now being challenged to open up our personal inner life deliberately, so that we can learn to live more authentically. If our life is enriched through self-knowledge, so the argument goes, then we must all become psychic explorers.

To aid us in our search for self-discovery today, there are a number of tools available. It has become common practice to assess people in business and professional life by the Myers-Briggs personality assessment rating. This method of assessment is also being used to explore one's spiritual potential. People find that the insights gained about the nature of their personality type can be one of the most revealing events of their lives. All sorts of puzzling feelings and reactions, which we could never understand before, suddenly begin to make sense. How we arrive at the beliefs we have, why our security is threatened by other people, and why we are stressed by particular situations begin to be understandable.

Certainly it is good that we gain insight into ourselves, become more objective about our feelings and see life as it really is. This helps to free us from addictive ways of behaving that come about because of an enslavement to our upbringing. Such insights help to lessen the unnecessary sufferings we impose upon ourselves and others, when we act and react out of ignorance of personality traits.

Yet perhaps it is all too good! The investigation of our personalities can tend to create a false confidence in our newly-discovered self-knowledge. Our inner selves are too complex to be neatly categorized. Our essential uniqueness is greater than we shall ever fully know. In addition, the tendency to label people psychologically actually imposes new limitations on others, as well as on ourselves. Suddenly, our mysterious 'being' has been reduced to a mere 'type'. What is often overlooked is that if God has made human beings in his own image and likeness, then without the knowledge of God to complement knowledge of ourselves, we are only driven into deep emotional frustration and dissatisfaction with living. Psychological 'tools' can only tantalize us with a greater hunger for spiritual realities. For while we are free to change many of the outward circumstances of our lives, we soon discover that we cannot change our personalities on our own.

This can be seen by examining exactly what a technique such as the Myers-Briggs test actually gives us. We learn that we may be more or less rationalistic, intuitive, judgmental, feeling, sensing, or perceiving. We find out if we are more introvert or extrovert. We can also learn about the consequences of being a compulsive perfectionist, a giver, a performer, a detached observer, a critic and devil's advocate, a hedonist, a lustful or bossy person, or a peacemaking type of person. But after we have discovered all this, then what? We are still left with our hunger for more. We long for greater personal growth, more 'success' and recognition, more security or inner satisfaction.

In the Greek legend of Theseus, retold by Andre Gide, Theseus explores the labyrinth that tries to detain him in its complexity. He hears someone ask:

> For so much trouble, so many struggles? And toward what? What is our purpose here? Why do we seek reasons for everything? Where are we to turn, if not towards God? How are we to direct our steps? Where are we to stop? When can we say: so be it; nothing more to be done? How can we reach God, after starting from man? I have tramped all the roads of logic. On their horizontal plane I have wandered all too often. I crawl, and I would rather take wings; to lose my shadow, to lose the filth of my body, to throw off the weight of the past! The infinite calls me! I know that my journey can have only one end: in God.

## The challenge of New Age thinking

Originating out of the human potential movement of the 1960s, the New Age movement offers a wide, if not also wild, series of antirational nostrums that can supposedly be attained by any individual: transcendence, blissful sex, world peace, and financial success beyond one's wildest dreams. So it appeals to the post-war baby boomers, the thirty- to fifty-year-olds, who went to the universities in the sixties and seventies, and are still searching for a way of life that gives them profound spiritual fulfilment, mystical experiences, ego satisfaction, great bodies, unending happiness and lots of cash for a narcissistic style of living.

With hardly any effort and no real thinking, New Agers promise you it all. Now the Aquarians have developed such consumer clout that through over 5,000 'metaphysical' bookstores in North America, and thousands more in Europe, books and tapes are rapidly introducing a wide readership to this mind-set. Indeed, most general bookstores have generous space now also devoted to this expanding literature. It is also penetrating public education, while holistic medicine is adopting shamanism, psychic healing, and other flaky health techniques. Nurses are being trained by New Age instructors in various meditative techniques, paranormal experiences, and motion theory, with the assumption that all this accords with the latest 'scientific findings'. New Age is also making an impact on television and in films, with shows of spiritual fantasy, interviews with gurus, and tabloid presentation of megastar enthusiasts such as Shirley MacLaine.

The professed desire of New Age thinking is for wholeness of body and spirit, and oneness with the universe. This may well be a natural reaction to the intense sense of alienation that is afflicting our society today. But the irony of the movement is that it is relentlessly egotistical. Spawned, as we have mentioned, by the human potential movement, it is now all a matter of living up to self-loving instincts of sheer selfishness. It is a perfect correlative for a neo-conservative era, where the norm is for the young, the rich, and the beautiful simply to ignore the unhappiness of the old, the poor, and the ugly. All those black immigrants, unemployed poor, and abused women are simply not living up to their potential. It's their choice, we are told. Or if we accept Alvin Toffler's predictions in *The Third Wave*, this New Age 'spiritual supermarket with its depressing razzmatazz and religious faking' is a desperate reaching out for something to cling to as the modern industrial order is replaced by a positive culture 'which will sweep away all the debris of a dying civilization and hopefully give birth to a new one.' Clearly we face the challenge of sweeping reconstructions of thought and spirit.

Like the gnostic movement in the early beginnings of Christianity, New Age is eclectic and syncretistic. It claims to have connections both with Christianity and the major faiths of the East. Dabs of sorcery, occult, and pantheism are added to the mixture. With these ingredients, a synthetic mixture of religion and magic is being produced that denies an intelligent faith, routine living, even conventional law and order. Instead, it quests for personal experience of the extra-sensory, the feeling of spirituality, and the realization that life does not 'happen to us'. Instead, the claim is that we ourselves are our own 'happenings'. We create our own reality. The distaste for any body of doctrine makes it hard to identify New Age tenets, but there appear to be at least four strands in its mind-set.

## The desire for wholeness

Living longer, feeling better, and having more bodily energy is leading a new generation to want to live holistically. How do we manage our own lives? How mobilize positive beliefs and expectations? The answer is sought in such approaches as cognitive therapy, relaxation training, and all that advances bodily health and the enjoyment of healthy pleasures. But in place of cultivating affections for God and our neighbour, the emphasis is on our own pleasure. It is more skin touching than the touching of the heart. It is giving each other baths, scheduling body massage, and fantasizing lustfully, rather than learning who is that unique person in a body whose spirit we must reverence and be committed to in loyal friendship. It is the idyllic love between a dog or cat and its owner, where the relationship is always controlled, not the give and take of true human friendship, with its unpredictability, aware of the uniqueness of the other. 'Investing in yourself' ends up being self-indulgence. All these so-called holistic self-improvement programmes carry the seeds of their own failure, because they are so unrealistic as to how our inward nature can be changed, to become another person than the one who stands in need of improvement.

The sense that 'all is one' is pleasant enough for those who live lonely lives of quiet desperation. Many have experienced this sense of cosmic totality with mind-altering drugs. The effect of such altered states of consciousness is to blur all distinctions between subject and object, of perceiver and perceived, into an all-encompassing whole. As we have seen, this type of experience is being treated more cautiously these days, as the dangerous nature of drug-taking has become more apparent. Indeed, this is no different from the primitive pantheism of nature religions, also induced by mind-altering drugs as popularized by such writers as Castaneda. So it is not really 'new' at all! As C. S. Lewis has astutely observed, it is pantheism:

> It is the attitude into which the human mind automatically falls when left to itself. No wonder we find it congenial. If religion means simply what man says about God, and not what God does about man, then Pantheism almost is religion. And religion in that sense has, in the long run, only one really formidable opponent—namely Christianity.

While pantheism is a very seductive religion in an age of cultural disintegration such as we face today, we still have to ask ourselves, why have we lost this sense of wholeness in the modern world? Is it not because we live merely functionally, playing out professional roles, full of activity, but with little relational life and personal love? Efficiency is the new morality, not personal loyalty. Our society is characterized by motion without direction, speed without reflection. Everything expands endlessly—the Gross National Product, our pay-packets, mobility, ambitions. Knowledge is for knowledge's sake, and the information explosion is a technology lacking an ultimate purpose.

As a result, every human activity seems to have broken from its moorings, riding forward at an ever-accelerating pace, like a rudderless ship riding before the storm. Indeed, all our institutions and professions are being questioned to discover their authenticity and true purpose for society. Deep uncertainties lie before us, politically and socially, as familiar landmarks are erased, leaving us only with the sweeping winds of change. We don't want anarchy, and yet how can we preserve our wisdom in such radical times of change?

## The self as God

The human potential movement has a tendency to make human beings into gods. After the fad for the 'death of God' movement in the sixties, 'I am–ism', the assertion of the supremacy of the self, became fashionable. As a guru assured Shirley MacLaine:

*Intuitive perception comes through the right brain. When you touch that, you are then working with your God self and will understand that you already know everything there is to know. Therefore, you are your own best teacher and your own guru, so to speak... All your previous lifetimes of experience reside in your God self.*

*That is what serves as your counsellor, your guide, your teacher.*

This God-potential in the self gives New Agers the assuring sense that they are capable of doing whatever they set their minds to. As Shirley MacLaine has put it: 'If I could know me, I could know the universe.' For New Age thought seeks to transcend time and space, the rational and the moral. This takes 'positive thinking' on wings indeed. To affirm, 'I am the universe, reality is me,' smacks of megalomania, to say the least.

With all its enthusiasm and its extraordinary promises, has the New Age delivered the goods? Clearly not. Closed in upon the self, the universe still remains that prison that Theseus experienced in the labyrinth. Without the reality of God, there is no 'out there'. Such a perspective can give no basis or authority for ethics. Because of this, New Age beliefs are indifferent as to how my way of behaving may affect other people. New Agers shift mercurially through adultery and other doors of self-gratification. New Age beliefs turn their back on truth and reality as it is commonly accepted by society.

The results of this can be alarming. To opt for your own godhead leaves you with no recourse to any principles of objective reasoning. It is an ultimate turning inwards upon yourself that leaves out any objective criteria whatever. It is like someone who is mad, completely alone in his or her delusions of grandeur, never open to be persuaded by any external convictions. In practice, many New Agers cannot go to the logical extremity of their own position. If they did, they would cut themselves off from any reality of daily living, with bodies that need feeding, spirits that need loving, and personalities that still need the acceptance of others, regardless of their claims to extra-terrestrial voyaging. It simply points up the lengths to which the human spirit will go to satisfy the hunger for deep spiritual reality. The superficialities of our plastic age clearly cannot begin to satisfy this human need.

## The mastery of spiritual realities through techniques

New Age beliefs assume mastery of spiritual and psychic. For example Jose Silva claims to have taught his mind-control course to over one million students in the seventies alone. This is a form of meditation that improves memory, eradicates bad habits, improves health, beats cancer, enables you to practise extrasensory perception, and helps your self-esteem to soar. All this in a four-day course! Examining Eastern mystics, such as Tibetan monks, humans are claimed to be able to control the temperature of their bodies, demonstrate heart-rate changes, and show remarkable controls of mind over matter. Biofeedback techniques assume that almost any internal body processes can be brought under control. Deep states of hypnosis have also been experimented with, to induce physiological changes. With a combination of scientific experimentation and a wishful imagination, claims are made that you, the reader, can come 'into direct contact with an all-pervading higher intelligence, learning in a moment of numinous joy that it is on your side'. So claims are made to give you the confident use of new energy, and the feeling of being in the loving presence of higher powers.

There are numerous inbuilt contradictions and inconsistencies in the movement. There is a revolt against the aridity of technocracy; yet there is also the full use of all manner of techniques to create power and energy. Its mysticism is really a lust for personal power, which is what magic really is. Power is what is sought and promised, not love and friendship. There is no notion in all this of a personal God.

Where it suits its practitioners, it is respectably

'scientific'. So writers such as F. Capra find a compatibility between the new science and Eastern mysticism. We are being promised that all around us are potential sources of energies, still to be discovered, but these will only be discovered and utilized when 'seed men', with very different attitudes to those of Western thinking today, have been able to experiment with new forms of consciousness. So the New Age demands a new mutation of what it means to be 'human', a great risk indeed for the welfare of humanity. A fundamental transformation of human consciousness is thus demanded, more radical even than communism's 'New Man'. In fact, it resembles a Hindu notion of humanity more than anything we think of as a person in the West. For it is an amalgam of Hindu philosophy and Western technocracy.

## Ecological harmony with nature

'Deep ecology' today represents an earnest desire to live in such harmony with nature that we fit into our environment rather than being transcendent over it. This seems a misfit with the Promethean powers sought by the other strands of New Age. Yet it does identify with the pantheism that suggests humanity is part of a higher 'planetarization of consciousness'. So New Age communities want to demonstrate on the one hand their immersion into Nature, yet on the other to show the powers they have to produce bumper harvests and record crops in their control over nature.

All that is hoped for is that eventually some mysterious 'planetarization' will take place in human consciousness—not conscience; that the ideal paradisal state will then ensue. But in all this, little is directed towards dealing with the actual environmental problems of our habitable globe. For you cannot take the posture of pantheism, of being 'in nature' as part of nature, and at the same time assume transcendence 'over nature'. It is only humanity, made in the image and likeness of God, who can really grapple with the earth's stewardship, both in actual responsibility for what has happened to the planet, and to prescribe the remedies needed.

So then, just as gnosticism promised salvation through mystical, initiatory rites of 'knowledge', but could do nothing to save the collapse of Roman pagan society, New Age today is only highlighting the return of paganism into a dying culture. It gives no clear remedy for its disintegration. It has no fundamental categories of life and action, by which to grapple with the environmental crisis, the loss of childhood in society, the breakdown of the family, and the sustenance of personal and community life. Rather it is reaping the whirlwind of Descartes' terrible dictum, 'I think, therefore I am'. At least in African tribal culture there is a community spirit which says 'We think, therefore I am'. In Christian faith we can go further to say 'I respond to God, therefore we are'. Then we are held accountable to God for the well-being of the earth, and for relationships at every level within the family of humankind. Instead, New Age beliefs are a revolt against God, an 'Aquarian Conspiracy' indeed of the dark forces of evil, to usurp God's sovereignty. This 'conspiracy', like many before it, threatens the possibility of true happiness more than we dare think.

As Augustine reflected upon the confusions of his day, when Rome was about to fall, he observed: 'Only they can think of God without absurdity, who think of him as life itself'. Again, we remember the same writer's famous dictum: 'God made us for himself, and our hearts are restless until we find our rest in him.' That God should create us in his own image does indeed create an enormous temptation in humanity to mistake our own God-given nature for divinity itself. Our souls are indeed deeply mysterious, for in them is a great void that only God can fill. No wonder, then, that modern people, with all their newly acquired skills and knowledge, are more vulnerable than ever before to be tempted by the evil one, 'you shall be as gods!' This is the hiss of the serpent. A Faust could sell his soul for great powers of sorcery; modern men and women can do the same.

I was just typing out this passage in the book when a lady interrupted me with a visit. She had very recently given her heart to God, wholly and joyfully so. But as she began to realize the fullness of what she was doing, she reflected that as a little child she grew up in her grandparents' home, because she was an illegitimate child. She never knew her real father, though later she was protected by having a step-father, who knew little of her past. The secret of her origin remains with her, although it has left a great void in her heart. Now the God who gives life and love has become more precious than a father ever could be. His presence now fills her deepest need, and has fully legitimized her as no legal action nor surrogate father could ever do.

Again, I think of Paul, a friend whose mother tried to commit suicide, and instead was invalided for the last ten years of her life, as a bitter, suffering woman, unable to mother her two sons. Alcoholism and all the appalling consequences of disfunctional family life have taken heavy toll of Paul's emotions. Yet he, too, has seen the life of God become so loving to his wounded heart as to give him a deep sense of personal acceptance and inner affirmation, such as he had never had all through his previous life. Sorcery may possibly heal bodies, but only the love of God can heal hearts wounded by sin and pride.

Without God in our inner being, changing and healing the emotional wounds of childhood, mankind is doomed to lives of quiet desperation and unhappiness. So we leave now the diverse ways in which our society has experimented with utopian dreams of happiness, philosophical endeavours for peace of mind, the 'paid friendship' psychology, and the contemporary madness of New Age paganism, to trace wherein true happiness is to be found. Jacques Ellul has put it plainly:

*The hope of Jesus Christ is never a dash of pepper or a spoonful of mustard. It is bread and wine, the essential and basic food itself, without which there is only the delirium of knowledge and an illusion of action.*

# 7

# Is the Universe
# a Happy Place?

*It is quite certain that there is no good without the
knowledge of God; that the closer one comes, the
happier one is, and the further away one goes, the
more unhappy one is.*

Blaise Pascal

Our search for happiness, as we have outlined it so far, is
more modern than ancient. It embodies an expectation of
'achievement' that was not found in the ancient world of the
Bible, or in pre-technical societies generally. In the modern
world, we think of measuring our achievements in a way
that has not been done before in history. This also holds
true when we think of 'achieving happiness'. 'How much
have I achieved?' we ask each other.

In the world of the Bible, such an outlook would have
been seen as false. Achievements were qualified by a sense of
what was right and just for the whole community. The people
of those times had a strong instinct for the harmonious well-
being of others. Achievement was attained in good relationships: between husbands and wives, parents and children,
servants and masters, subjects and monarch.

Today's version of achievement also has a far more individualistic ring. We think of it as what one individual can do

by himself or herself, or in competition against others. In ancient times, status and rank mattered more, and everyone had a place or level in society. Achievements were seen to be those actions which were in harmony with your position in the community. The community at large prescribed in advance what the limits for achievement might be.

A final difference between then and now was that achievement was never excessive. It was always related to the necessities of life, since the ideal was to be neither rich nor poor. Ideally, this meant that the unhappiness of excess was confined to the greedy few, rather than to a culture as a whole. It was accepted that wisdom was to live a balanced life, both for yourself and in relation to others. This guiding principle enabled the Israelites to have a secure place within society, and before God.

Unhappiness is caused when we step out of place. This can happen, for example, when we act as though we have godlike powers to decide our own destiny. This was the choice taken by Adam and Eve in the Old Testament's creation story. They were tempted into eating fruit from 'the tree of the knowledge of good and evil'. In other words, they decided to live without God. To do this means to take the decisions that only God can make into our own hands.

## Adam and Eve, Babel and Abram

The expulsion of man and woman from the garden of Eden—whether this is taken in symbolic or historical terms —was because of arrogance. They chose to be godlike, living by their own powers, instead of staying in their place in the universe, as humans living under God's power. Because of this basic rebellion against God, we are now cursed to achieve in vain, and to work in exhaustion and suffering.

The Book of Genesis has another story which illustrates human ingenuity to persist in self-achieving. This is the story of the Tower of Babel. Even the materials for this colossal ziggurat were man-made bricks, and the building went on at a sacred site where people thought they could meet with their gods. The tower became a symbol of the human quest for self-identification. Behind the building of the tower was the spirit of autonomy:

> *Come, let us build ourselves a city, with a tower that reaches to the heavens, so that we may make a name for ourselves and not be scattered over the face of the whole earth.*

This call echoes the original intention of God when he created human beings: 'Let us make man in our image, in our likeness.' The difference between the two calls is that in building the Tower of Babel, the builders wanted to create 'a name' for themselves. They were not so much attempting to achieve prestige and glory as to gain control over their own destiny, and to gain self-knowledge. They wanted to become the product of their own creation, which is the essence of sin. For us to realize our own being without God is the supreme rebellion. The result was the reverse of all they hoped for. Instead of making a name for themselves, they lost the power to communicate. And their work prompted, rather than prevented, their dispersion over the earth. Utter confusion followed their attempt at independence from God:

> *So the Lord scattered them from there over all the earth, and they stopped building the city. That is why it was called Babel—because there the Lord confused the language of the whole world.*

They were left only with babble—confusion, lies and the inability to relate and communicate with each other, let alone with God. This is a graphic image of what happens when we deny our place as human beings before God.

Juxtaposed with this story is a later episode in Genesis: the call of Abram. As in the creation account, God again speaks:

> *The Lord had said to Abram, 'Leave your country, your*
> *people and your father's household and go to the land*
> *that I will show you.*
> *I will make you into a great nation*
> *and I will bless you;*
> *I will make your name great,*
> *and you will be a blessing.*

In contrast to the story of Babel, God, rather than the tower-builders, takes the initiative. Instead of trying to 'make a name' for himself, Abram is blessed by God. This means that God promises Abram life in its fullest sense—human life with all the glory and dignity that God had always intended it should have. Through his submission and obedience to God, Abram would also gain what the tower-builders had lusted after: a great name and that his children should become a great nation.

This stark contrast between the two stories shows us the misery of humanity turned in on itself, and its glory when given up to God. Those who are 'blessed' in Abraham are set free from the curse of wanting to be like God, and of creating their own story. Faith is seen as accepting God's initiative for our lives, trusting in what God has promised. This theme of faith runs right through the Bible. As a later prophet, Isaiah, says:

> *Lord, you establish peace for us;*
> *all that we have accomplished you have done for us.*

This faith in God is the opposite of independent action. God's story of our lives takes place, according to one of the prophets, '"not by might, nor by power, but by my Spirit," says the Lord of hosts.'

It is this Old Testament foundation of human identity in God that sets the scene for the revelation of Christian faith in the New Testament. Again, we discover our full humanity not through our own achievements, but because of what Jesus Christ has done for us—dying on the cross to bring us back to God. Once more, to have faith means to renounce our attempts to go it alone. We stop trying to assess our lives, and the lives of others, in terms of our individual achievements and successes. Instead, we put all our weight on the prior achievement of God which set us free to accept all the goodness he longs to give us. With faith, we can cry out: 'I do believe; help me overcome my unbelief!'

All of this means that we regain our true place in the universe. This is what the apostle Paul calls being 'in Christ'. We are given back our true identity in all the blessings that flow from Jesus to his disciples. We accept that we are a part of God's creation, instead of trying to displace God as our creator. The result is that our lives change. Paul pictured this change as receiving the 'fruit of the Spirit' of Christ in our lives: 'love, joy, peace, patience, kindness, goodness, faithfulness, gentleness and self-control'. These qualities are not evidence of our own natural spirit, but the gift of the Spirit of God within us.

This is where the journey of searching for happiness comes to an end, and where the new perspective of receiving from the giving God can begin.


## Ancient Greece and Rome: behind the mask

The primal biblical stories of Adam and Eve, the Tower of Babel and the call of Abram tell us about the origins of being and the sources of reality. The ancient Hebrews were not alone in having such stories. The ancient Greeks, whose culture has had a profound impact on our own, told a set of very different stories.

In his tragic play, *Hecuba*, Euripides tells the story of a great queen who loses in the Trojan wars her husband, most of her children, and her political power. She is made a slave, and yet in the midst of all her unhappiness, she remains strong in her moral integrity. She had left her youngest child to the care of her dearest friend, who had promised to look after him. But after the wars are over and Hecuba can return to Thrace, she sees a naked body washed up on the shore. It is so badly eaten by the fish that at first she does not recognize who it is. But as she looks at it more closely, she is horrified to discover it is her own child. Her friend had murdered the boy for money, and thrown his body into the waves.

Hecuba suddenly realizes that all the foundations of her moral life have been destroyed. Looking around, she groans, 'Everything that I see is untrustworthy.' If this is what a trusted friend can do, what will happen to the rest of life! In her despair, she turns to revenge, and puts out the eyes of her former best friend. It is predicted that Hecuba will turn into a dog. Her transformation from being the best of humans to the worst has taken place because she has become wholly incapable of putting trust in others any more. Her openness and trust has been replaced by a closing of her character, as she turns in on herself. In ultimate distrust, Hecuba has really decided: 'I won't be human any more.'

*Agamemnon* is another play, written by the founder of Greek tragedy, Aeschylus. The play tells the story of a king who is leading his army to Troy. However, the expedition is becalmed at sea, and Agamemnon is told that the gods are demanding a sacrifice. He will have to kill his own daughter in order to complete the expedition. So he is faced with a choice of one or other of two great evils: disobedience to the gods and the loss of his moral role as a king, or the sacrifice of his daughter and the death of his role as a father.

Greek tragedy is set within such horrific choices. These

choices confront the characters not when they are doing evil, but when they are trying to do good and to live well. The message is that it is when good people are trying to do their best that bad things happen. It is in the deep seriousness of duty and commitment, of love and of moral values, that the Greeks saw the tragedies of life.

What the Greeks did not recognize was that man and woman were left alone by the gods to be human. The gods were of no help, and often set up profound obstacles to being human. Played out on the stage, such dramas called the entire community to enter into the horrendous moral dilemmas, without a solution other than to go on in despair.

It is in this Greek setting of tragedy that we have the origin of the word *prosopon*, from which we derive our word 'person'. A prosopon was the mask worn by the actor, which defined the role he played on the stage. In acting out his role, the player took on a significant identity in the play, and tasted a freedom that he might never know in his normal, unmasked life. This was because the Greek view of the world denied significance to human beings.

For the Greeks, the cosmos was essentially impersonal. Even the gods had to fit into it as best they could. The cosmos was like a brutal machine that would crush all who dared to defy its laws. There could be no independence of being, no personal uniqueness, no true freedom. The place of humanity in this scheme of things could only be expressed in tragedies such as Hecuba and Agamemnon, in which the gods are completely unmoved by human suffering. So, for the Greeks, personhood—the prosopon—was defined by the tragic situation we find ourselves in.

This way of thinking, many thousands of years old, still maintains a powerful grip on the imagination of our culture. Albert Einstein was once asked what was the most important question he could ever ask. He replied: 'To know if the universe is a friendly place.'

The Romans were less philosophical and more pragmatic

about human nature. For the Romans, to be a person did not mean wearing the mask of tragedy. Instead, it was the legal status of a man in society. Legally, a man was declared by Roman law to be entitled as a 'person' to have authority in his own family, to offer sacrifices to the household gods, and to serve the emperor. He was thus the legal representative of law and order within the Roman empire. However, this view of the person, although different from the Greek tragic view, had one fundamental in common. To be a person was in fact impersonal, because the person was defined according to the law, rather than in relating to other persons. Neither the Greek nor the Roman worlds can justify personhood in an ultimate sense.

This is not just ancient history—it is our dilemma today. Our secular society has cut itself off from its Judeo-Christian roots, in which the person is one who relates to God and to others. It has instead turned to a modern version of the Greek and Roman views, speaking impersonally of legal 'rights', or of personal 'role-playing'. In trying to become our own creator and our own destiny, we have returned to the sin of Adam and Eve, and the Tower of Babel. This is the source of our own lethal autonomy, which isolates us so effectively from each other, and which robs us of community. This is the burden we place on our governments: to keep us all together, as isolated individuals demanding our own rights, acting like particles of drifting sand in a desert of loneliness.

## Living without love

This alienation of person from person is the story of the human race. The novelist George MacDonald tells the story of a Victorian family which had returned from church on the first Sunday of Advent. In the service, the minister had preached on the verse: 'Whom the Lord loves he chastens.'

The little girl, Sophy, strangely believed it and longed for God to punish her so that she would know he loved her.

Little did she realize how sunless and loveless her life had been so far. Her father neglected her and her step-mother rejected her. Nor was there any real love between Mr Greatorex and his second wife, a vain, empty-minded woman whom he could not change to meet his expectations. She only vaguely realized that she was no pleasure to him. All his efforts to make her fit into his own mould passed over her completely. Now she was pregnant, and fondly hoped that if she could present him with a son—for clearly he had no interest in his only daughter—then somehow a new domestic bliss might come into the loveless home.

Many times that Advent season, Sophy had dwelt upon the thought of the baby Jesus who was born each Christmas Day. She believed that he could present himself into every home as the same baby Jesus. On Christmas morning she crept out of her room, down the staircase and into the spare room where a single candle was burning. Lying there on the bed was the most beautiful doll Sophy had ever seen. Was it for her? Was it a Christmas gift?

Gently, Sophy carried it to the candlelight, and then the truth struck deep within her that it must be the baby Jesus himself. But why was he so still? As she sat, 'she began, as was her wont, to model her face to the likeness of his, that she might understand his stillness—the absolute peace that dwelt in his countenance.' However, her doubts began to intensify with his stillness. He did not breathe, and he was cold—oh, so very cold!

Awakening late, the household had been looking for Sophy, and found her in the spare room. Her father found her with his dead son wrapped in her coverlet.

'Jesus is dead,' she said slowly and sadly, but with perfect calmness. 'He came too early, and there was no one up to take care of him, and he's dead—dead—dead!'

With a cry that was half sob, half shriek of utter despair

and loss, she was taken up in the embrace of her father who comforted her: 'No, no, Sophy! Jesus is not dead, thank God. It is only your little brother that hadn't life enough, and is gone back to God for more.'

The effect of the little girl's faith and grief over Jesus, that was in fact her little dead brother, was the beginning of a new relationship between daughter and father, husband and wife, and the friendship of others too. The child in each was brought to new life. MacDonald comments, 'Such were the gifts the Christ-child brought to one household that Christmas.' This could only be a Christian story, not a Greek tragedy, for only God-made-flesh could ever bring such transformation of relationships.

The modern novelist, Iris Murdoch, has dwelt on the same theme of living without love, and therefore without personhood, in her story, *The Word-Child*. Hilary Burde, the central figure, admits that he is 'unfit for ordinary life'. The drama of the war would have suited him fine, because inner turbulence has plagued him all his life. Hilary was the child of a prostitute. He never knew his father and was abandoned in an orphanage as a child. So he grew up with the resentment of 'anti-life'. A perceptive friend says to him, 'I think you've got a secret sorrow, Hilary.' 'I've got about two hundred,' he replies. But he refuses to divulge even one of them.

Well-meaning people try to convert him with their simple faith, but he rejects it:

> *Their religion seemed to me to be over-lit, over-simple, overly threatening. There was nowhere to hide. I rejected the theology but was defenceless against the guilt which was so fruitlessly beaten into me. Those who regarded me as a thoroughly bad lot were in no way unreasonable.*

In his delinquency he is saved by the discovery of words:

*I discovered words and words were my salvation. I was
not, except in some very broken-down sense of that ambiguous term, a love-child. I was a word-child.*

Studying English literature at school, and then at Oxford,
words become Hilary's escape route through life. He admits:

*I loved words, but I was not a word-user, rather a word-
watcher, in the way that some people are bird-watchers.
I had no religion and no substitute for it. My days gave
me identity, a sort of ecto-skeleton. Beyond my routine
chaos began and without routine my life (perhaps any
life?) was a phantasmagoria.*

Religion is impossible for Hilary. In this way, the novelist
cleverly recites the narratives of Hilary's affairs, adventures,
and mistresses. There is no purpose, other than what turns
up from one day to the next. Life begins on Thursday, but
there is no Sunday, just a leap from Saturday to Monday,
until near the end of the story when there are two Sundays
together, both full of tragedy and without any form of
redemption.

The word-child Hilary felt as if he had 'been turned si-
lently out into the desert, there was no one now to whom I
could speak at all of the things which were hourly and mi-
nutely devouring my heart'. So for the first time in many
years he sat alone in church, crying out his thoughts. 'Was
another cycle of misery, intensified, more dense, beginning
for me? Would even cynicism help me?' The one glint of
hope came to him: there was one woman he could make
happy. Then as he left the church he saw the Christ-child
leaning from his mother's arms to bless the world.

At the end of the novel, there is still confusion about
whether the word-child ever did get to know the Christ-
child. Yet what both writers are hinting at in their stories is
that personhood must be inspired and renewed at a

transcendent level—at a level above and beyond ourselves—
by the coming of a personal God. Only then can human
beings become more fully human, inspired by divine personhood. Every generation needs renewal to step outside the
fatalism of an impersonal, classical tradition, into the realm
of divine love and personhood that is true happiness.

## The three-personned God

Being a person in the fullest sense is impossible to justify in
classical thought, or indeed in any religion except biblical
faith. Only when God is known as a person can we say that
personhood is the basis of being human. An impersonal God
can be no basis for personal existence.

But the Christian faith takes us beyond even this. The
uniqueness of Christian faith is that God became human in
the person of Jesus Christ. Through his Spirit, we are able
to enjoy his presence within us, and to know him personally.
No Confucian can ever claim to know Confucius personally;
no Buddhist can claim to know Buddha personally; no Mus-
lim can claim to know Allah personally. This belief, which
lies at the heart of the faith, is unique to Christianity.

This is the secret of true happiness for every Christian—
enjoying a personal relationship with God, because Jesus
Christ lives in our lives by the power of his Spirit. No other
faith can repeat what Jesus promised to his disciples: 'If anyone loves me, he will obey my teaching. My Father will love
him, and we will come to him and make our home with him.'
Later in this same passage, Jesus prays that his disciples, and
all who come to believe in God through their witness, should
be as united with each other as the Father and the Son are
united in the Trinity. This incredible unity in relationships
leads to happiness. As Jesus prayed: 'That they may have
the full measure of my joy within them.'

Christians themselves have probably never fully realized

the depths on which they can draw from such Trinitarian and personal spirituality. The Western church has its roots deep within the ancient Latin church, received largely through Augustine. This tradition has focussed on the oneness of God, rather than on the more personal emphasis of the three persons of the Trinity. This over-emphasis on God's unity has enabled philosophers to get away with simply understanding God rationally, rather than knowing him for themselves. In western culture, God has become an object to describe rather than a person to know and love.

The Latin language also translated the Greek word *ousia* (which was used to describe the unique 'personhood' of God) with the word *substantia* (the 'stuff' or 'substance' of God). This tended to leave the Latin mind with a depersonalized view of God, which has in turn been handed down to us. The western world therefore prefers to see God in terms of function—how he works in the world—rather than seeing him as a personal being who relates personally with each one of us.

However, there is another tradition which we can draw on. The Eastern church split off from the Western church partly because its stress was on the three persons of the Trinity, rather than on the oneness of God. If we begin with this stress on the three-personned God, rather than with his oneness, then we are confronted with a greater sense of the personal God. This is because we start to see how the three persons of the Trinity relate to one another and to us. Our approach to God changes dramatically from being a concept to become a relationship.

This is the emphasis of the Old Testament. The people of Israel 'knew God'. This implies a personal relationship that is even more intimate than the way a husband and wife may 'know' each other. 'Knowing God' in the New Testament takes on a further dimension. To know Jesus Christ is to know the Father too, as John emphasizes so clearly in his

Gospel. This can only be true because God has sent his Spirit into our hearts. As Paul the apostle says:

> *You did not receive a spirit that makes you a slave again to fear, but you received the Spirit of sonship. And by him we cry, 'Abba, Father.' The Spirit himself testifies with our spirit that we are God's children.*

Paul comes back to this theme in another of his letters:

> *Because you are sons, God sent the Spirit of his Son into our hearts, the Spirit who calls out, 'Abba, Father.' So you are no longer a slave, but a son; and since you are a son, God has also made you an heir.*

The verb 'calls out' is a vivid expression of deepest emotion, often used of inarticulate anguish, as when Jesus cried out on the cross. So from the depth of our being, we are now able to enter into a new, glorious relationship with God. Our relationship with him could not be nearer or more personal. It shares something of the mystery of the eternal friendship within the Godhead, of God as personal being: Father, Son and Holy Spirit.

Losing sight of this relational emphasis within the Holy Trinity has been a tragedy for the western world. Westerners have settled for the unhappiness of mere rational certainty instead of pressing on to relational certainty. This is not to belittle thinking or our rational selves, which are given to us by God. Rational belief must be the starting-point for our relationship with God. We can only come to know God personally if we first know the truth about him. Rational thinking is a great place to start off from in our journey of faith, but disastrous if we never leave it.

In a human relationship, there is much more than merely collecting information about the other person. I may be informed about the other person but still not be able to relate to them. It is love that enables us to relate. And when we receive love in return, we know the joy of receiving something that is far greater than information about the other person. What is true of our human relationships is true in a greater sense of our relationship with God. The ultimate that we can say about God is that 'God is love', which must be experienced personally if it is to mean anything at all. If God is love, then unless we know this love for ourselves, we will know nothing of any value about him.

The illusion of scholarship is that it assumes that knowledge about God is a substitute for knowing God personally. There can be no ultimate source of happiness in this distorted thinking. Knowing God personally is the only appropriate way of knowing God.

## Over the bridge, above the darkness

All this may seem to be talk that is 'theologically airborne', flying blissfully above the reality of everyday life! How does the idea of relating personally to God work out in the context of our own lives? Perhaps the best way to illustrate this is through the story of Evelyn.

Evelyn grew up in an English village. Her father was professionally successful, her mother came from a socially privileged family, and she had an older sister. Sadly, Evelyn's father showed affection only for the older sister, and her mother always took the side of her husband when Evelyn complained of being neglected in the family. Left alone, Evelyn felt profound rejection. Going to church on Sundays was like having good table manners. It was the 'done thing', and meant no more than that. All deep emotions at home were covered over in a polite silence that disabled Evelyn from talking about her feelings. As an adolescent, Evelyn rebelled, but her parents never understood why she did this.

When she was thirteen, Evelyn was called before the

whole class at school, by an authoritarian teacher, to stand and read aloud to them. She was overcome by fear and fainted, and her lips became sealed. She lost her voice. From that day on, she never sang again. She could only smile in a sad and foolish way, allowing others to interpret her silence as they thought fit. Inside, she became more and more emotionally confused. Above all, she felt rejected, living by herself in a void.

Evelyn went to live on her own in London. She escaped from the arms of one boyfriend, only to go to bed with another. She remained wordless, once telling her latest lover, 'I have no voice—only my body that I can give.'

She could not sing, and she rarely knew what to say, for any sort of intimate communication was impossible. What could she say when she feared to reveal anything about herself?

Then Evelyn began to read the novel based on Jesus' life, *The Robe*. As she read about Jesus, she warmed towards his humanity. She felt she could speak to Jesus, for he too had experienced rejection. Yet at the same time he called God 'Father'. This was a contradiction for Evelyn, whose father had shown no interest in her. Why should God care about her?

And yet Jesus had turned to God as his Father naturally, with intimacy and integrity. Perhaps then, in his healing relationship of trust and love, Jesus might in turn help her to know God for herself, as her Father too. One day she poured out her heart to a friend who was a Christian. He asked her if she wanted to pray. As they waited together in silent prayer, Evelyn slowly began to pray to Jesus, hesitantly at first, and then openly.

She broke the silence with an anguished cry: 'O Jesus, give me a voice to pray to you.' She poured out the pent-up longings of a lifetime, in her need to communicate and to be intimately understood. Evelyn realized what had happened to her for the first time. She had been wordless, with no

voice, only her body to give away. But as she ended the silence of her heart for so many years, she experienced what
the apostle Paul meant when he said that 'the Holy Spirit
himself prays for us with groans that words cannot express.'
As one of the psalms says, she was given a new voice to sing:

> I waited patiently for the Lord;
> He turned to me and heard my cry.
> He lifted me out of the slimy pit,
> out of the mud and mire;
> he set my feet on a rock
> and gave me a firm place to stand.
> He put a new song in my mouth,
> a hymn of praise to our God.
> Many will see and fear
> and put their trust in the Lord.

As Evelyn had begun to see, the process of learning to know
the personal God is very simple. Our prejudices against religion fall away, we begin to distinguish clearly between God's
character and the character of our parents, and the desire to
love God is awakened in us. We long to become like Jesus,
to pray as he prayed, to know his Father as he so intimately
knew him, to have the Spirit that he had. We seek to be forgiven and accepted by him. Then we see that Jesus himself
is the bridge over the unfathomable abyss that separates us
from God. The jump to God becomes less of a fearful leap
in the darkness, and more like a gentle bridge, crossing by
the humanity of Jesus himself. All the time, his Spirit
breathes new life into us, giving us the desire to trust him as
a child alone can trust.

The Christian writer, C. S. Lewis, describes this process
of relating to the mystery of the Holy Trinity:

> An ordinary Christian kneels down to say his prayers.
> He is trying to get in touch with God. But if he is a
> Christian, he knows that what is also prompting him to

*pray is also God: God, so to speak, inside him. But he
also knows that all his real knowledge of God comes
through Christ, the Man who was God—that Christ is
standing beside him, helping him to pray, praying for
him. You see what is happening. God is the thing beyond
the whole universe to which he is praying—the goal he's
trying to reach. God is also the road or the bridge along
which he is being pushed to that goal. So that the whole
threefold life of the three-personal Being is actually
going on in that ordinary little bedroom, where an ordinary man is saying his prayers.*

That, then, is one explanation of how we may enter into the
mystery of the three-personned God, even though this mystery will always remain to surprise, shock or shatter us—as
John Donne prayed: 'Batter my heart, three-person'd God.'

Perhaps the best introduction to knowing God is to discover him through the person of Jesus. After all, Jesus was
God, living as a human on earth. Because we are used to relating with other humans, Jesus is our most natural link with
God. By reading the Gospel accounts of Jesus' life, we begin
to follow in the footsteps of his first followers. We discover
that, like us, the disciples asked all sorts of questions about
Jesus, because they found him perplexing. After all, to walk
alongside the God-man is a great mystery. But as their
friend, they clearly knew that he was with them.

Then after his death and resurrection, Jesus ascended
back into heaven. After waiting for the feast of Pentecost,
his Spirit came to them in a new, even more intimate way
than they had ever experienced when he was physically with
them. In this way, he fulfilled his promise, 'never to leave
them, nor forsake them'. For he now came to them as their
guide, counsel, defender, comforter, the one-always-with-
them. This experience of the first disciples is also the experience of all modern disciples. This is the secret of becoming a
real person, of becoming truly human. With such new

insights, we can now begin to envisage how we, too, can overcome the deadening alienation of our impersonal culture today.

## Glasnost of spirit

Perhaps we are beginning to see that without knowing God personally, we are not capable of being persons as we would like to believe. Perhaps we are also beginning to see that we, too, are like Hilary, the parents of Sophy, or Evelyn. The gift of the Christ-child is needed by us all, to transform our unreality. It is only as we give ourselves to Jesus Christ, as we surrender ourselves, that paradoxically we become more ourselves, more personally the real 'I'. The reason is that in our vulnerability, Christ never absorbs us in the way a pagan god was believed to absorb the personality of the worshipper. Instead, he fulfils our unique personality far more than we ever dreamed possible. He frees me to be more like my true self—a real person, enhanced and affirmed by his recognition of my uniqueness, and loved by him.

However, we need to count the cost. To believe that only God can make us real persons means that we play for the highest stakes with our destinies. The motto of the Renaissance was, 'Live alertly.' But Jesus teaches us to 'Live freely,' and therefore to 'Live fully.' This is what Jesus taught in John's Gospel, in contrast to the deadly religion of his day:

> *If you hold to my teaching, you are really my disciples.*
> *Then you will know the truth, and the truth will set you*
> *free. I tell you the truth, everyone who sins is a slave to*
> *sin. Now a slave has no permanent place in the family,*
> *but a son belongs to it forever. So if the Son sets you free,*
> *you will be free indeed.*

The false religion of the leaders who confronted Jesus, and

who ultimately had him crucified, concealed a lust for power. Their religion gave them no sense of personal freedom, nor true happiness, any more than religious bureaucracy can do today. So they had to remain concealed as unreal people behind the religious masks they were wearing. An unreal society cannot provide us with happiness, if while it promises us Utopia it persists in living in unreality. Being set free from our absurdities and inconsistencies requires a certain glasnost of spirit, and the moral courage to face our failures.

## Freedom from the absurd society

The modern home is built of many conveniences and comforts, cemented together with pleasure and selfishness. The gadgets are fun, the automobile is new and glistening, mass education is available to study whatever one wishes, the career promises endless financial rewards in upward mobility, and holidays are to be had the world over. Yet beneath this thin veneer of satisfaction there is hostility and violence. We do not feel completely safe anywhere any more.

Too many people carry a daily load of fear and anxiety, and visits to the counselling profession are as common as daily visits to the supermarkets. Too many couples are getting divorced, while children live wounded family lives. Others are caught in the savage traps of drugs, alcohol, illicit sex, and compulsive habits. Material progress seems to mock us with the unhappiness it brings, and there is a sense of the destructive potential of emotional anarchy, ready to burst apart the structures of society.

We can see what glasnost—not political but emotional glasnost—might do for the societies of the West were it to be permitted. So instead of accepting glasnost with joy, the leaders of the West are beginning to sense that they might not be ready to permit it in what used to be called 'the free world', if its upheavals were to loose anarchy upon the whole world.

A whole family of absurdities possesses the modern world: an unrestrained idolatry of reason, a consuming love of impersonal machines, awe of the scientific and technical, an addiction to materialism and consumerism. Our culture has an indirect approach to living which detracts attention from the essentials of the human spirit. In place of the essentials, we give immense time and energy to roles, procedures, prestige and profits. Rarely do we perform out of a sense of duty, righteousness, or love. As a result, there is great wastage of human emotions and human lives. The systems of society are not human enough. The overheads are too costly to the human spirit. People are therefore left passively with the cowered spirit of a slave, or the rebellious spirit of an outsider.

That is why there needs to be a new honesty, in the West as well as in the East. We need a new openness to change—not for the sake of change, but to repent. For shame has been largely lost, and without a personal sense of shame, there can be no exposure of false values, false gods, personal conceits and false self-images. Clearly, the absence of a sense of sin—being personally accountable to God—or of being obligated in life, to act as a steward in living, is the cause of great disillusionment.

Freedom from absurdity, then, is really freedom from idolatry. To worship idols of our own making is really a deceitful way of worshipping ourselves. We think that we can manufacture all that we need, including our own happiness. But even a moment's thought shows us that we can never be totally self-sufficient. We inherit our traits of personality from family life, and we are also inheritors of our cultural history. We are not just the product of the self. We receive and share with all the human race. The boast of self-sufficiency is a delusion which we may worship. But without God in our lives, we are doomed to live in delusions.

We need to go back again to the child in us. In the very first consciousness of childhood, there is an awareness of some benign Spirit—God—who is watching over us, guarding our human condition. The poet Thomas Traherne tells us:

> *How like an angel came I down!*
> *How bright are all things here!*
> *When first among his works I did appear,*
> *Oh, how their Glory did me crown!*
> *The world resembled his eternity,*
> *In which my soul did walk;*
> *And everything that I did see*
> *Did with me talk.*
>
> *The skies in their magnificence,*
> *The lively, lovely air;*
> *Oh, how divine, how soft, how sweet, how fair!*
> *The stars did entertain my sense,*
> *And all the work of God so bright and pure,*
> *So rich and great did seem*
> *As if they ever must endure*
> *In my esteem.*

Wordsworth described this sense of awareness of God in childhood as 'trailing clouds of glory'. However, he adds:

> *Shades of the prison-house begin to close*
> *Upon the growing boy.*

The presence of God becomes blurred as we grow up, so that God is eventually eclipsed in many people's careers. For many people, it is in old age, in our second childhood, with our failing faculties, that the maker of our lives becomes apparent once more. Then perhaps we realize the ghastly mistake we have made, in worshipping ourselves and the idols of our own hands. Our freedom, then, lies in the spirit of the child. After all, it is children, Jesus tells us, who inherit the kingdom of heaven.

## Freedom from addictive living

If happiness is to exercise personal freedom, then our personal integrity also lies in such freedom. The absurdity of our society is that it gives us accolades for our accomplishments, when in fact many of them are simply addictions in disguise. In much of our lives we circulate between the addictions to control and to be angry. And when our addictions are forcibly removed, we experience restlessness as a withdrawal symptom. This happens when we are between jobs, or retired, or in some other significant change of life. Then we begin to see how hooked we are in the daily pattern of our lives, craving once more for the narcotic of normal routines and habits.

The addiction to control is apparent in the successes of many people. A friend of mine, who was the director of a large hospital, abruptly gave up his position in mid-career to reflect upon the essentials for a more authentic way of living. He remembered how as a young child he had recurrent dreams of falling into a deep, dark well. Chaos was always near the surface of his consciousness, and so he grew up with a desperate need to control. He accomplished this brilliantly in scholarship, so that his intelligence always kept things tightly under his control. By breaking free from the addiction to control, he helped to save his marriage, and became more concerned for genuine human relationships. He also gained a deep, new love for God, which replaced his insatiable quest for self-achievement.

Many people feel themselves to be homeless and without roots in the world today—like the Jews in the Middle Ages, or the Chinese now scattered in the world. Such groups often compensate for their deep sense of insecurity by the controlling instinct of choosing the 'right' profession. This gives them a sense of security in a chaotic world, only to find that there is a heavy price to pay. They live estranged lives, cut off from family, friends, and God, because of their addiction to work, money and prestige.

At the opposite end of the spectrum of emotional addiction is Margaret. Her drug is anger, because she is never in emotional control. Fear of her strong-minded mother kept her submissive, with all initiative taken from her. Now in mid-life, she weeps as she reflects that she may never bear children, for she has feared marriage as an initiative she could not take. Why has her career been so checkered and uncertain? Her timidity and lack of self-assurance has left her deeply frustrated, angry with her mother, angry with herself. Yet on the outside she appears as a milk-toast type of person. No one would suspect the volcanic potential behind her mild-mannered mask.

If we are searching for personal integrity and happiness, we must face up to the anarchy of the emotional government within us. Suppression of concealed anger will do us no good. As William Blake recognized:

> *I was angry with my foe:*
> *I told it not, my wrath did grow.*

Only the love of God can satisfy the insatiable hunger we may have for recognition, for acceptance, and for love. Only in Christ can the smouldering fires of anger be put out.

## Freedom from self-deception

Above all else, this is what causes our addictive lives: we deceive ourselves. We excuse our compulsive actions by explaining them as perfectly normal. 'Oh, it's only natural that

I react in the way I do.' 'But this is the way I was brought up—my home was perfectly normal!'

But is anything really normal? If we are all the children of Adam and Eve—either literally or symbolically—then is it not fair to say that there is actually something rather abnormal about the human family? Some say that we only have to be true to ourselves to succeed in overcoming our faults. In Shakespeare's Hamlet, one character is given this very piece of advice:

> *This above all: to thine own self be true,*
> *And it doth follow, as the night the day,*
> *Thou canst not then be false to any man.*

What a thin promise this is! A marriage between myself and my true self. But as the artists of human nature explored further they realized that this was just not possible. Robert Louis Stevenson depicts Dr Jekyll and his murderous alter-ego, Mr Hyde, as nearer to the truth about our schizophrenic tendencies. The Russian novelists such as Dostoevsky and Tolstoy explored deeper into the human psyche, to reveal the ugliness within our inner natures, as did Freud a generation later. W.B. Yeats saw more clearly than Shakespeare the impersonations we put on:

> *Those masterful images because complete*
> *Grew in pure mind, but out of what began?*
> *A mound of refuse or the sweepings of a street,*
> *Old kettles, old bottles, and a broken can,*
> *Old iron, old bones, old rags, that raving slut*
> *Who keeps the till. Now that my ladder's gone,*
> *I must lie down where all the ladders start,*
> *In the foul rag-and-bone shop of the heart.*

Yeats is telling us that, unlike Jacob who dreamed of a ladder up to heaven, we in the twentieth century have lost our ladder in the midst of secular unbelief. The reputable modern psychologist, O. Herbert Mowrer, admits:

> *For several decades we psychologists looked upon the whole matter of sin and moral accountability as a great incubus, and acclaimed our liberation from it as epoch making. But at length we have discovered that to be 'free' in this sense, that is to have the excuse of being 'sick' rather than sinful, is to court the danger of also being lost.*

The very nature of our sinful hearts is that they deceive us, and move us away from recognizing our self-deception. As a result, the true seriousness of sin is glossed over and forgotten. If we refuse to face the fact of our sinfulness, we will go on living a kind of fantasy half-life, prey to idolatry and addiction.

Without God in our lives, without realism about sin in our hearts, without God's forgiveness and acceptance, we are doomed to live falsely. If we believe that God is dead, then the mask is justified as the only reality that we can have. In all honesty, we can only take a flight back to the empty horror of Greek tragedy. The nineteenth-century philosopher, Friedrich Nietzsche, who coined the phrase, 'God is dead,' admitted: 'Every profound spirit needs a mask.' Or as Emerson also said of the artist: 'Many men write better in a mask than for themselves.' Oscar Wilde went further: 'The truths of metaphysics are the truths of masks.'

When God is dismissed, reality begins to collapse in on itself. There are no absolutes, there is no moral accountability, there are no universal truths, there are only appearances and masks. This is the 'weightlessness' of humanity that Nietzsche envisaged for a godless world. Freud concluded that the fate of the human race was to be *Unhappiness in Civilisation*, the title he proposed for his last great book. Freud's publisher persuaded him that he should change the title instead to *Civilisation and its Discontents*. His own first title was more honest.

The profound unhappiness of Freud gives us clues to the unhappiness of the modern world. Freud, like many today, was unhappy because of his addiction to controlling people and situations. Although he lived in Vienna, the great musical capital of the world, he explicitly tells us:

> *With music I am almost incapable of obtaining any pleasure. Some rationalistic, or perhaps analytic, turn of mind in me rebels against being moved by a thing without knowing why I am thus affected and what it is that affects me.*

Where rational understanding was not possible, Freud wanted no part of it. Music triggered deeply painful memories of his religious nanny, who loved him more profoundly than any love his parents ever gave him, so it reminded the child within him of her loss and of his profound sense of helplessness. Religion reminded him too painfully of the helplessness of his own childhood. Whether it was music or religion, Freud hated being swept off his own rational pedestal into the ocean of his own emotions.

Our acceptance of God in Christ is not the terrifying helplessness experienced by Freud, but a renewed awareness of coming to life in the love of God. It is a glorious exchange from the dreariness of self-deception to the new realism of living for Another, who knows us better than we can ever know ourselves.

The freedom to become more personally real comes only from true religion. This must be a faith that releases us for more genuinely human relationships. Only the God-man can give this to us. Only where perfect love meets us in the human condition, can such a possibility be open to us. When this happens, he redeems our wounded childhood, restores the image and likeness of God within us, and enables us by his Spirit—in residence in our lives—to be renewed in our motives and attitudes. Blaise Pascal was surely right when he observed:

> *There is no good without the knowledge of God; that the closer one comes, the happier one is, and the further away one goes, the more unhappy one is, and that ultimate unhappiness would be certain of the opposite (to him).*

# 8

# Happy Families

*What about my mother?*
*Everything has always been referred back to mother.*
*When we were children, before we went to school,*
*The rule of conduct was simply pleasing mother;*
*Misconduct was simply being unkind to mother;*
*What was wrong was whatever made her suffer,*
*And whatever made her happy was what was*
  *virtuous—*
*Though never very happy, I remember. That*
  *was why*
*We all felt like failures, before we had begun*
*I think that the things that are taken for granted*
*At home, make a deeper impression upon children*
*Than what they are told.*

T. S. Eliot

This quotation is from T. S. Eliot's play, *The Family Reunion*. The person speaking is Harry, the eldest son of a widowed mother. Harry is supposed to be coming home to take up his inheritance of the family estate, but the emotional pressures of his family force him to escape instead to become a medical missionary.

Then Harry discovers that happiness does not consist 'in getting what one wanted, or in getting rid of what can't be got rid of, but in a different vision.' It is the vision of seeing through the inheritance of family emotions, the release of burdens imposed by the past, the healing of memories long since buried in one's psyche. As the consciousness of his unhappy family grows within him, Harry unlocks the door to discover many family skeletons. He learns about his father's weak spirit, which caved in to his mother's strength; how his father committed adultery with Harry's aunt and tried to kill his mother; how his father deserted the family when Harry was eight years old. He understands 'the endless drift of shrieking forms in a circular desert' of his own boyhood emotions.

So as Harry now leaves home for good on his mother's birthday, he cannot really explain what is happening to him. He cannot say where he is going or why he has to leave, except to admit:

> *This last year, I have been in flight*
> *But always in ignorance of invisible pursuers.*
> *Now I know that all my life has been a flight*
> *And phantoms fed upon me while I fled.*

With newly-growing insights, Harry now knows 'that my business is not to run away, but to pursue, not to avoid being found, but to seek'. According to the bland sociological surveys of happiness, some sixty per cent of Americans are said to have responded that they were happy in their marriages. No doubt Harry's family would also have replied in the affirmative, indicating that they really did not know what happiness was. The many millions of divorces each year in the western world reveal the starkly real statistics of family unhappiness and breakdown. One of the saddest aspects of such family tragedy is that the statistics of divorce among Christians are not all that different from the rest of society.

## Marriage as walking in the presence of God

If being a real person implies consciously living before God, as we saw in the previous chapter, then the integrity of a man and woman living together needs the further consciousness of God in both their lives. Part of the problem of having a broken human nature is that we easily deceive ourselves. This is why it is so important to have soul-friends, who sometimes know us better than we can ever know ourselves. A true friend helps us to break through the barriers of self-deceit. A marriage partner can be a true soul-friend in this sense.

Western society has placed an exaggerated emphasis on individualism. This does not help us to live more truthfully with ourselves, but often traps us in our own false perceptions. Modern counselling techniques can mislead us even further, as we turn to our 'paid friend' for advice about our problems. The paid friend may well act from the impure motive that 'the customer is always right'! Such a friend can never help us honestly to confront the most painful aspects of our personalities.

This may help us to understand why it is that the family was never more expertly advised, psychoanalysed and researched, yet never has it fallen apart more dramatically than in the last generation. If we need God's help to enable us as individuals to taste reality, then our marriages need God even more. In our narcissistic culture, how can two people, infected with self-love, learn to love each other? This is where we need the dynamic of God's transforming presence. Some of the early church fathers used to argue that marriage was more of a sacrifice than celibacy. They said that denying the sexual urge was nothing compared to dealing with the male and female cross-currents that sweep through a marriage.

We can only freely give ourselves to someone else when we are 'real persons'—just as Harry was beginning to see in the play. True marriage requires us to show trust, loyalty, stability, permanence and self-sacrifice. None of us naturally has these qualities, since we are descendants of flawed parenting, in one degree or another. So how can we create a happy family, in reality? This can only come about through the person of Jesus Christ. He is the only person who can make it possible for us to become ourselves—to become a true person in an impersonal world. This is the true happiness of the human race, to be like Jesus in his humanity.

In turn, Jesus points us to the mystery of the Trinity, where each divine person is mutually self-giving, depending on each other and yet holding their distinct identity. This means that community and relationships are at the heart of God's being. If becoming a person can only arise through communion with God, then in the same way the marriage of two persons arises and is sustained only in God. So perhaps it is not so far-fetched after all to say that 'marriages are made in heaven'!

At this point, someone might rightly argue: 'I happen to live on earth, and it is here that I want to have a happy marriage!' That, argued an early church preacher, John Chrysostom, is why Jesus performed his first miracle at the wedding in Cana of Galilee. There he not only blessed the marriage with his presence, but he turned the water into wine. This miracle was a sign that Jesus is the miraculous source of joy in marriage. His presence transcends our best efforts to make relationships work. To this day, the Eastern or Orthodox church wedding service makes repeated allusion to this incident in the ministry of Jesus.

In our own marriages, full of human limitations, Jesus can multiply our sources of happiness beyond all recognition. I see it myself in my own marriage, and with our own four children. This thirty-seventh year of my marriage is the happiest yet, and hopefully the festivities will echo in some way through the generations to follow us.

Is this presumptuous? It was not to the Israelites in the

ancient world, as they recited Psalm 128. This is what they sang in praise to God:

> *Blessed are all who fear the Lord,*
> *who walk in his ways.*
> *You will eat the fruit of your labour;*
> *blessings and prosperity will be yours.*
> *Your wife will be like a fruitful vine*
> *within your house;*
> *your sons will be like olive shoots*
> *around your table.*
> *Thus is the man blessed*
> *who fears the Lord.*
> *May the Lord bless you from Zion*
> *all the days of your life;*
> *may you see the prosperity of Jerusalem*
> *and may you live to see your children's children.*
> *Peace be upon Israel.*

This hymn is full of symbolism. It is worth looking at each key word or phrase in turn. 'Blessing' is the happiness we seek, the ultimate good for our lives. To 'fear the Lord' implies both trust in God and obedience to his word and will. To 'walk in God's ways' reflects all the demands made on Israel by Yahweh, the personal God of the Old Testament. Psalm 25 echoes this thought by saying: 'Show me your ways, O Lord, teach me your paths; guide me in your truth and teach me, for you are God my Saviour.'

The vine was the symbol of fruitfulness or blessing, so a 'fruitful' wife was both a blessing to her husband and the bearer of his children. The olive, like the vine, was symbolic of all that was long-lasting. This included well-being and happiness, and also children. Children were recognized as a cause for long-lasting happiness, so they are included in the vision of the happy family. 'Around your table' converts every ordinary domestic meal, with the family gathered round, into another divine celebration of joy. 'Zion' is the symbol of God's heavenly presence, and 'Jerusalem' is its earthly counterpart. This is true in the same way that our ideal of what God can do in our lives is counterpoised by the actual human condition we find ourselves in.

When Old Testament psalms such as this one were sung in the New Testament church, they took on new meaning, although the old promises were still there, ready to be fulfilled in the lives of the worshippers. For the New Testament, 'Israel' is now the Christian church, and 'Zion' has visited earth in the coming of Jesus Christ. Our marriage is now to him, and a true Christian family is a tangible evidence of his kingdom, or kingly rule, on earth. The Orthodox church wedding ceremony includes the crowning of the bride and groom, which expresses the truth that marriage symbolizes God's rule on earth. Transformed by God, our marriages can be 'crowned with happiness'.

In reality, however, we often take each other, and God, for granted, and fail to see how our lives could really be. If we have not realized that the source of personhood and community lies in the being of God as Father, Son and Holy Spirit, then the odds are that we will have a low view of human life and of relationships. This is why we need to ask how marriage can be remade as God originally intended it to be.

## Marriage as a mystery

Why talk about the 'mystery' of getting married? If a man and a woman like each other, decide to settle down together and get married, what is so strange about that? Living happily ever after may not be so common these days, but as we have a much greater life expectancy, perhaps we shouldn't expect too much of only one marriage. Marriage is simply two people agreeing to get together.

This argument unwittingly follows the ancient Roman

attitude towards marriage. In Roman law, a marriage was simply an agreement between two free parties. Its famous dictum was *nuptias non concubitus, sed consensus facit*: 'marriage is not in the intercourse but in the consent.' This gave Roman women much greater individual liberty than women in other societies, even though they were still not legally regarded as a person in the way that men were. So the whole basis for marriage, then and now, was by mutual agreement between the two people.

In ancient Israel, the basis for marriage was to have children. At that time, there was no clear faith in an after-life, and so children represented the future hope both for the nation and for individuals in it. However, by the time of the New Testament this had changed. Because Jesus had died and risen again from death, the link between child-bearing and the future hope had been severed. The future hope was now in a full after-life. This is why the New Testament does not speak about child-bearing being the basis for marriage. From a Christian point of view, mutual agreement and the procreation of children are wrong reasons for getting married.

Because our culture devalues the reasons for getting married, it also has a limited view of the permanence of marriage. This again is true to our cultural roots. The Romans and Jews, with their different legal frameworks, allowed for divorce. The Christian vision of marriage is radically different. It sees that marriage is between two unique persons, whose personhood is acknowledged to come from God. Because of this view of persons, the whole concept of marriage being 'until death us do part' begins to make some sense.

In the teaching of Jesus, the permanence of marriage is never a legal matter. Jesus said that divorce was not allowed, 'except for marital unfaithfulness'. This does not mean that adultery is the one legal basis for divorce among Christians, because Jesus never encouraged his followers to think or act in legalistic terms. It is when we do not act and behave as

Jesus' followers that adultery can take place, followed by legal proceedings for divorce.

Such standards, which exclude the possibility of adultery and divorce, appear today to be impossibly hard, just as they did to Jesus' disciples then. Their response to Jesus' words was to despair: 'If this is the situation between a husband and wife, it is better not to marry.' Jesus' response was to say that not everyone can take this teaching. But the teaching does treat adultery and divorce with the seriousness it deserves. Unfaithfulness in marriage is a tragic betrayal of freedom within the relationship. Divorce can be the only outcome, unless grace and forgiveness can intervene.

Is marriage broken by death, leaving the surviving partner free to marry again? This was clearly the view in ancient Roman and Jewish times, but again this cuts across the Christian view. Paul the apostle taught that Christian love 'never fails', and as a result he does not recommend widows or widowers to remarry. He does not actually forbid remarriage for those whose partner has died, but his view seems to be that this is not God's purpose for marriage. It could be said that the hard teaching of the New Testament is hopelessly out of touch with modern life. On the other hand, it could also be said that the madness of modern life is hopelessly out of touch with God! It seems that our pursuit of happiness is proving to be much more radical than we bargained for. In marriage we thought we were just 'getting together'. Instead we find that we are joined together 'in Christ'.

Christian marriage is no less than the unity of two people, living out the reality of Christ's coming, death and resurrection in their lives together. True marriage is to experience the life of God's kingdom in our daily domesticity. 'This is a great mystery,' declares the apostle Paul, for it is so much more than two people getting together. Its profundity, he argues, lies in the fact that the unity of marriage enters into the mystery of the unity of 'Christ and his church'. In other words, marriage is a picture in miniature of the whole realm of the Gospel. The love, forgiveness, presence, power and friendship of God are all involved in marriage.

For this reason, a Christian marriage is a like an opened door, through which we see new visions, and walk out into a vast panorama we never knew existed. This is not magic, for it introduces us to new relationships of intimacy and friendship, rather than of impersonal power and fantasy. The apostle Peter speaks of the mutual submissiveness of wives and husbands, just as Jesus himself was submissive in his time on earth to death. Peter makes a strong connection between Jesus' attitude and the attitude we need to have. As Christ lived for others in his relationships, so we must serve others, not only in marriage, but in all our friendships and other relationships.

## Marriage as the power of intimacy

The creation account in the Book of Genesis contains a beautiful picture of God walking with Adam and Eve in the cool of the evening, in the garden they had created and cultivated in harmony with each other. This picture symbolizes the life of Christian marriage, in its intimacy of friendship. The word 'intimacy' means nearness, coupled with honesty, affection and love. The obsession with sex in our society has conditioned us to assume that intimacy must always mean sex. However, this limited definition robs intimacy of all its power and richness.

If we have no intimate relationship with God, then we can have no true intimacy within marriage either. This is an echo of the double commandment in the Old Testament to love God and others too. True intimacy begins when we cry out to God in the words of Psalm 27: 'My heart says of you, "Seek his face!" Your face, Lord, I will seek.' This explicit desire for deep communion with God runs right through the psalms, and it was also characteristic of the early Christian community. It is a call to us, too, to leave behind us the false self of our own independence, to celebrate how wholly dependent we are upon God. Because God never takes advantage of our intimacy with him, we know that we are safe, more secure, and truer in his presence than anywhere else. This intimacy with God helps us to reach out to our marriage partner in developing a more intimate life together. The result is that the friendship of a husband and wife should be the most intimate and most spiritual friendship two human beings can ever enjoy together.

This intimacy between a husband and wife is sexual, too. Sexual intimacy is a mirror in which we face each other, so that whatever weaknesses, fears and loneliness we have is reflected in sexual intercourse. This is where false sex can be devastating. Our weaknesses are ruthlessly exposed, without the true understanding and compassion of the other person. Obsessive lust can reveal the absence of true intimacy. Sexual intimacy can also be deceptive, suggesting a short cut to love and closeness, instead of being the climax of a whole environment of happiness in marriage. If one partner is always condemning the other, or if there is no gentle understanding, no gracious acceptance of the other, then sexual intercourse can be a violent thing, a form of legalized rape. It becomes a cause of further alienation, expressing the dependence of one partner and the lonely giving and resignation of the other.

Sexual intimacy, or the absence of it, can also point the way towards greater intimacy with God. Our sexual condition can help us to recognize how guarded we are, or how self-seeking, manipulative, or fearful we are, instead of being trusting, selfless, kindly, reverent and free in the bonds of love.

Intimacy is a living experience, rather than a state which we can arrive at. Intimacy is marked by cycles of encounter and withdrawal which ideally involve trusting in absence, as well as communing in each other's presence. Prayer, too, reflects the cycles of our intimacy with God. Sometimes we need patience and faithfulness, as we experience a desert of spiritual dryness. At other times God is so near us, surrounding us with his presence, that silence becomes the most appropriate way of enjoying the intimacy. Happy couples can take a long walk, without a word spoken, for the quality of silence says it all. Being silent in prayer is another dimension of being quiet with the other person.

Prayer, practised over many years, brings great changes in our person. Human intimacy does similar work in us. For a Christian, it should be almost impossible to judge which changes have been brought about by the marriage and which have been brought about by the love of God. Being in love with God helps us immensely to be in love with our partner.

Intimacy brings a deeper understanding of God and of our partner. One of the great passages of the Old Testament, Psalm 139, expresses the intimacy of God's love for us:

> O Lord you have searched me
> and you know me.
> You discern my going out and my lying down;
> you are familiar with all my ways.
> Before a word is on my tongue
> you know it completely, O Lord.
> You hem me in, behind and before;
> you have laid your hand upon me.
> Search me, O God, and know my heart;
> test me and know my anxious thoughts.
> See if there is any offensive way in me,
> and lead me in the way everlasting.

Such inmost knowledge can cut both ways. Without love it would be a terrifying experience. Or it could be the deepest level of intimacy and trust. This interchange between God's intimacy with us and our intimacy in marriage is beautifully illustrated in another Old Testament poetry book: the Song of Songs. At one level it celebrates sexual intimacy. From verse one, it plunges straight in with the fervency of love: 'Let him kiss me with the kisses of his mouth.' Later, in the interplay of presence and absence, the lover expresses her yearning for her absent lover:

> All night long on my bed
> I looked for the one my heart loves;
> I looked for him but did not find him.

And later: 'I called him but he did not answer.' The symbol of their intimacy is a garden. The bridegroom says: 'You are a garden locked up, my sister, my bride,' while the bride responds, 'Let my lover come into his garden and taste its choice fruits.' 'I have come into my garden, my sister, my bride; I have gathered my myrrh with my spice.' The conclusion is clear: 'I am my lover's and my lover is mine.' All these descriptions are given richly sensuous images. Scents and flowers, animals and trees, herbs and spices, as well as descriptions of the body, give a lyrical quality to the joy of intimacy.

Yet it is clear from other Old Testament passages that intimacy is also a quality between God and his people. In spite of the unfaithfulness of Israel to God, pictured in the prophet Hosea's broken marriage, God promises:

> I will show my love to the one I called 'Not my loved
>    one.'
> I will say to those called, 'Not my people,' 'You are
>    my people';
> and they will say, 'You are my God.'

Even more daringly, the prophet Isaiah says of God:

> As a bridegroom rejoices over his bride,
> so will your God rejoice over you.

It is no wonder that Christians later interpreted the message of the Song of Songs as the love of Christ for his bride, the church. Just as we derive our reality and uniqueness from the life of God the Trinity, so true human intimacy derives its reality and validity from God's love given to us.

## Marriage as the focus of trust

I have a friend who has had a miserable marriage, because his wife has never given him her trust. All the time she wildly imagines him being unfaithful to her in a thousand trivial ways. Although his marriage has become loveless, he has remained faithful to his wife, simply because he has experienced the faithfulness of God. This reveals the profound importance of trust in a marriage. Trust begins with personal integrity which is then shared in marriage too.

In the strictness of my own father's wisdom, he instilled into me a deep respect for the opposite sex, so that there was no physical play or caress with any women until after I had married my wife. What a rock this can be in the shaky marriages around us. Many people start their marriages wondering how many affairs their partner has already had, and wondering if they can compete with the possibilities that might threaten them in the future. In contrast, trust is like the precious soil in which a relationship can grow and put down secure roots. This trust can be blown away or eroded. If this happens, it can take generations before trust can once more be established in a family. So while trust is a creative agent, bringing about growth, distrust destroys and inhibits relationships.

Just as happy people create their own inclination towards further happiness, so trusting relationships create further trust. Faith in each other is a lifelong process, beginning with trust in God. We discover that our trust in the other person is founded in how we see him or her trusting in God.

What really makes us trustworthy is not ourselves, but our faith in God. The Book of Proverbs expresses this dependence on God for trust in this way:

> *Trust in the Lord with all your heart*
> *and lean not on your own understanding;*
> *in all your ways acknowledge him,*
> *and he will make your paths straight.*

We can begin to understand this vital principle when we reflect on how we have been emotionally wounded in the past. It is in the nature of a young child to trust, first the mother, and then the father too. As Unamuno, the Spanish philosopher, observed: 'The child is an infinite believer.' However, as we become more emotionally mature, we begin to see that we have been hurt by the inconsistencies of our parents. Mother loved, but she loved manipulatively. Father cared, but he did not give us enough time and attention.

The imperfections of our parents cause us to generate compensatory emotions that go on influencing us throughout life. One person might say: 'I am a workaholic, because I realize now I had to win points to get the approval I craved from my parents.' Someone else might realize: 'I dream and idealize a lot, because I was left so much to my own company.' These and many other distorting compensations we carry into our marriage, only to learn that our dynamics of trusting each other are profoundly affected by the way we related to our parents. In fact, this process often begins a stage earlier. A woman might marry someone who reflects the emotional responses she had with her father. A man might marry a woman who echoes his relationship with his mother.

How can we escape from the emotional addictions we carry in ourselves? It is only through a living faith in God that we can make a new start in our emotional life with each other. That is why the initiative of God towards us is so vital for a new start in life and marriage: 'We love God because he first loved us.' Only by experiencing the love of God can we both walk in his ways in our marriage, and trust each other with what God is doing in both of our lives. Paul the apostle gives us this assurance: 'He who began a good work in you will carry it on to completion until the day of Christ Jesus.'

## An essential unit in the community of happiness

If sexual intimacy mirrors our inner life, then family life mirrors our outer life. When one little girl was asked by her mother to pray before the family and some guests started eating, she became tongue-tied and shy. 'Just pray by reciting what I told you this morning,' the mother persuaded her. 'O God,' stumbled the little girl, 'why did I ask all these people for lunch? Amen.' How many little voices have been silenced to censor such embarrassing moments!

More seriously, our families are the index of our own personal and marital happiness. Unhappy homes have a tendency to breed further unhappy homes in succeeding generations. One young man recently told me about his emotionally disturbed mother, who attempted suicide but succeeded only in permanently injuring herself. In the last ten years of her life, her two teenage sons bore the brunt of her bitter and depressed spirit, while their father turned to the bottle and left them to it. To build up happiness in his life, this man will now face a long, slow rebirth of all his emotions, growing as a Christian through the support of others.

The world today desperately needs to build communities of love and peace. And yet the family is often the last place where people expect to find these qualities. The popularity of religious cult communities reveals the extent to which many people have turned their backs on the family.

In Christian thought, the family has always been seen as an essential unit in the community. The early church fathers said that the home should be a 'little church' or, as the New

Testament describes it, 'the church that is in your home'. It is in the home that Christian identity is formed and encouraged, and where Christian relationships are worked out. It is here too that the husband should act as priest within his own household, as the example and nurturer of his wife and children. The home provides a safe and secure place for children to ask their biggest questions about faith and to discover for themselves the love of God in Jesus Christ.

In earlier chapters, we saw that our emotional life is centrally important in the growth of our personal life and faith. So much of our unhappiness reflects disharmony in our emotions and relationships. Human selfishness is so real in all of us that it requires no social encouragement, as in the breakdown of marriage, to pass it on to our children. The collapse of love, and the growth of irresponsibility and indifference to children, will ultimately have to be paid for in society. Like the decline of Rome, collapse takes place when there is softness and corruption within the structure of the family. This is why every family needs to be renewed in its relationships—both to one another and to God.

Part of the problem is that the church over the centuries has given mixed signals about the family. The virtue of celibacy has been extended into the vowed life of monasticism and the single priesthood. Marriage has been seen in cultural rather than biblical terms, which has sometimes demeaned its God-given value. The mystery of sexuality has caused much confusion in the history of the church. Even the place and character of children have been misinterpreted. Until the seventeenth century, children were seen as miniature adults. Their emotional development was not understood as it is today.

Christian growth and education has often been seen as a job for the church, which has robbed the home of its crucial importance for its shaping of Christian character. Parents are not viewed as the primary educators of their own children, either in the world or in the church. So a radical reform of the Christian faith is needed, to bring about an essential re-focus on the importance of the family.

Whatever we think about child baptism, it did reflect a serious interest in the role of the family in bringing up children. Child baptism is the equivalent of circumcision in the Old Testament and in the modern Jewish household. It reinforces the idea of family solidarity. The baptism of the child is directly related to the faith of the parents. Children are baptized by the faith of their parents, and on no other basis. This is, in fact, highly realistic, relating to the way that families work. Social studies on the religiousness of adults have shown a very clear correlation between what they now believe and the spiritual environment of the home in which they were brought up. It is the loss of tangible, lively faith in the home that exaggerates the external, rationalistic and professionalized expressions of religion that are so deadening today. The loss of socializing the faith in the home leads to its loss in society at large.

As Harry says in the play with which we started this chapter:

> *I think that the things that are taken for granted at home, make a deeper impression upon children than what they are told.*

It is this environment of faith in the home that western society needs so desperately to recover. So what are some of its characteristics?

## Accepted and accepting

If kindness is giving territory to the uniqueness of other people, then it also reflects an assured sense of one's own identity. Earlier in the book we examined the essence of what it means to be a person. Christians, living as whole, remade people, are 'in Christ'. They know that their personal life is rooted in God the Trinity. Forgiven as a sinner, accepted by Christ, secure in God the defender come life or death, he or she is a person in the fullest sense.

Because of this profound sense of acceptance, we understand and come to terms with our own uniqueness. For most people, this is a great hurdle to overcome. Many of us handle our uniqueness wrongly. Either we become arrogant— 'Thank goodness I'm not you!'—or we feel threatened— 'Poor me, I am so lonely without you!' The joy of the Christian life is that God recognizes and accepts my uniqueness, much more than my parents could ever have done.

I vividly remember some years ago, sitting in a private room in Washington DC, expressing this to a high official in the White House. He wept for joy to hear this good news, when all his social connections (and at the back of it all, his own father) never gave him this recognition. The truth that 'Jesus loved me and gave himself for me,' was an incredible transformation for him. I become more myself by knowing and loving, and being known and loved by, God the Father, Christ the Son and the indwelling presence of the Holy Spirit. I learn the secret of happiness by being accepted by God.

This revelation enables us to show kindness to others. Once we are recognized and accepted by God, we become free to accept others. This can be true in spite of our inherited characteristics. We may have drunk judgmentalism in our mother's milk, or received a streak of meanness from our father. The Old Testament addresses this issue, quoting a piece of ancient near-eastern pop psychology:

> *What do you people mean by quoting this proverb about*
> *the land of Israel:*
> > *'The fathers eat sour grapes,*
> > *and the children's teeth are set on edge'?*
> *As surely as I live, declares the Sovereign Lord, you will*
> *no longer quote this proverb in Israel.*

Redemption and grace stop the flow of cause-and-effect in our parenting. As we think about it, a major cause of personal unhappiness in our lives arises from the ways in which we are quickly aroused to emotional resentment and prejudice against other people. This often takes place because their responses to us arouse the wounded feelings that our parents or other family members inflicted on us. We can judge this by the massively negative emotions aroused within us by little pin-pricks that we should be easily able to take. God's acceptance of us can put a stop to our inherited reactions.

In the New Testament, Paul frequently tells his readers to 'be kind to one another', 'consider one another in love', and so on. Without this awareness of 'one another', our personal relationships can be shadowy, superficial and unreal. Warm acceptance, and a compassionate and kindly approach, should be the marks of all that we give to others—and to our own children too.

## An environment of prayer

What are the true foundations for a happy family life? Some of them must be: for children to see their parents on their knees in the privacy of their own room; a spiritually disciplined life that is accepted as the daily norm; the absence of prolonged marital discord coupled with complete honesty with each other, a deep awareness of personal loyalty to God and to each other. None of these qualities may actually be talked about in the home. Instead, they are felt with the keen sense of personal radar which we all have.

In such an environment, children can begin to explore and learn to take risks. They can grow emotionally, exploring their own inner lives, living without fear. Later, if the child takes a definite stand as a Christian, there will also be a deeper challenge to struggle to change at heart; tackling inward dispositions as well as facing the difficult questions of faith. These inward struggles for wholeness as a person lie at the heart of what it means to be a Christian. Wholeness is not found in disorder, but in the tranquillity of an ordered life. This does not mean the absence of struggle and effort, but the absence of anarchy and emotional fogginess and confusion.

As a result, happiness and fulfilment in our lives never come ready-made, but the emotional environment we give to our children can contribute enormously to their growth. This environment, in turn, reflects the stage of maturity we have been able to reach as men and women in Christ. If we remain 'stuck' Christians, we cannot expect our children to become 'growing' Christians.

The prayer of parents is therefore profoundly important for authentic family happiness. The life of one of the great leaders of the early church, Augustine, illustrates this well. In spite of Augustine's youthful rebellion, he could never forget the prayers of his mother Monica for him. Immediately after his experience of Christian conversion, he went to tell her. He later recorded her response:

> *How she rejoices! We related to her how everything happened; she exulted and gloried and was now blessing you (O God) who are able to do above what we can ask or conceive, because she recognized that with regard to me you have given her so much more than she used to beg for when she wept so pitifully before you. You had changed her mourning into joy, a joy much richer than she had wanted and much dearer and purer than she had looked for.*

Ever since, 'a mother's prayers' have been almost proverbial of what authentic Christian parenting is all about. This bond of Christian love between Augustine and his mother transformed their already close relationship. A few days before Monica died, they stood together by the open window, looking towards the sunset. Just as Paul the apostle had once written of being 'transported into the third heaven' in a mystical experience of God, so mother and son were united in their desire for God. Their experience, as Augustine expressed it, took them:

> *Up to the sky itself from which the sun and moon and stars shine upon this earth. And higher still we ascended, by thinking inwardly and speaking and marvelling at your works, and we came to our minds and transcended them to reach that region of unfailing abundance where you feed Israel forever on the food of truth.*

Five days later, Monica died, but Augustine's memory was for ever engraved by the transforming reality of their communion together in 'delighting in God'. As I was typing these words, a young friend phoned to tell me about the wonderful summer holiday he had just had with his father. They had for many years been estranged from each other. He said, 'How wonderful it has been for us both to seek new understanding of each other as we have prayed together and sought healing from each other's wounds.' Prayer within a family takes on new focus and gives new prospects, when the love of God flows through it all.

## Family unity in suffering

We have to admit that happiness has no integrity unless it has burst through the clouds of sorrow. In the Old Testament Book of Job, Satan questioned the integrity of Job's faith in God because he had never suffered. In the same way, we can question the substance and basis of our happiness if it has not been put to the test of suffering. Without some element of suffering in our lives, it is difficult to distinguish a pleasurable life from a happy life. In chapter two we looked at the differences between pleasure and happiness. Pleasure can be no more than a gourmet's appreciation for delicacies, whereas a happy person can readily settle for a much simpler diet. Because of this, suffering is less of a threat to happiness, while it spells death to the pleasure-seeking life.

The truly happy person is not affected by many types of irritation and stress. One American psychologist surveyed 659 people to count up some 21,000 examples of everyday irritations and annoyances. Some of those questioned said that these annoyances disturbed their pleasure, though none would really add up to forms of unhappiness. Because they had no lasting influence, they were regarded as minor. Yet when such annoyances are compounded by the strains of family living, what would cause one family annoyance might easily add up to long-term unhappiness in another family.

Great suffering is usually identified with unhappiness for most people, if it also generates feelings of hopelessness, meaninglessness and despair. When these feelings become rooted in the family character, then unhappiness seems to be permanently established. But even in these circumstances, some people will discover inner resources to cope with suffering that would be intolerable to others. It is how we react to suffering, rather than the magnitude of what we have to bear, that distinguishes one person from another. For some people, it is precisely the impact of suffering that strengthens their character and faith in God. This was what Paul himself found in his sufferings:

> We also rejoice in our sufferings, because we know that suffering produces perseverance; perseverance, character; and character hope. And hope does not disappoint us, because God has poured out his love into our hearts by the Holy Spirit, whom he has given us.

Family suffering is a time of reckoning, when the genuine-ness of goodness and character, faith and hope, love and for-bearance with one another are most severely tested. There may be a suicide within the family. This must be one of the greatest afflictions parents or a marriage partner may be called upon to endure. As one father walked with me recent-ly by the lake where his seventeen-year-old son deliberately drowned himself, he spoke of being 'a man of affliction'. Di-vorce can bring far more anguish to young children than par-ents ever realize. Loving rebellious children unselfishly can bring great suffering to parents. Having to accept a Down's syndrome baby into a family can bring much anguish.

However, the ultimate test of family happiness must be found in the words of Paul: 'Godly sorrow brings repent-ance that leads to salvation and leaves no regret, but worldly sorrow brings death.' Brought before God, and left in trust before him, suffering can lead to creative consequences we will never regret. Failure to trust God leaves us in despair and ultimately leads to the grave. Paul added: 'See what this godly sorrow has produced in you: what earnestness, what eagerness to clear yourselves, what indignation, what alarm, what longing, what concern, what readiness to see justice done.' This response from his readers brought Paul joy. The by-product of suffering brought true happiness.

One of the greatest gifts given to the spirit of a family is the gift of being triumphant, transcendent, transformed by the creative consequences of suffering, endured and con-quered in the presence of God. In the early pages of the Old Testament, Joseph was cruelly treated by his brothers, who sold him into slavery. But years later he was able to tell his brothers: 'You meant it for evil, but God meant it for good.' Joseph saw that although he was given evil he was able to turn it into goodness.

This is also what the cross symbolizes. The cross shows us a union of opposites: returning forgiveness when evil was given; giving life when death was inflicted; showing love in the face of hatred. The crucifixion of Jesus was no naive rejection of the reality of evil, but a confrontation with evil that destroyed it. Evil was destroyed by the love, submission and death of Jesus. The cross is therefore the key to every family situation, as well as for all human history. God has gone ahead of us to provide, in the suffering and death of his Son, all the special grace we may individually need to cope with evil and the abuse of love. For this reason, our happiness is ultimately not in our circumstances, nor in our temperaments, nor even in our families, but in God alone. Happy indeed is that family that stands united in sharing such a common faith, hope and love in God. Suffering will not tear it apart—each member interpreting and reacting to it differently—but will leave it standing, united and transformed.

Suffering achieves its greatest act of transformation when it forces us to see how helpless we are, without God's help to overcome our own natural reactions of bitterness and despair. Suffering then becomes God's megaphone, as C. S. Lewis puts it, not merely to nudge our personalities towards God, but to warn us that our lives are wholly unreal unless God actually enters into them. Suffering at this level can then take on the character of being a positive good that was wholly unexpected, and previously unacceptable to us. It drives us home to the God who longs to turn our disasters into triumph.

# 9

# Truly Human

*Man never attains to a true self-knowledge until he has previously contemplated the face of God. The knowledge of God and the knowledge of ourselves are bound together by a mutual tie.*

John Calvin

*Know yourself and you will have a wholesome fear of God. Know God and you will also love God. You must avoid both kinds of ignorance, because without fear and love, salvation is not possible.*

Bernard of Clairvaux

*To know God and yet nothing of our own wretched state breeds pride; to realize our misery and know nothing of God is mere despair; but if we come to the knowledge of Jesus Christ we find our true equilibrium, for there we find both human misery and God.*

Blaise Pascal

As the quotations above show, there is a recurrent recognition by the great minds of the Christian faith that we cannot separate the knowledge of ourselves from the knowledge of

God. The two hang together. Yet, as we have seen, this is not the view of modern man.

Above the gate of the ancient Greek Temple of Apollo at Delphi was an inscription: 'Know yourself.' It warned people on their way into the temple of their position before the gods. 'Know that you are human and nothing more,' might express the spirit of this inscription. Since the gods were the measure of things, it was a warning against presumption and a call to the virtue of temperance.

Knowing who we are as humans has been one of the great vexed questions, searched after and written about down the centuries. Later thinkers, such as Socrates, isolated self-knowledge. 'Know yourself' became a form of self-examination, interrogating ourselves about our own nature. Plato argued that to know yourself was the very essence of knowledge. Yet it was so great a task that only Zeus, chief of the gods, could master it. Then Protagoras went further in saying that 'man is the measure of things', a saying that has become a secular creed for modern times.

However, since the Holocaust, the Jews and many other peoples have had difficulty in accepting this belief. If the Nazis of the extermination camps are the measure of our humanity, then we are left in darkness and despair. So what is it that we want to know? Do we want to classify ourselves zoologically? To know our ultimate destination? To search for the essence of our humanity?

The problem is that no amount of self-knowledge can entirely express our full humanity, precisely because we are incomplete beings. Animals occupy a closed, instinct-driven world in which they are complete, but humans are different. The presence and influence of other persons in our life make us more than we are on our own. This means that 'consciousness-of', is the human equivalent of 'instinct-in' in animals. We do not behave simply according to our instincts, but look to others to follow and imitate. Humans have a surprising degree of receptivity—or even gullibility—in being open to other people in their lives. Rather than being a finished product, we are always in a state of dynamic change: becoming more or less 'human', or 'personal', or indeed 'spiritual'.

Most people have some fear of death. But our deepest fears should be reserved for everything that keeps us from becoming more human, more personal, or more spiritual. So self-understanding cannot be merely a matter-of-fact. The essence of being human consists in the values we place on ourselves in being human beings. As a result, knowing ourselves involves much more than self-observation, or self-description. It also means assessing and judging our character. However, we have already seen how easily we can deceive ourselves, because of our broken humanity which connives with evil. So in fact, self-knowledge requires no less than revelation. We can only know the truth about ourselves from an outside source.

## The truth which shatters

In one of the stories of Flannery O'Connor, a black couple, Ruby Turpin and her husband Claud, are in the doctor's waiting room with a crowd of other patients. Mrs Turpin is a self-opinionated woman. She is never entirely comfortable until she has surveyed those before her, put them mentally in their places and seen herself rise to the top in doing so. She is in the process of doing this with her fellow patients, when her gaze is met with hostility by a fat, pimpled, nineteen- or twenty-year-old girl. The girl scowls as she raises her eyes from her book entitled *Human Development*.

Mrs Turpin remarks to the woman next to her that she once knew a girl who had everything a child could possibly want, but was still a spoilt, ungrateful brat. At this point, the book flies across the room and hits her. The girl hoarsely whispers: 'Go back to hell where you came from, you old wart-hog.' After the doctor, nurses and others have rushed to the scene to settle the girl with a syringe and have taken her off in an ambulance, Mrs Turpin goes home. But she feels dead inside.

Lying on her bed, the vision of herself as a razor-backed hog with warts on its face haunts her. 'I am not a wart-hog from hell,' she moans. One evening soon after, she goes out to the pig yard and hurls defiance against the Almighty: 'Go on, call me a hog! Call me a hog again! From hell!' A garbled echo returns to her. A final surge of fury shakes her and she roars, 'Who do you think you are?'

Then the evening sky begins to burn with a transparent intensity. A long purple streak spreads across the sky. As she looks in its direction, she sees in a way she has never seen before:

*She saw the streak as a vast swinging bridge extending upward from the earth through a field of living fire. Upon it a vast horde of souls were rumbling towards heaven. There were whole companies of white-trash, clean for the first time in their whole lives, and bands of black niggers in white robes, and battalions of freaks and lunatics shouting and clapping and leaping like frogs. And bringing up the end of the procession was a tribe of people whom she recognised at once as those who, like herself and Claud, had always had a little of everything and the God-given wit to use it right. She leaned forward to observe them closer. They were marching behind the others with great dignity, accountable as they had always been for good order and common sense and respectable behaviour. They alone were on key. Yet she could see by their shocked and altered faces that even their virtues were being burned away. She lowered her hands and gripped the rail of the hog pen, her eyes small but fixed unblinkingly on what lay ahead. In a moment the vision faded but she remained where she was, immobile.*

The fat, smug ego is the relentless enemy of God and of the happy life. It has to be put in its place. This can only be done by having a transformed imagination, something that can only come about through a 'revelation'. Mrs Turpin has to place everybody in her universe within a hierarchy: 'nigger', 'white trash', 'common', 'stylish', 'good'. She compared them all to herself, rather than to God. She was the measure of her own world. She thought she knew herself very well, but faced with God she realized that she knew virtually nothing.

Mrs Turpin did not know Bernard of Clairvaux's observation, that the first step into pride is comparison, and the subsequent steps lead into a self-focused life. Her sense of gratitude was not for God's gifts, but for her own virtues. Everything was absorbed by Number One, by Me. Nothing could penetrate that world of her unshakeable convictions but the humility of being exposed and shattered by the ugly girl with her outspoken rudeness, significantly called Mary Grace. Was it really God's grace after all, to use this unpromising Mary to break Mrs Turpin's view of things? It was this humiliating act that allowed God's revelation to take place in her heart.

## When God breaks in

But truth is often stranger than fiction. These two true stories reflect the way in which God can break into the closed world of the self. Paul was a young dentist whose dental practice enabled him to travel widely all over the world. He treated wealthy Canadian patients, as well as giving free treatment to the poor in Third World countries. He literally travelled from the Arctic to the Amazon in the course of one year, as well as attending his patients in downtown Toronto. Although his life was packed with drama, exciting travel adventures, wealth and personal idealism, yet in his heart he felt the emptiness of it all.

Then Paul began to dream. Although Paul usually forgot his dreams on waking in the morning, he began to remember his dreams and started to keep a diary of what he had dreamt. In one of his most vivid dreams, he saw a large aspirin bottle, labelled: 'Guaranteed to mask pain for a while!' The label also included a caption: 'Joy of life in remedy bottle.' It listed the drugs mixed together: alcohol, promiscuity, masturbation, materialistic attitudes, workaholism, thrill-seeking, attention-seeking, competitiveness, self-indulgence, etc.

Then Paul saw that he had emptied all the contents, and that the bottle was now empty. This posed a dilemma for him. What do you do when the pain is still there, caused by a low self-esteem, the absence of love in one's heart, the loss of personal assurance, and emotional confusion? In his deep distress at seeing the empty bottle, the words of Paul the apostle came to him:

> *Therefore, as God's chosen people, holy and dearly loved, clothe yourselves with compassion, kindness, humility, gentleness, and patience. Bear with each other and forgive whatever grievances you may have against one another. Forgive as the Lord forgave you. And over all these virtues put on love, which binds them all together in perfect unity.*

All this has been the consequence of Christ's death on account of our sins, and now of our experience of resurrection with him. As he awoke, Paul thought to himself: that's like the story of the Prodigal Son. 'When the son returned to his father, he was not rebuked, for the father knew that the son had already learned what was necessary now to trust the father. So he then clothed the Prodigal in his love.' That for Paul has been the gift of revelation, as the most significant turning point of his life, away from self to be moving now towards God.

The second story is about George, a medical man who gave up professional research to go into property business. With two partners, he created a vast financial empire of over half a billion dollars in some six years. But then disaster struck. The bank they had bought failed, and the property market softened. George lost everything, including his home. His religious faith, which had always been a rationalistic, brittle thing, simply broke apart.

In his despair, he began to see the truth about himself. He lived a very wilful life, and the fear of chaos had always haunted him from childhood. That was why he always had to be in the saddle, controlling everything within his reach with great brilliance and clarity of mind. He had always been able to anticipate the actions of others, especially his rivals.

It was only when he was confronted by God, broken and forced to give up his pride, that he began to see clearly for the first time the vast difference between living a self-directed life and living for God. He chose to move towards God rather than continue the journey deeper and deeper into the trap of himself. The Book of Psalms opens by describing this choice which we all make: the choice to move towards God, or away from him. Psalm 1 begins with a graphic contrast between two entirely opposed ways of life:

> *Blessed is the man*
> *who does not walk in the counsel of the wicked*
> *or stand in the way of sinners*
> *or sit in the seat of mockers.*
> *But his delight is in the law of the Lord,*
> *and on his law he meditates day and night.*

The 'blessed' person is the true worshipper, who turns towards God, while the 'wicked' follow their own devices regardless of God. This same choice is open to everyone. The consequences of our choice are serious, because God has made us in his image and likeness. If God made us for himself, as Augustine recognized at the beginning of his *Confessions*, then we will always be restless until we orient our lives towards God and rest in him alone. Augustine also said, 'Narrow is the mansion of my soul; enlarge it that you may enter in.' This is exactly what happens once God has met us, spoken to us, challenged our ways and thoughts, and revealed himself to us.

## Living in awe of God

Awe of God is basic to our lives. Without it, we live unhappily, unaware that God can make such a vast difference to us. Living without awe of God is like living as a beggar, when instead we could live in the king's palace as the heir. Our sense of awe wakes up when we begin to take notice of the mysteries of life. We begin to see that life is too vast and too mysterious to be flattened into cheap explanations.

Perhaps we have actually known that God has encountered us personally. Nothing else explains the conviction we have that we have heard him speak to us. Awed by this, we have naturally developed an awareness of the transcendent. In other words, we see beyond the material world to spiritual reality. We are reverent and grateful to God, showing him what the Old Testament frequently calls, 'the fear of the Lord'. This is a blend of real fear at the presence of God, combined with a powerful awareness of his 'otherness' to ourselves. Our sinful condition can also make us uncomfortable in the presence of God's moral perfection. Awe is therefore a natural human response to God. It helps to melt away the human spirit of arrogance and wilfulness, replacing them with gratitude for God's love and mercy. Our faith turns away from the search for personal security, which we all instinctively seek when we feel threatened, and leads us to abandon ourselves to God alone. As awe of God enters the core of our being, it becomes a whole new principle and power within our inner life, turning us towards God.

At times, the experience of awe before God may fill and dominate us completely. Our other values, arrangements, cares and concerns are eclipsed before the wonder of God's own presence with us. Then it is as if our fragmented lives are integrated, fulfilled and satisfied as they have never been before. With God as the absorbing focus of our lives, we can act and love, trust and desire, in ever-deepening channels that flow into the ocean itself. This in turn raises our relationships with others to a new plane. In place of our fears of other people, we now enter into their lives as never before. We discover that the mysteries in others, which used to leave us baffled and frustrated, now enrich our inner selves. We become enlightened in our relationship with God and with other people, and the Christian faith makes sense as nothing else ever could.

If the awe of God shatters our drive towards self-security, then the strongly growing desire towards closeness with God frees us from our drive towards self-fulfilment. We realize that the spiritual life matters infinitely more than all the material possessions or human status we once may have enjoyed. We are delivered from the me-generation to become aligned with God. Instead of seeking praise for ourselves, we begin to worship God. Self-abandonment leads us away from our own ego towards the unknown journey with God. We begin to take his word—the Bible—seriously, as it becomes our light and guide in our daily prayer and communion with God.

All of this means that we are inwardly nourished by the awe of God, and enriched by his closeness to us. Our human dignity of being made in the image and likeness of God takes on new meaning. The frenzied living for ourselves which we once used to value so highly now disappears before the far more vital longing to keep company with God in faith, hope and love. It is as if we are at home with God, for his presence and his friendship become a greater reality for us as we grow to know him better. There is a new openness in our inner lives, a new emotional effectiveness, a dynamic gentleness that is a blessing to others who are attracted to the serenity of spirit they see in us. We gain a new sense of loyalty, steadfastness and fidelity that are not our own.

Our relationships take on a completely new dimension as we deepen our relationship with God. We begin to sense with a keener sensitivity the needs of people around us. Events in our own lives take on a pattern, as if we really were walking with God in our midst, guided continually by his presence. We find ourselves saying words that truly comfort. We are able to see into the heart of things for other people. In these ways, our relationship with others grows and deepens, freeing them to be in Christ as they might long to be. We are able to enter into their sufferings so that they are no longer alone in their grief and pain.

We become something of a bridge between other people and God. Our personal involvement with them brings them the warmth of human love, while at the same time raising them up and beyond their problems to the love and healing of God. This new vision of life is in marked contrast to the blindness and insensitivity of self-interest and pride. To become a 'presence' for others opens up a new dimension of being, and at the same time we know the joy of God's presence in our lives.

## The fear of God's presence

Our instincts tell us to beware of abandoning ourselves to the care of someone else. Many men experiment with one sexual liaison after another, always afraid of what personal commitment might involve. Women can similarly become inwardly cold when a man gets too close to them. If this is a common experience sexually, how do we approach commitment to God? Many people never break through this barrier to faith, but carry on living in fear of self-abandonment. They create the illusion that they are the sum total of their own accomplishments. They believe that the approval of others only shows how great they are, seeing the loss of self-will as a form of rape.

Why is it that we fear to allow God to take control of our lives? For some of us it is because we have suffered from the emotional manipulations of others. There is evidence that Freud's father sexually abused his own children. To reject such a father is closely associated with the rejection of God, which is exactly what Freud did. For many people, disbelief in God is the closest revenge they can take against a manipulative parent. Freud himself vocalized the logic of this rejection:

> Psychoanalysis has made us familiar with the intimate connection between the father-complex and belief in God; it has shown us that a personal God is psychologically nothing other than an exalted father, and it brings us evidence every day of how young people lose their religious beliefs as soon as their father's authority breaks down.

The Christian psychologist Paul C. Vitz has said, 'From Freud's example, one has reason to suspect that behind many an atheist, agnostic or sceptic of today lies shame, disappointment or rage directed at the father. For many people, disbelief in "God the Father" is the closest to revenge that they can get.' Atheism is an expression of neurosis in a way that belief in a personal God can never be, for it is an irrational and emotional reaction to personal hurts and disappointments. It reveals distrust in other people and the impressions they convey about their God. That is why awe of the love and holiness of God must come first in the awakening of our hearts.

We need to throw open our entire personalities to God. If we find it difficult to trust others with our inner selves, then we will find it difficult to trust God. And yet this is just what we must do. It is much easier to trust God with selected areas of our lives, holding back from trusting him completely. We need to bear in mind the wise counsel of Francis de Sales, the seventeenth-century Bishop of Geneva, when he dedicated his book, *Introduction to the Devout Life*, to his close friend Philothea:

> *You want to live a life of devotion, because you are a Christian. Everyone paints devotion like an artist painted all his portraits of women, after the appearance of the women he loved. So one will prescribe spiritual disciplines and fastings perhaps as number one exercise, and neglect to deal with hidden anger within him. Another will focus on prayer and yet keep on saying all sorts of damaging things about other people. Another will place philanthropy on a pedestal and yet have a resentful, unforgiving spirit. Another gives generously yet never settles his debts.*

In a true relationship, God enters into every need and every area of pain in our lives. There is no blanket, generalized approach to God. He calls us by name, and his relationship to each one of us fits our own person uniquely. That is why there is such comfort and assurance in being related to his Holy Spirit. No one can be more intimate in his relationship with our spirit than God's Spirit. He is closer to the true core of our being than our own heart throb, nearer to us than our own presence. Yet he is the 'Holy' Spirit, and therefore other than ourselves. He is not be to confused with our human parents, as Freud and others have neurotically identified him. He is God, and not human. He is 'other' than our sinful selves, holy and righteous in all his ways. So Francis de Sales rightly adds:

> *Genuine, living devotion, Philothea, presupposes the love of God, and thus it is simply the true love of God.*

We allow ourselves to tune in to the personal life and love of God, not to an abstract principle or an impersonal deity. We begin to realize more deeply that knowing God and knowing ourselves is a single process. God introduces us to our true selves, so that we come to recognize ourselves, and our God for the first time.

## Faith, obedience and the Bible

True faith is not simply about thinking the right thoughts— although right thinking plays a part in our faith. The heart of true faith is that we enter into an experience of God which takes up our whole being, emotions included. In place of the animal, instinctive life, where we behave addictively, we start to realize how a relationship with God, who is above and beyond us, can transform our whole lives and our relationships. Paul recognized this when he wrote: 'I can do all things through Christ, who strengthens me'.

The more we surrender our lives to God, the more true we become to ourselves. This may seem like a contradiction. If I stop concentrating on myself, then surely I will lose out? In fact, we find that the reverse is true. As we give up concentrating on our selves, our lives begin to reflect more clearly what it means to be human, as God intended us to be. Our lives become richer and more free as we give ourselves to God and to others. Relinquishing the self leads to maturity of the self in God. One hymn expresses this vision of a transformed humanity in this way:

*Take my life and let it be*
*Consecrated Lord to thee;*
*Take my moments and my days—*
*Let them flow in ceaseless praise.*

*Take my hands and let them move*
*At the impulse of thy love;*
*Take my feet and let them be*
*Swift and beautiful for thee.*

*Take my will and make it thine—*
*It shall be no longer mine,*
*Take my heart—it is thine own,*
*It shall be thy royal throne.*

Abandoning ourselves to God does not mean that we become quiet and passive. To be a Christian means actively to follow Jesus Christ in faith, just as the first disciples of Jesus did. Discipleship is a dynamic, open and practical road for us to follow. Sharing in such a personal faith gives unity to the diversity of human beings, bringing us together with others. As we are inspired and taught by others, we find that the closer we get to Jesus, the more we share in common with those on the road with us.

In spite of the distances of time and culture, we also discover that we can learn from the great men and women of faith who lived before us. We can understand the heartbeat of Augustine, Bernard of Clairvaux, Julian of Norwich, Teresa of Avila, Martin Luther or John Calvin, just as we know our own fears and our longings. Jesus Christ is the common denominator between all Christians. This gives us a powerful sense of tradition, in the best sense of the word. We know that the roots of our faith can hold us firmly in all the insecurities of the modern world.

On a deeper level, we discover that our roots go straight down into the Bible, the word of God. Reading the Bible, we enter into an amazing new world of thoughts, prayers, stories and relationships. This is a world in which we can grow closer to God. But it can also be a foreign world to us, and to those whose faces are set against God it is a closed world. With our secular, modern spirit, we need to become attuned to the Bible, in order to appreciate its power to transform our minds and hearts. We can only become familiar with this new world by spending time in it.

Reading the Bible can be done, of course, out of a sense of curiosity. However, with God himself at the focus of our lives, we can rise above mere curiosity and focus in on the true purpose for reading the Bible. The Bible encourages in us the desire for God as the source of human happiness. This requires that we give up foolish, immoral reading, or reading to acquire power, or reading that is self-indulgent. The monks of the Middle Ages used to practise 'divine reading', which meant that they expected their lives to be transformed as a result of what they read. We too need to read the Bible in our hearts, rather than simply to discover facts or satisfy our curiosity.

The Bible is the law of God, which encourages us to obey God and to live for him. The Bible shows us the will of God, which we can accept with great delight. In the Bible, we discover the revelation of unseen things; mysteries which we approach in awe and reverence. As we read this book, like many before us, we cannot depend on our own strength or understanding, but instead need to be humble and allow God's Spirit to instruct and guide us. Jeremiah, the Old Testament prophet, assures us of God's promise: 'You will seek me and find me when you seek me with all your heart.' And Jesus once said: 'If anyone loves me, he will keep my word.' This is the key to reading the Bible.

## Reading from the heart

A Roman Catholic scholar, Hans von Balthasar, recently observed that the weakness of his own church in the past was that it neglected the Bible, while concentrating too much on the teaching of the church. On the other hand, Protestants, he observed, have been too busy trying merely to understand the Bible. In place of these two extremes, we need to be like Mary, Jesus' mother, who received the word within her, so that she actually gave birth to the Word of God. The faith of Mary sets the pattern for all true believers. It is not how much we read, nor even what we understand in our heads, but receiving in the same spirit in which the scriptures were first written. To understand what David says, we must listen to his spirit. To read Paul's letters, we seek his spirit too. We try to listen to the Bible, hearing what God is saying to us through it.

Faith and obedience to God go hand in hand with personal involvement in the Bible. Obedient reading of the Bible means that we do not read it selectively, choosing only the passages that reinforce our moods and temperaments. True faith in God means that I distrust myself in order to trust in God. In this way, self-distrust—or humility—and obedience go together and reinforce each other. Humility enables us to be wise about ourselves and to learn to resist our weaknesses more firmly. This then leads us to trust in God and to obey him rather than ourselves.

Good literature requires good readers, who can discern its qualities and receive them. In the same way, the moral value of the Bible generates spiritually discerning readers, who see its power to transform their lives. 'Good reading' of the Bible enlarges our capacity to receive more of its depth and riches, to see with other eyes the wondrous things that God reveals to those who 'have eyes to see, and ears to hear'. This also comes into being as we couple reading the Bible with prayer. Prayer opens our lives to all of God's word and will. For it is prayer that enlivens our attitude towards the Bible, and that keeps open the channel of communication between ourselves and God. We are open to receive; open to respond.

We respond to God from the heart. This is the focus of

the Bible, which tells us that while 'man looks upon the outward appearance, God looks upon the heart'. It is specific-
ally the heart that God calls to turn back to him. One Bible
passage says: 'If you seek the Lord your God, you will find
him if you look with all your heart and with all your soul.'
And one of the prophets says: 'Your hearts must be fully
committed to the Lord our God.' This is also echoed in the
Book of Psalms:

> *Teach me your way, O Lord,*
> *and I will walk in your truth;*
> *give me an undivided heart,*
> *that I may fear your name.*

The heart is above all the place of encounter between a
human being and God. It is the sphere of the mind, of our
thinking faculty, as well as of our affections and our will. It
represents the core of the whole person—feelings and emotions, as well as mind and spirit. It is the source of all our passions and desires. It is also the source of deception. As
Jeremiah put it: 'The heart is deceitful above all things and
beyond cure. Who can understand it?' In answer to this
question, God said to Jeremiah: 'I the Lord search the heart
and examine the mind, to reward a man according to his conduct, according to what his deeds deserve.'

We are reluctant to open our hearts to God and to receive
his word within our hearts, and this is well understood by the
Bible's writers. By entering the world of the Bible, we soon
become familiar with all the obstacles used to keep God at a
distance: avoiding the truth, conflicts in personal relationships, self-alienation, hardness of heart, and, above all,
pride. The human heart is very possessive. It wants to control, and fiercely resists its own capitulation. So we struggle
to avoid giving God our whole heart. The paradox is that it
is only in our self-surrender that we are truly blessed. John
of the Cross, the mystical writer, expresses this truth:

*In order to experience pleasure in all,*
*Desire to have pleasure in nothing.*
*In order to arrive at possessing all,*
*Desire to possess nothing.*
*In order to arrive at being all,*
*Desire to be nothing.*
*In order to arrive at knowing all,*
*Desire to know nothing.*

This is why Paul the apostle could say: 'May I never boast except in the cross of our Lord Jesus Christ, through which the world has been crucified to me and I to the world.' Christina Rossetti, the Victorian poet, struggled with these words of Paul in her desire to overcome the world, the flesh and the devil. In one of her poems, she feels sad, weary and footsore, but then sees that her sufferings are nothing compared to the sufferings of Jesus. At this point, the devil accosts her with further arguments:

*'Thou shalt win Glory.'*
*'In the skies,*
*Lord Jesus, cover up mine eyes*
*Lest they should look on vanities.'*
*'Thou shalt have Knowledge.'*
*'Helpless dust!*
*In thee, O Lord, I put my trust:*
*Answer thou for me, Wise and Just.'*
*'And Might'—*
*'Get thee behind me. Lord,*
*Who has redeemed and not abhorred*
*My soul, oh keep it by thy word.'*

This is the secret of the heart's loyalty to Christ: to keep listening to God. Jesus proved this during his temptation by the devil in the desert at the outset of his ministry. He resisted temptations by relying on the word of God. The great

call to Israel in the Old Testament is the *shema*, which means
'hear'. The *shema* is still repeated daily by devout Jews the
world over: 'Hear, O Israel: the Lord our God, the Lord is
one. Love the Lord your God with all your heart and with all
your soul and with all your strength.' Jeremiah also under-
lines the importance of listening to God: 'Listen to my voice.
Then I shall be your God and you will be my people.' Solo-
mon wisely asked God: 'Give your servant a listening heart
so as to be able to discern.' This appeal to hear God continues throughout the Bible: 'All who are on the side of
truth,' Jesus told Pilate at his trial, 'listen to my voice.'

As we listen to music, we allow it to flow over us, and we
enter into the atmosphere it conjures up. In the same way, as
we trust God with our whole heart, we begin to listen to him
appreciatively, intelligently, and with genuine willingness.
This listening to God also has a future dimension. The Song
of Songs contains these words: 'I slept but my heart was
awake.' To listen is also to expect. We wait in anticipation of
his future coming back to earth. Like love, listening to God
has its own reason for being. It implies a whole-hearted self-
abandonment, an unpossessiveness that never sleeps, never
stops listening, obeying and loving.

## Gentleness of spirit

The wholeness of the Christian life lies in surrendering,
dying, and rising to new life in Jesus Christ. This wholeness
comes about when we realize for ourselves that we need
Jesus as our rescuer and companion, redeemer and friend
for life's journey. Because each of us is unique, we will never
really know ourselves. We are a mystery to ourselves, and it
is only God who sees into this mystery, knowing us
completely.

Because of this, we surrender to God our self-knowledge
and our self-significance, all the things we struggle so

desperately to hold on to in our egoism. Then we can begin to understand what Paul means by being 'in Christ'. This is not as mystical as it may sound, for it means that Christ has priority over our lives, our careers, our relationships, and over the meaning of our identities. As we reorient our lives away from ourselves and towards God, we discover that we are oriented towards joy, happiness and well-being. We become authentic people, for we are in contact with the Original (*authentikos* is a Greek word, meaning 'original'). The genuine person measures up to true personhood in Christ.

Personal authenticity coincides with a holy life. We can never achieve a perfect life by our own efforts, but as we rest in God's love, seek God's will, and identify with God's life, then we are holy as he is holy. Purity of life, in our thoughts and attitudes, becomes our quest. We grow in prayer, because friendship with God becomes our dominant concern. We seek God, serving others to the utmost, in care, compassion and the desire for healing and encouragement. Stretched beyond ourselves, we rest in our communion with God.

Our communion with God produces new qualities of life in us. We turn to God in worship, thanking him daily for all things, pleasant or not. We learn a new quality of silence. Silence is the garden of the soul, where space and time are devoted to the presence of the Lord, and a deeper understanding of the truths of God. We gain a wide vision of God, so that narrowness and meanness are excluded from our relationships with God and others. A wide view of God gives us a perspective on life that is not cramped by our everyday circumstances. This allows us to be patient in the face of the daily frustrations of life. Detachment from the everyday gives us a higher view of our lives. If we want to see the night sky, we have to leave the bright lights of the city behind and climb a darkened mountain. Only self-detachment has this sort of clear vision.

Out of these qualities, gentleness becomes the sustained

environment of our inner lives. Jesus once said, 'I am gentle
and humble in heart.' The New Testament calls us to follow
Jesus in this, by being 'completely humble and gentle'.
Gentleness is the fruit of obedience and listening. If I refuse
to listen, violence possesses my soul, and I live in stress and
stubbornness. I plan my own life, impose my own desires,
and disrupt others' interests. I refuse to hear anything that
might disrupt my own plans. But when I listen, I become
gentle. I give space for others, and allow others' plans to
come before my own. I share kindness in order to let others
be themselves.

The gentle spirit hears new things and sees new perspectives beyond those of self-interest. In fact, the gentle spirit
hears 'the still small voice' of God in ways that the noisy temperament will never hear. So gentleness becomes a special
way of hearing others, and of hearing God in stillness and solitude. Gentleness becomes an important mark of our spiritual ministry to others. As Francois Fenelon prayed:
'Gentleness is thy work, my God, and it is the work thou
hast given me to do.' Gentleness is a major feature of spiritual growth and wholeness, and we should therefore cultivate
it seriously. Peter once said that the true inner self is 'the un-
fading beauty of a gentle and quiet spirit, which is of great
worth in God's sight.'

There can of course be a facade of gentleness that is not
genuine. But the test of true gentleness is that it relies deeply
on the love of God, and is therefore closely associated with
confidence in God. Confidence in God allows us to be gentle
with others as we no longer struggle to assert our own plans
and willpower over them. In the ancient Greek language,
the word for 'confidence' is *parrhesia*. This is made up of
two words: pan, meaning 'all', and rhe, the root of the word
'to speak'. This expresses the confidence and boldness of
having said it all. Everything has been expressed and exposed before God, so there is nothing to hide, and no concern about being made vulnerable. This is why the first

Christian believers were able to proclaim the good news about Jesus so fearlessly. The writer of the Book of Hebrews expresses Christian confidence in this way: 'Let us then approach the throne of grace with confidence, so that we may receive mercy and find grace to help us in our time of need.' Because of Christ, we 'have parrhesia towards God', says another New Testament passage. This means that 'whatever we ask of him, we shall receive it' according to his will.

This holy boldness in turn reinforces our gentleness of spirit. We do not need perspiration if we have inspiration. We do not need to be aggressive and anxious if we have open access to the Father, the indwelling presence of Christ in our hearts, and the guidance of the Holy Spirit. Instead of being so pushy, ambitious and restless, we can place our trust and confidence in God. This means that there is no need for the barrenness of a busy life. Instead, our identity lies in Christ, not in our function before others. Gentleness keeps us from being caught up in the illusions of the world. We are not homeless or alienated, because we are indwelt by the Father, Son and Holy Spirit, who give us this gentleness of spirit. This indeed is the whole, happy and joyful life of the children of God.

The spiritual writer, Francois Fenelon, had this to say about Christian gentleness:

> *Don't lose any opportunity, however small, of being gentle towards everyone. Don't rely on your own efforts to succeed in your various undertakings, but only on God's help. Then rest in his care for you, confident that he will do what is best for you, provided that you, for your part, work diligently but gently. I say 'gently' because a tense diligence is harmful both to our heart and to our task and is not really diligence, but rather over-eagerness and anxiety.*

*Soon we shall be in eternity and then we shall see how little it mattered whether some things got done or not; however, right now we rush about as if they were all-important. When we were little children how eagerly we used to gather pieces of broken tile, little sticks, and mud with which to build houses and other tiny buildings, and if someone knocked them over, how heartbroken we were and how we cried! But now we understand that these things really didn't amount to much. One day it will be like this for us in heaven when we shall see that some of the things we clung to on earth were only childish attachments.*

*I'm not suggesting that we shouldn't care about these little games and trifling details of life, for God wants us to practise on them in this world; but I would like to see us not so strained and frantic in our concern about them. Let's play our childish games since we are children; but at the same time, let's not take them too seriously. And if someone wrecks our little houses or projects, let's not get too upset, because when night falls and we have to go in-doors—I'm speaking of our death—all those little houses will be useless; we shall have to go into our Father's house. Do faithfully all the things you have to do, but be aware that what matters most is your salvation and the fulfilment of that salvation through true devotion.*

# 10

# The Truly Happy Life

*Beatitude is, in my opinion, a possession of all things we believe to be good, from which nothing is absent that a good desire may want. Now the one thing truly blessed is God himself. Whatever else we may suppose him to be, this pure life, the ineffable and incomprehensible good, is Beatitude. He is the one lovable who is always the same, rejoicing without end, in infinite happiness.*

Gregory of Nyssa

We saw in the first chapter how we can understand more about ourselves according to our type of personality. We looked at ourselves in terms of our compulsive traits, seeing the weakest aspects of our inner lives. Later in the book, several of these personality types have been illustrated in the stories of people who have revealed their inner thoughts and feelings and their struggles with themselves. With them, we long to believe that our expectations of happiness can be transformed, so that we can become happy in a way we never thought possible. This chapter looks at how our personalities can experience 'more than we can ask or think', as Paul the apostle once expressed it.

The essence of God is that he is personal. No other religious faith communicates this truth about God. This makes it possible to believe that God can relate to us, and that he

can reach out to us and transform our nature. When we see
our old personality being changed, then our happiness is
truly a transforming happiness. Christ has come into the
world. Christ has died for our sakes. Christ has risen again.
Now by his Holy Spirit he lives in our innermost selves, so
that we become transformed into his image and likeness.
This means that in many ways we become like God, and yet
in others we remain unlike him. God's Spirit is called the
'Holy' Spirit, to remind us that we are not to be confused
with his unique identity, nor are we perfect as he is perfect.
We remain sinners, while he is the Holy God. However, as
'Spirit', he is able to enter into our spirits. He becomes
closer to us than any human friend could ever be.

The Christian faith teaches that all my human nature
needs to be redeemed by Christ. One early writer, John of
Damascus, said: 'Had there been anything of me not assumed (by the Word of God) it would not have been saved'.
We believe that Jesus Christ did assume, or take on, our
human nature in every part. However, he did this without
falling into the compulsions, the defence mechanisms, and
all the sinfulness and deceitfulness of our own lives.


## Jesus is the happy life

The truly happy life—life as God intended—became reality
in the earthly life of Jesus Christ. We can test this if we com-
pare the human character of Jesus to our own personalities,
as we saw them in chapter one. The perfectionist, as we saw,
tries to do things perfectly because of his or her compulsive
desire to avoid showing anger. Jesus was different. He could
be angry when he saw injustice and evil. He spoke of being
perfect, but he saw perfection as abandoning ourselves to
God, seeking to do his will. While the human perfectionist
judges others, Jesus accepted those around him, especially
those who were judged and despised by others. Jesus clearly

accepted others, rather than rejecting as we do. The perfectionist is an anxious person, always afraid of what may go wrong. In contrast, Jesus said: 'Do not worry about your life, what you eat or drink; or about your body, what you will wear.' The perfection Jesus spoke about is in marked contrast to the obsessions of the perfectionist.

The giver identifies strongly with Jesus as the servant of others. However, as we saw, this type of personality hangs on to others, looking to them for affirmation and praise. This was not the way in which Jesus was a giver. The secret of Jesus' great kindness to people was that he helped them and yet always gave them space to be themselves.

The performer, like the giver, identifies with Jesus' call to his disciples to work with him in service. However, Jesus never called people to work for work's sake. Instead, he called them to 'follow me!' This call was to himself. It was not a call to workaholism and a sense of achievement, but to an abiding relationship with him. Achievers fear failure, and yet Jesus' life was a failure by most human standards. He spent some thirty years in an obscure village, and only three short years in his public ministry, which was misunderstood by the great majority of the people who saw and heard him. Performers also crave for power. But Jesus, faced by temptation in the wilderness, resisted the three temptations to seek power. He ended his life by hanging, powerless, on a cross, saying, 'Father, into your hands I commit my spirit.'

The romantic is attracted to Jesus because he seemed to be a great charmer who attracted others. However, while the romantic is afraid of being ordinary, Jesus was so ordinary that even his own family could see nothing special about him. Jesus was so steeped in ordinariness that most people never recognized him to be their Messiah. Romantics can suffer tragically, because they are unrealistic about themselves. But Jesus' sufferings were experienced on behalf of humankind, not because Jesus was unrealistic about himself.

The observer loves knowledge for its own sake, but Jesus

stood against this attitude. He was constantly in conflict with the religious and legal authorities of his day. The trap of the observer is to be distant from the needs of others. This is why the experts of Jesus' time criticized him for healing the sick on the Sabbath, accepting social outcasts, or infringing the fine points of the law. Jesus rejected this. He spoke in stories or parables, so that the simplest might understand if they had a heart to see and hear. Above all, Jesus taught the truth with his own life.

The responsible show great loyalty, but they also make great demands upon other people. They like their lives to be organized and tidy; they hate paradox and mystery. It was people like this who crucified Jesus, because they hated the mercy he showed to the common people. They saw Jesus as a threat to their legalistic religion. Their self-righteousness was a cover for their fear of disorder. They felt profoundly insecure in the face of something that was so personal and intimate. The apostle Paul was later to fight this 'letter that kills', in order to communicate the Spirit who gives life. Our transformation by God does not come about through the law, but because of God's love and grace. This is why Jesus could forgive a woman caught in adultery, when the legalists were ready to stone her to death.

The fun-lover likes to have a good time. Jesus also enjoyed himself, to the point where he was criticized as 'the friend of tax-collectors and sinners'. At a wedding at which the wine ran out, he miraculously turned the water into wine. One of the marks of Jesus' discipleship is a great sense of joy. However, the fun-lover is motivated by a fear of pain, which he or she tries to escape. In contrast, Jesus never ran away from trouble, nor left people in their sickness or sorrow. Instead, he healed the sick and comforted the brokenhearted. Jesus always faced the human condition head-on. Jesus did not hide behind laughter, in the way that the fun-lover does. Instead, he used wit appropriately, as in some of his parables. He also warned his disciples of future persecution, hardship, and the judgment that lay ahead of them. The realism of Jesus is a strong counterbalance to the superficiality of the fun-lover.

The strong boss, who faces violence head on, is afraid of weakness. Yet the secret of Jesus' life was that he was wholly submissive to his Father. His humility was no weakness, but absolute strength. One of the positive aspects of strong bosses is that they fight against injustice, and show themselves to be externally strong characters. Jesus, too, confronted injustice and corruption, to the point of driving the money-changers and merchants out of the temple court. His language was certainly not watered down when he charged the scribes and Pharisees with being 'white-washed sepulchres', 'blind guides' and even 'a brood of vipers'. There was no compromise with Jesus against all injustice and dishonesty. Yet at heart Jesus was not a strong boss. Strong bosses are ruled by their aggression and assertiveness. Jesus instead spoke of giving his disciples peace. This would be a peace unknown to this world, and which this world cannot give.

Finally, the mediator is patient. Jesus, too, encouraged those who heard him to wait in patience for the promises of God. God's purposes will be fulfilled, but the times are in his hands. The temptation of the mediator is to be lazy, and this is where the mediator and Jesus part company. Mediators also lack self-assurance, something that Jesus promised to give to all those who follow him. So in contrast to the mediator, who fears and avoids conflict, the followers of Jesus are fully equipped to fight the good fight of faith.

## God's prescriptions for happiness

Some people might object to being classified as a personality 'type'. After all, I'm me! Others identify more easily with the types we have looked at. They do not feel so defensive, but they may well feel uncomfortable about these new insights into their personal weaknesses. In either case, we need to recognize that the uniqueness of the person can really only be handled and sustained by God. Because we have been created in his image, he is the source of our personhood.

Individually, we are not up to the task of trying to handle our own uniqueness. Either we are arrogant, saying, 'Thank God I am not you!' Or we say, 'Poor me, I am so anxious, because I am alone, unrecognized, even by those who should know me best.' And so we tend to wobble between these two extremes in seeing our uniqueness. We are incapable of accepting and handling our unique dignity and character. In fact, the defences and addictive attitudes described in the first chapter only illustrate the false ways in which we deal with ourselves. We seem to be unaware of our true essence, unable to express that essence authentically, and therefore unable to embody who we really are in the sight of others.

The transformation which God works in our lives is that we become real people. We have true relationships with other people, because we are becoming more like Jesus Christ. This is the great paradox of the Christian life, that the more we abandon ourselves to God, the more genuinely real and unique we become as individuals. This is the polar opposite of those who have been brainwashed by an ideology, and who lose all sense of being individuals. Jesus does not destroy our person, he always enhances and deepens it.

This discovery of our true selves is most strongly expressed in the sayings of Jesus known as 'the beatitudes'. Each beatitude begins with the word 'blessed', which could also be translated as 'happy'. True happiness, according to Jesus, comes about when we turn away from the commonly-accepted prescriptions for happiness to abandon ourselves to God.

> *Blessed are the poor in spirit,*
> *for theirs is the kingdom of heaven.*
> *Blessed are those who mourn,*

*for they will be comforted.*
*Blessed are the meek,*
*for they will inherit the earth.*
*Blessed are those who hunger and thirst for*
  *righteousness,*
*for they will be filled.*
*Blessed are the merciful,*
*for they will be shown mercy.*
*Blessed are the pure in heart,*
*for they will see God.*
*Blessed are the peacemakers,*
*for they will be called sons of God.*
*Blessed are those who are persecuted because of*
  *righteousness,*
*for theirs is the kingdom of heaven.*

These beatitudes do not signal the elimination of the self, but the integrity of the self in God. Jesus was describing a fulfilled life which could only grow to be better and better. The truly happy life has the resources of a great river that flows endlessly, bringing strength and hope to ourselves and to others. One of the psalms speaks of the abundance which God gives to us:

> *They feast on the abundance of your house;*
> *you give them drink from your river of delight.*

This life is eternal in character. Paul, writing in the New Testament, said:

> *I always pray with joy being confident of this, that he*
> *who began a good work in you will carry it on to com-*
> *pletion until the day of Christ Jesus.*

It is no wonder that one psalm-writer could sum it all up by saying:

*Blessed is the man whose God is the Lord.*

The beatitudes of Jesus show the way in which we can experience transforming happiness in our own lives. The beatitudes were never meant as a sort of new Ten Commandments, which we have to strive to keep. Instead, they express the source of our personal well-being and blessing. The beatitudes are counter-cultural, because they correct and challenge the ways in which we understand happiness. They come up against our distinctive types of personal defence and weakness. They are not simply beautiful, poetic sayings. They rebuke and correct us, calling us to break with our old way of life.

If we reflect further, we can also see that each beatitude addresses the weaknesses of the different types of personality we looked at earlier. Not only do the beatitudes speak to these types, but they also promise the gifts of God to redeem us from ourselves. We will look at each beatitude in turn.

## Blessed are the poor in spirit

The perfectionist has to learn that Jesus was 'poor in spirit'. Where we may boast of our striving for perfection, Jesus had only humility. He calls us to follow him in humility. When we come to the end of our own virtues and realize our inner poverty, it is then that we can start to experience 'the kingdom of heaven' in our lives. We start to live under God's rule. To rediscover the life of Jesus in our own times is to come before him, poor and naked, and to live his life, not ours. Unless we can see the profound radicalism of the spiritual meaning of his poverty, we cannot hope to enter into all the other aspects of the truly happy way of living.

Poverty always spells weakness, vulnerability, humiliation, and having no prospects for improvement. For this reason, poverty is closer to our true condition than the much-admired qualities of the rich or the powerful. Poverty forces on people the reality of the whole of their lives. The poor in spirit, those who recognize their inner helplessness, are ready to confess the words of the famous hymn, Rock of Ages:

*Nothing in my hand I bring;*
*Simply to Thy cross I cling;*
*Naked, come to Thee for dress;*
*Helpless, look to Thee for grace;*
*Foul, I to the fountain fly;*
*Wash me, Saviour, or I die.*

The first beatitude shocks us with this blunt realization that true happiness is reserved for children and the poor. It is not for the superstar, nor for the superman. It is not for those intent on self-fulfilment nor for the 'successful'. It contradicts all the assumptions of secular culture—that I can gain self-knowledge and pull myself up by my own shoestrings. It strips us of all the illusions and idolatry of the world, to face our basic personal need. This is the way of Jesus, 'who though he was rich, yet for our sakes became poor'. He lived as a village carpenter's son. He chose his companions from among the poor and the despised. He held a common purse with his disciples, and he allowed Judas, who was to betray him, to hold it for him. Perhaps there was no other way to expose the absurdities of human pride.

Francis of Assisi, like Jesus, lived out this beatitude. He embraced poverty as a follower of Christ. Like Jesus, he used his poverty to be totally available to those in need around him. His lack of possessiveness made him fearless. He was not afraid of losing anything, because he had nothing to lose—no reputation, no possessions, no clinging to any aspect of life.

Christian poverty is not an end in itself. It is a means of identifying more closely with the joy of Jesus Christ. It enables us to remove anything that gets in the way of our relationship with God. Poverty is also a means of increasing our sensitivity towards others. We are able to be alongside them in their pains and their distresses. The instinct to have or to achieve is toppled off its throne, and instead we receive a strong sense of communion with others and of living in community.

Celano, in his Life of Francis, says that the brothers who lived with Francis 'desired to meet, and together they were happy; on the other hand, absence was painful for them, separation was bitter and parting sorrowful'. The detachment of poverty liberated their spirits to love each other and to enjoy all things. Jacopone da Todi, the follower of Francis, expressed it in this way:

> *Poverty, deepest wisdom, you are slave to nothing,*
> *And in your detachment you possess all things.*
> *The man who desires possessions is himself possessed,*
> *Having sold himself to the things he loves.*
> *God does not dwell in a heart that's confined,*
> *And a heart is only as big as the love it holds:*
> *In the great heart of Poverty*
> *God has room to dwell.*

Until we are 'poor in spirit' we can never have room to receive Christ within our hearts. Until we are 'poor in spirit' we never recognize the riches that God has to give us. When he was elected Governor-General of Canada, Georges Vanier felt deeply inadequate for the heavy duties he had to face. He wrote to a friend: 'I feel it is only in weakness that I can glorify God.' It is only when we are weak and 'poor in spirit' that we can experience the overwhelming power and wealth of God.

## Blessed are those who mourn

If the first beatitude cuts sharply across the ways of the

world, then this second saying follows hard on its heels. No one would ever naturally connect mourning with happiness. Mourning is the one thing people want to avoid doing. However, like that about poverty, this saying talks about mourning in a spiritual sense. In the first place, we all need to mourn for our own sins and for the negative contribution we bring into the world. As long as I refuse to recognize my part in the fallenness of the world around me, I will never be a blessing to others. Pride will prevent me from receiving God's forgiveness and mercy, and from transmitting it to others.

Spiritual mourning reinforces 'poverty of spirit'. To mourn in this sense means to be conscious of living in a fallen world, where people live such lonely, broken lives. It is an openness to life as it is, without falsification and without cosmetically touching up the serious flaws in human nature. True mourning cures us of superficiality. It deepens us and makes us more reflective as people.

Returning to our personality types, the giver has a great deal to learn from the saying, 'blessed are those who mourn'. The trap of the giver is pride, believing that you have enough inner resources to give away to others. In contrast, spiritual mourning implies personal distress and loss. To mourn is to be stripped of self-sufficiency and to identify with the needy on their own level, not from above them. In becoming human, Jesus stooped to our level of need. He became the ultimate mourner, suffering with us in our distress.

It is only when we begin to face an illness that we can find a cure. This is what Jesus did in facing up to our fallen condition. He lived in the depths alongside the needy, the sick and the poor. He saw the foulness of sin, our rebellion against God, and our indifference to the sufferings of others. He understood all the causes of human unhappiness. He wept and mourned over it all.

Mourning enables us to see the millions who die of starvation in our world not as impersonal statistics, but as unique human beings. We can learn to see them as people loved by God, and for whom Christ died. This kind of mourning leads us to side with the poor, and to take action alongside them.

Mourning also helps us to see the dangers facing our planet. We are only one generation away from causing irreparable damage to the Earth's biosphere. This could decide our extinction or survival as the human race. Without mourning on our part, can future generations ever hope to be blessed, and to bless the earth in their turn?

Mourning shatters the illusions of self-sufficiency and breaks through the blindness of self-containment. It helps us to see that suffering is a part of being human. However, mourning has its dark side. It can either lead us into bitterness and despair, or it can drive us towards greater sensitivity and responsibility and a deepening love for God and for others. Mourning leads to happiness when through it we sense our place within the human family, and our need for God's love.

Our mourning can only be taken up into joy when we bring it back to Jesus Christ. Jesus had these words to say about his followers' mourning:

> Now is your time of grief, but I will see you again and you will rejoice, and no one will take away your joy. In that day you will no longer ask me anything. I tell you the truth, my Father will give you whatever you ask in my name. Until now you have not asked for anything in my name. Ask and you will receive, and your joy will be complete.

In our self-absorption, we may never have seen the fullness of joy that we can experience when we begin to know the character of God. As we draw near to him in our distress, we learn to ask him for the things we need. This is an experience we can enter into now, for our present existence, as well as being a future hope. This mourning cleanses us of our false expectations and superficialities, where we try to flatten everything into a manageable world in which we are in charge. Mourning also cleanses us of pity, which can be a subtle form of pride, or of self-pity which is a form of blindness to life as it really is. It heals us of depression and sadness, as if they were intrinsic to the kind of person I believe myself to be.

Mourning helps us to escape from the many different kinds of self-imprisonment. Instead we begin to see things on a bigger canvas. We live in the presence of God, seeing things from his perspective. By our own poverty of spirit, we begin to gain a new realism about life and the way we ourselves live.

## Blessed are the meek

We are now beginning to see that the beatitudes are like steps cut into a mountain. They lead us up to where Jesus is enthroned, giving us a broader, more eternal perspective. Each step leads us upward and forward, each providing further transformation of our lives before God and before ourselves in the light of God. We start by learning to live as 'poor in spirit', and therefore open to see our own sinfulness and that of others. This leads us to mourn for our condition. From this, we step forward to reflect on the essential need for humility.

Jesus speaks these words especially for the performer. The trap of performing types is to display their efficiency by constantly seizing the initiative. Jesus releases us from this addiction by revealing himself as the willing servant, humbled to the point of death, submitting his will to the will of God. This type of humility is clearly not a sign of weakness, but of great strength. True humility is realizing that God can make a much better job of my life than I could ever do by myself. Humility is to orient our lives towards God, so that we understand and obey him in a greater and greater sense.

Someone has characterized the beatitudes as 'be-attitudes'. Our identity lies more in 'being' than in 'doing'. We learn that to 'be in Christ' is far more important than 'being in myself'. We begin to reinterpret our lives as receiving from God, rather than being a series of self-achievements. Perhaps we can only ever see this when we have been 'broken' by God, perhaps through failures or disasters that he has allowed us to experience. It may be that we can only find true humility through humiliation.

Humility begins to grow within us when we go into the desert to be alone with God, to enter into the heart of God. This is not to be confused with the alienation of spirit where we are alone with ourselves. Instead, this is a solitude that gives space for God within us. We learn to exercise silence before God, to be like Mary, the mother of Jesus, as she 'pondered all these things in her heart'. 'Humility,' as John of Climacus says, 'works alongside obedience.' Humility is therefore the hallmark of our relationship with God. In a passage from the Book of Isaiah, God says: 'This is the one that I esteem: he who is humble and contrite in spirit, and trembles at my word.'

To be humble is learning to know ourselves in the light of the knowledge of God. As John of Climacus said: 'The man who has come to know himself is never fooled into reaching what is beyond him. He keeps his feet henceforth on the blessed path of humility.'

## Blessed are those who hunger and thirst for righteousness

To the romantic Jesus expresses his hunger and desire to live only by the words of God. Jesus helps us to hunger and thirst after righteousness, not for romantic notions of unreality. The romantic gets trapped in his or her own small world. It is only by relating outside ourselves to God that we can avoid this trap. Nothing else will do.

The more open we are to God, and the weaker our self-will becomes, the more desire will grow and flourish within us. Desire and reason do not make good bed-mates, for where reason tries to control the world, desire is aware of the vastness of life, which it knows it can never control. So the desire for God grows as self-will diminishes. This desire is the longing to be freed from selfishness and sin, and to live in harmony with the will and purposes of God. Self-concern, with all its fantasies, is left behind. This experience is an echo of one of the psalms:

> *As the deer pants for streams of water,*
> *so my soul pants for you, O God.*
> *My soul thirsts for God, for the living God.*
> *When can I go and meet with God?*

It is perhaps at this stage of our spiritual pilgrimage that we begin to develop an appetite for reading the Bible devotionally—that is, out of love for God. We may also be inspired by some of the great classics of Christian writing. We begin to realize that we are not alone in our restlessness of spirit, but in company with others who have also taken God seriously. Read the quest of Francis of Assisi as a young man, or the search of Ignatius of Loyola in the early years of his conversion. By identifying with the agonizing quest of John Bunyan or John Wesley, you too will stand in awe of the infinite longings of the soul for God. This longing is profoundly expressed by John of the Cross:

> *O lamps of fire!*
> *In whose splendours*
> *The deep caverns of feeling,*

*Once obscure and blind,*
*Now give forth, so rarely,*
*So exquisitely,*
*Both warmth and light to their Beloved.*
*How gently and lovingly*
*You wake in my heart,*
*Where in secret You dwell alone*
*And by your sweet breathing,*
*filled with good and glory*
*How tenderly you fill my heart*
*with love!*

What should we do with our desire for God? We begin by reminding ourselves daily that God provides all that we need for our lives. This then means that we feed daily on the Bible, which tells us about his righteousness—or right-relatedness to him. We allow the Bible to redirect our lives, making its authority the standard by which we relate to God, just as Greenwich mean time helps navigators know where they are at sea. For our emotions, too, can be at sea unless the authority of God's word is hidden within our hearts.

One of the great spiritual writers, Madame Guyon, speaks about 'experiencing the depths of Jesus Christ'. For this to occur, we must first get rid of selfish desires, and replace them with desire for God. This occurs when we start to 'pray the Scriptures', linking the Bible with meditative prayer. In our personal encounter with Christ, we begin to distinguish how we have naturally tried to please him, instead of allowing his love to enter our hearts so that we begin to love him with his gift of love to us. We begin to ask him for more of his love to love him more. When this happens, we begin enjoy him for himself, present within us. A new stillness enters our hearts, where there is no longer any need to express ourselves. Like lovers, we simply hold hands in the silence.

A new simplicity enters the soul. We learn to pray with a

believing heart, with an emphasis on trust rather than on understanding. Periods of dryness may follow, to test whether it is faith, rather than feelings, that controls your relationship with God. As our lives are transformed by God, we experience a deepening desire to enter into the heart of God. To hunger and thirst after righteousness in this way is another step up the mountain to God.

## Blessed are the merciful

To the observer, Jesus expresses mercy. He is mercy. The observer has an insatiable desire for abstract knowledge. He or she lives in an impersonal world, out of touch with other people. But it is in mercy that we most relate to fallen people like ourselves. Jesus once said that those who had been shown the greatest mercy by God were the ones who loved him the most. If we experience the mercy of Jesus, we will naturally share mercy with others, rather than hiding from them as mere observers.

Every step we take upwards towards Jesus is also another step forward in search of other people. Every new insight of God's love for us is another motive to love others too. Personal spirituality can only make progress if it is in partnership with social spirituality. Receiving mercy from God can only mean that it will overflow, as a full cup runs over. For this reason, those around us benefit from our being in love with God.

Today we know what it is to be 'professionalized', experts at our job. But sadly our world suffers because we are not 'mercied' in our professions. We fall into the trap of being efficient technicians of life, starved of the personal dimension of being 'mercy-full'. Those who have been filled with all the previous beatitudes of Christ now overflow in mercy to those around them.

Some years ago, broken and wounded by others, and

deeply convinced of my own self-concealing sinfulness, I cried out to God in the words of one of the psalms:

> Have mercy on me, O God,
> according to your unfailing love;
> according to your great compassion
> blot out my transgressions.

As I began to reflect on this verse, I let its truth penetrate deep within me. What does this word 'mercy' convey but the reality that God, too, has gut feelings of the most intimate tenderness towards me. These are the feelings a mother has when she is carrying a child within her womb. Does God have this kind of tenderness towards me? And is his love so imperishable that, when others deal treacherously with us, he never fails to be loyal? If this is true, then what else can I ever have that is more precious than the possession of his Holy Spirit within me?

This is how he shows us mercy and enables us to be merciful in turn to others. How happy is our life when his Holy Spirit takes residence within us! Martyn Lloyd-Jones, the Welsh preacher, once said:

> We are not meant to control our Christianity; our
> Christianity is rather meant to control us. I am to be
> dominated by the truth because I have been made a
> Christian by the operation of the Holy Spirit within.

Paul expressed it in this way: 'I live; yet not I, but Christ lives in me.' A whole new attitude to living unfolds within me. This new life reveals more and more the gifts of God, and less and less the human efforts we vainly try to make. We are reborn in God, leaving behind us the continuity of our earthly and parental life.

How are we merciful? Only to the extent that we are becoming aware of the mercies of God. Jesus spoke about forgiveness in the Lord's prayer: 'If you forgive others when they sin against you, your heavenly Father will also forgive you.' This is not a conditional statement, reflecting some deal that God makes with us: 'You forgive first, then I'll forgive you.' Instead, this is the evidence that God's forgiveness possesses our lives so powerfully that we are given the strength to forgive others in turn.

In each of Jesus' beatitudes, God's blessing comes in the first line, and is then followed by the effect of this blessing on us in the second line. Our lives show the evidence of God's blessing. So as we are shown forgiveness and mercy by God, we become merciful ourselves. It can never happen the other way round. God's grace transforms our lives so that we become givers of God's grace to others. It is our communion with God that enables us to have empathy, kindness, intimacy and identification with others, which flow forth from us like rivers in an oasis. Compassion then fills our life, because the compassion of Christ has transformed our hearts.

## Blessed are the pure in heart

To the responsible, Jesus speaks of being 'pure in heart'. The responsible are over-cautious, hiding behind others. They can never expose themselves, nor deeply know themselves. But the 'pure in heart' are those who 'see God'. Because of their profound sense of being accepted by God's love, they can live transparently, not hiding behind the mask of being dutiful.

One of the psalms echoes this beatitude of Jesus:

> *Create in me a pure heart, O God*
> *and renew a steadfast spirit within me.*

We cannot expect to receive from God unless our spirits are in harmony with his Spirit. It is interesting that Jesus, at this point in the beatitudes, turns to focus on the heart. Because the heart is the seat of all our emotions, affections and willpower, this means that the impact of being blessed by God eventually reaches down to the very core of our persons. We are being transformed through and through. This is not an option for having more of an emotional than an intellectual life, but of being wholly for God. If we are naturally more 'the feeling type', then our transformation by God will bring about deeper thought within us. If we are 'the intellectual type' then we will grow in our emotions before God.

As God penetrates the core of our lives, we realize that it is in the heart that all the issues of life are decided. All our weaknesses, sins and troubles arise because of our faulty, uncleansed hearts. To receive a 'pure heart' implies the cleansing that God alone can give, since it is also the source of our own self-deception. When God makes our hearts pure, we stop deceiving ourselves. We become single-hearted and single-minded before God. Our lives become focussed on one aim.

Another meaning of the word 'pure' reveals that the heart is also cleansed. To become 'pure in heart' is therefore to be like Jesus. To have purity of heart is to become godly, expressing the holiness of God, so that in turn we may 'see God'. This is the choice before us: to be self-seeking or God-seeing.

But how can we 'see God'? In the Old Testament, Moses asked to see God, only to be told that 'no man can see God and live'. In fact, Moses did 'see God', but only in a partial sense. God always has to 'empty himself' as the incarnation demonstrates, for us to see God. He comes alongside us and takes on our humanity, in order for us to see him, in the same way that the intensity of the sun is scaled down to the ray of light through the window. To Moses, God appeared as 'the compassionate and gracious God, slow to anger, abounding in love and faithfulness.' These were the words Moses heard as God passed by.

Learning to see God as he is in his own being will be reflected in our own hearts. We learn to see God as he really is, and not as we have imagined him to be. The evidence of this is the change which takes place within our own hearts. The apostle John spoke about this when he said: 'We know that when he appears, we shall be like him, for we shall see him as he is.' Then he adds: 'Everyone who has this hope in him, purifies himself, just as he is pure. No one who continues to sin has either seen him or known him.'

Where the heart is turbulent and restless, where it is mixed in motive, and conceals anger, pride, or fear, then the vision of God cannot be seen. We cannot understand God's true character. Purity of heart, said Soren Kierkegaard, is to will one thing—to hunger and thirst after God alone. Kierkegaard compared the heart to the ocean. Its depth determines its purity, and its purity determines its transparency. When the heart has great depths, no surface storms can affect its clarity. The deep, transparent heart seeks only for God.

## Blessed are the peacemakers

Only after this prolonged focus upon personal and inward spirituality can we now turn to the outward expressions of social relationships. God's children, 'his sons', are to be known as God is known, as reconcilers, or 'peacemakers'.

This beatitude speaks especially to the fun-lover. Jesus offers us his peace, which is wholeness of life. Fun-lovers live superficially, afraid to face suffering and to enter deeply into the ambiguities and hurts of an imperfect world. However, Jesus is our peacemaker. He does not give as the world gives, but gives instead his peace, fullness and wholeness of life. He enables us to accept pain and suffering, doing it for Christ's sake.

We are now reaching the high point of the truly happy life. This is a life so transformed that it stands in utter contrast to the life which comes naturally to us as human beings. It reflects an entirely new way of living with ourselves and of behaving before others. If the pure in heart gain integrity, then peacemakers gain their wholeness and health. When Dante, the Italian poet, was exiled from his home in Florence, he decided to walk from Italy to Paris, to search for the real meaning of life. Late one night, he stopped at the gates of a Franciscan monastery to seek shelter. He was asked by the friar who opened the gate to him, 'What do you wish?' Dante answered in one word: 'Peace.'

This is the desire to have a completely new foundation as a person. This is what it means truly to be a child of God.

Our lack of peace is reflected in every area of our lives. Many people today are aware that they do not have the full assurance of their sexuality. Inadequate parenting has left them wounded, confused, fearful of intimacy, double-minded, and addicted to all kinds of emotions. Their sense of inner emptiness and fear is projected outwards in deformed relationships and actions. This is turn generates unrest and disturbance in society at large.

One young man told me how he was recruited into the South African police force. He had a strong desire to be a 'peace-keeper'. But at the age of eighteen he was wholly unprepared for the terrors that awaited him. One night, he found himself with a few other police enveloped in the hatred of a black township uprising. As he stood guard in the hut where a handful of police had taken refuge, a terrible fear possessed him. He had been well educated, and came from a home where much love was shown, but alone in the darkness he imagined a thousand evil eyes upon him, and his one instinct was to blast away with his gun with murder in his heart. He fired out into the night again and again.

At sunrise, the sickening reality dawned that bullets, his bullets, had mown down human beings. They now lay for ever dead. Guilt besieged him for many years. How could he ever become a peacemaker? How is it that love and hate live so close together within one pulsing heart? This man is learning slowly how deeply the experience of God's forgiveness has to penetrate through his whole being.

Among Jesus' last words, he left us this legacy, which in a sense reflects his whole life:

> *Peace I leave with you; my peace I give you. I do not give to you as the world gives. Do not let your hearts be troubled, and do not be afraid.*

## Blessed are those who are persecuted because of righteousness

It may seem strange to pass from peace-making to being persecuted. But the radical life-style of the true Christian is so contrary to the ways of the world that it cannot help being a threat to others. This was the experience of Jesus, and it was the experience of the early Christians in the Roman Empire. In a world that substitutes power for relationships, lust for love and magic for the true love of God, we will always have to fight to express the truth of what it means to be truly human. In the struggle between good and evil, we will inevitably suffer.

To the strong boss, Jesus promised his Spirit in the midst of persecution, with all the violence of evil we may have to face. As this type of personality is trapped in the fear of appearing weak, facing the ridicule of those who persecute goes against all the grain of personality. But Jesus, who was himself reviled, and 'led as a lamb to the slaughter', is able to strengthen us in our weakness of personality.

And so we can go back to all the Beatitudes, seeing how each stands or falls in relationship to the previous

'Be-attitudes' that we have before God, in God, for God, and through God living in us. Truly then, the Beatitudes test the personal integrity of our lives and of our interpretation of true happiness.

# 11

# Desiring God

*Maturity, at least for me, seems to lie in the discovery that happiness and circumstances don't have all that much to do with each other; that happiness is more a matter of choice and habit than we suppose, and less dependent upon the accident of circumstances. For me, too, it seems allied with giving the fundamental grief and despair room and expression, using them as a kind of necessary ballast but not taking so much of them on board that they swamp the vessel.*

Monica Furlong

When we are young, we assume that if only we can get the circumstances of our lives right, then we will automatically be happy. This is not very far from the belief that pleasure and happiness amount to the same thing—a belief with deep flaws, as we saw in an earlier chapter. As we travel through life, we begin to realize that grief and deep disappointments lie beneath the surface of our lives. If these underground emotions came to the surface all at once, they would shatter our existence, but fortunately they come upon us gradually —more so for some than for others.

As we have seen, the legacies of childhood set the pattern for the way in which we interpret and live our adult lives. This is graphically illustrated in the case of one girl, whose mother died when she was seven years old. Ever since, she has always felt that she has a tenuous grip upon life. It is only now, in middle age, that joy is beginning to develop in her heart, as she begins to realize that God has truly given her the gift of life. In spite of her unhappy childhood, the love of God has brought her healing and reassurance.

## Depths of desire

Perhaps it is a basic rule of life that the deeper the emotional deprivations of the heart, the simpler our joys appear. C. S. Lewis, whose mother died when he was ten, tells us:

> *With my mother's death all settled happiness, all that was tranquil and reliable, disappeared from my life. There was to be much fun, many pleasures, many stabs of joy; but no more of the old security. It was sea and islands now; the great continent like Atlantis had slid under the waves.*

As a growing child, three simple experiences set the pattern of joy for the rest of Lewis's life. He describes these experiences in his autobiography, *Surprised by Joy*. The first occurred one summer's day, when he was standing beside a flowering currant bush:

> *There arose within me without warning, and as if from a depth not of years but of centuries, the memory of that earlier morning at the Old House when my brother had brought his toy garden into the nursery. It is difficult to find words strong enough for the sensation which came over me; Milton's 'enormous bliss' of Eden (giving the full, ancient meaning to 'enormous') comes somewhere near it. It was a sensation, of course, of desire; but desire of what? Before I knew what I desired, the desire itself*

was gone, the whole glimpse withdrawn, the world turned commonplace again, or only stirred by a longing that had just ceased. It had taken only a moment of time; and in a certain sense everything else that had ever happened to me was insignificant in comparison.

The second glimpse came through Squirrel Nutkin though I loved all the Beatrix Potter books. It troubled me with what can only be described as the Idea of Autumn. It sounds fantastic to say that one can be enamoured of a season, but that is something like what happened: and, as before, the experience was one of intense desire. It was something quite different from ordinary life and even from ordinary pleasure; something, as they would now say, 'in another dimension'.

The third glimpse came through poetry. I had become fond of Longfellow's Saga of King Olaf: fond of it in a casual, shallow way for its story and its vigorous rhythms. But then, and quite different from such pleasures, and like a voice from far more distant regions, there came a moment when I idly turned the pages of the book and found the unrhymed translation of Tegner's Drapa and read:

> I heard a voice that cried,
> Balder the beautiful
> Is dead, is dead—

I knew nothing about Balder; but instantly I was uplifted into huge regions of northern sky. I desired with almost sickening intensity something never to be described (except that it is cold, spacious, severe, pale and remote) and then, as in the other examples, found myself at the very same moment already falling out of that desire and wishing I were back in it.

Lewis then adds: 'The reader who finds these three epis-odes of no interest need read this book no further, for in a sense the central story of my life is about nothing else.' He goes on: 'The quality common to the three experiences is that of an unsatisfied desire which is itself more desirable than any other satisfaction. I call it Joy.' He then proceeds to distinguish this joy from happiness or pleasure, though like them it has the quality of wanting it again. But Lewis says that it could equally be called 'a particular kind of unhappi-ness or grief'.

## Desire and fulfilment

In C. S. Lewis' quest for joy, we can clearly see that the void left by his mother's death was never replaced in his child-hood, nor indeed perhaps ever in his whole life. His father certainly never replaced his mother's love. He was never able to relate adequately, as a sorrowing widower, to the two small boys left in his care. Even when he scolded them for some minor wrongdoing, he would cite the great orators like Cicero or Burke, as if he was taking part in a parliamentary debate, instead of addressing two small boys. Later in life, Lewis and his father drifted apart, never to be reconciled.

As a result, the three childhood incidents were profound-ly important to Lewis all through his life. They created in him a sense of desire and longing. Throughout his adoles-cence and youth, Lewis interpreted the void in his heart as a tragic awareness of 'the North', which he saw as 'cold, spa-cious, severe, pale and remote'. This was only changed when he became a Christian and was 'surprised by joy'.

In his book *Mere Christianity*, Lewis tells us that there are two mistakes people often make in the way they think about their desire. The first is the Fool's Way. The fool puts the blame on the things he desires. All his life, the fool thinks that if only he tried another woman, or holiday, or whatever, then this time he would really catch the mysterious something.

The second is the way of the disillusioned 'sensible man'. He decides that his desires are simply moonshine. He longs for what he can never really have. And so he represses the part of himself which used to cry for the moon.

In fact, this second approach is exactly what Lewis did. As a young man, he decided that belief in God was all moonshine. However, he gradually came to believe in an impersonal God, and then in the personal God of the Christian faith. He saw that God personally exists and relates to us, with us, and in us. He discovered that all his desires were related to the need we all have for God himself—not just for a mother's love or for some other intense childhood need. He said:

> Creatures are not born with desires unless satisfaction for these desires exists. A baby feels hunger; well, there is such a thing as food. A duckling wants to swim; well there is such a thing as water. Men feel sexual desire; well, there is such a thing as sex. If I find in myself a desire for which no experience in this world can satisfy, the most probable explanation is that I was made for another world.

This is not a proof for the existence of God. It is more like a wager, where we gamble our lives on the probability of God. We would be foolish to leave God out of our reckoning, never taking time to consider deeply why we are so restless with desire. Blaise Pascal, the seventeenth-century mathematician and philosopher, observed:

> There are three kinds of people: those who have sought God and found him, and these are reasonable and happy; those who seek God and have not yet found him, and these are reasonable and unhappy; and those who neither

*seek God nor find him, and these are unreasonable and unhappy.*

Desire is a powerful force within each one of us, not simply because of some human need for another human being, but because of our need of God. Augustine expressed his own restlessness and desire by saying to God: 'You created us for yourself, and our hearts are restless until they find their rest in you.' In Book Ten of his *Confessions*, Augustine searches and questions all created things for satisfaction, only to be told by them: 'We are not God, seek above us.' He goes on: 'I asked the whole frame of the world about my God; and it answered me, "I am not he, but he made me."' Then Augustine begins to ponder that the memory is a vast and boundless sphere, full of desires and hopes of happiness, as well as being full of fears and sorrows: 'Great is the power of memory, a fearful thing, O my God, a deep and boundless manifoldness: and this thing is the mind, and this am I myself.' Augustine recognizes that his desire for God is part of the way in which he has been made.

The writer of the Book of Ecclesiastes declared: 'He has made everything beautiful in its time. He has also set eternity in the hearts of men. I know that there is nothing better for men than to be happy and do good while they live.' We each have a God-designed vacuum within us, which God alone can fill and satisfy. This is the common message of great minds such as Pascal, Augustine and the writer of Ecclesiastes, among many others.

In modern times, psychologists have said that our unconscious mind, which powers our inbuilt desires, is simply another name for God. For Christians, it is a grave mistake to confuse God with our inner desires, even if God placed them there in the first place. But at least psychologists are coming to recognize that the unconscious mind, with its restlessness and its infinite desire, may be God-given and God-directed.

Our desires are of course double-edged. They can drive us into the arms of God, or into the clutches of evil. Many people trivialize their desire for God, and settle for something that is inferior. When this happens, we exchange God for cheap idolatry, whether we worship work, money, sex, or status. But they can never satisfy desire. It would be like trying to fill the Pacific Ocean with pebbles thrown into the waves. As Augustine said, the response of the ocean itself would be, 'But I too am a creature, that God made me.'

## The God-shaped vacuum

Our deepest desires can only be satisfied when we seek after God and eternity. To prove this claim for ourselves, we need to take two important steps. First, we must be ready to recognize that a natural desire within us points to a real object which can satisfy that desire. Secondly, that our desire for God is distinct from our desires for created things.

We desire a lot of things that the advertising industry brainwashes us to believe are indispensable. The 'right' perfume, deodorant, hairdo, suit of clothes, and shoes trivialize our desires and can devalue us as people. This happens when we are manipulated by 'the hidden persuaders' of fashion, the dictates of society, and the many fantasies about what people think of us. Our high desires for spiritual reality are transmuted into the sordid quest for consumerism and materialism.

However, there are other desires which do correspond to truly human values: the desire for friendship (because as human beings we were made for relationships), or the desire to give happiness to others (because our human nature makes us aware of the needs of others). Desires are not free-floating, like particles of dust in the sunlight with no apparent attachment to anything. Instead, our desires reflect the collection of values that we attach to our humanity. In other words, desires are authentically related to our very nature as human beings.

As we have seen, C. S. Lewis, more clearly than most writers, has sensed the uniqueness of God-inspired desire and of having God as the object of desire. In his book, *The Pilgrim's Regress*, he says that the experience of intense longing is distinguished from other longings by two things:

> *In the first place, though the sense of want is acute and even painful, yet the mere wanting is felt to be somehow a delight. This hunger is better than any other fullness; this poverty better than any other wealth. In the second place, there is a peculiar mystery about the object of this desire. Every one of these supposed objects for the desire is inadequate to it. It appears to me therefore that if a man diligently followed this desire, pursuing the false objects until their falsity appeared and then resolutely abandoning them, he must come out at last into the clear knowledge that the human soul was made to enjoy some object that is never fully given—nay, cannot even be imagined as given—in our present mode of subjective and spatio-temporal experience.*

There is an empty throne within the throne room of our hearts that only God can fill. In many cases this invisible emptiness inside us takes visible form. A dying man asked for a chair to be placed by his bedside, because he sensed that Jesus Christ was sitting beside him in the darkness throughout the night. When he died, his hand was found outstretched, resting on the chair, as if held by an unseen friend.

But as we have already seen, there is also a negative side to our infinite desires. There is the wretchedness and restlessness of our empty hearts without God. 'Who does not feel more unhappy at not being a king except a king who has been deposed?' asked Pascal. Because we have been given the possibility of sight, it is no surprise when we are inconsolable if we have no eyesight. Such examples of human misery, Pascal said, prove our greatness: 'It is the misery of a great lord, the wretchedness of a deposed king,' that reflect upon the human dignity of being made in the image of God. For Pascal, the truth about our condition was a strange paradox:

*So man's greatness comes from knowing that he is*
*wretched, for a tree does not know that it is wretched.*
*Thus it is wretched to know that one is wretched, but it is*
*a sign of our true greatness to know that we are wretched.*

The ability to think gives us dignity. The enjoyment of our place among others also gives us dignity. But our dignity supremely lies in the capacity and desire that God has given us to enjoy him and to seek for his esteem and friendship. This belief implies that we have a destiny rather than a fate. In other words, that we are not victims of chance and fate, but take an active part in our destiny, which is a spiritual drama. We are both exalted and fallen at the same time: sinful and yet given unique status in the universe of things. Our exaltation is related to our sinfulness, because sin is really the desire to grasp God's position for ourselves. This is why Jesus came, as the God-man, to redeem the evil of the man-God, who wanted to usurp the place of God in creation.

Without God as the supreme expression of goodness, love and personhood, human beings can have no true exaltation or dignity. In the modern world, we are reduced to an idealized figment of the communist imagination or we fall into secular despair, but we cannot be exalted as a personal being, uniquely loved for our own sake. The uniqueness of the Christian faith is that it orients man to hope in God, to respond to his love and to rest in God alone as the only source of ultimate happiness.

The God-shaped vacuum within us makes itself felt most when we ask ourselves—or our psychiatrist—'Who am I?' This is a question which animals never need to ask. Humans, with their openness to life and their profound sense of incompletion, are in sharp contrast with the instinctive, closed world of the animal realm. So the question 'Who am I?' reveals both our dignity and our folly. We cling to the symbols which give our life meaning and help us in answering this question. We depend upon emotionally-packed images, formed in childhood or reinforced in times of crisis during our emotional development.

The symbol for our inner life is 'the heart', a symbol taken up in the Bible. The heart is the focus of life-shaping changes in our existence. It has a direct impact on our growth as persons, happy or unhappy. Our lives begin with the influence of another's heart upon us. The mother's heartbeat is a constant feature of the unborn child's life: sixty beats a minute, 3,600 an hour, 86,400 a day and a staggering 24 million throughout the whole period of pregnancy. In the absence of mother, nurses have learned the trick of placing an alarm clock under the newborn baby's pillow. The Hebrew word *rechem*, meaning 'God's mercy', is drawn from the same imagery, since it literally means 'the womb'. This tells us about God's compassionate relationship with his people.

In the Bible, the heart is a powerful symbol for our inner selves. The heart can be joyful or sorrowful, proud or humble, as well as the home of our desires. 'A whole heart' signifies integrity, and it is 'from the heart' that the essential qualities of a person flow, either for good or evil. The heart is as much identified with thought and the mind as with the emotions and the will. So the 'listening heart' means the 'understanding mind'. The psalms and the Old Testament prophets use the language of the heart to say that 'the cleansing of the heart', or a heart transplant, is essential for our relationship with God to be restored. In the New Testament, God's love is poured 'into our hearts' through the Holy Spirit, while it is 'on the heart' that Christ writes our new identity, as we now belong to him.

Today, it is plainly recognized that stress is heart-related.

The physical condition of the heart can be linked with the emotional conditions of the inner life. This points to our need for healthy relationships with other people, and above all for a healthy relationship with God. To ask, 'Are you happy?' is ultimately to ask the question, 'How is your inner life before God?' As God made us for himself, how are we relating to him? The heart, or the inner life, is therefore a great teacher, pointing us back to the source of all happiness—to God himself. 'Listen to your heart,' we advise each other.

These, then, are some of the symbolic inklings we have of eternity, and of our divinely-destined path of happiness. The desire for joy lies deep within the human spirit, as deep as the soul's quest for happiness. It is certainly deeper than the body's appetite for pleasure. The drive for idol-worship is another sign. The belief that the unconscious mind is wise and good, and that it can be identified with God, is another signpost, false though its trail is. The God-shaped vacuum in every heart is an explicit signal of eternity. The desire for happiness is deeper and more powerful than we know.

## Looking for happiness in the right place

We live our lives on a human tightrope of infinite desires and yet of physical mortality. This keeps us in our place, although it frustrates us with a great deal of suffering. However, it is foolish to live with the denial of death, as modern culture tends to do. In our heart of hearts we know that we will all die. We also live absurdly if we forget the dignity of every one of our fellow human beings. We are naive, President Gorbachev said, if we repress the religious dimension of mankind. That is why we need windows of the soul, such as desire, happiness and joy, so that we do not lose sight of what our lives are truly all about.

Today, there are many religious and secular beliefs open to us. For this reason, we need a wise awareness of the important dimensions of life. This will help us not to confuse physical pleasure with true happiness or the spiritual reality of joy. In the introduction to her autobiography, the writer Elizabeth Goudge speaks of this when she compares her adult romantic interest in roses with her childhood delight with the snow. She says:

> *I appreciate roses more than snow, but that was not the case at the beginning. Then, in company with all children and most dogs, I thought snow the wonder of the world. The snow-light filling the house with magic as the white flakes drifted down in the windless silence, the splendour where the sun came out and the hills and fields and trees sparkled under the arc of blue sky, the thought of the things one did in the snow, tobogganing and snowballing, and building a snowman: it was all ecstasy. And some-where tucked away at the back of one's mind was the knowledge that every crystal in the vast whiteness, though too small for the human eye to see, was fashioned like a flower or a star. How could snow not be the wonder of the world?*

Looked at from one point of view, snow is the wonder of the world, provided you have a child's appreciation of magic and can withdraw quickly from the cold into the warmth of the indoors. It is a wonder, as long as you do not carry the responsibilities of having to clear the roads for traffic, nor understand the host of problems that a winter blizzard can bring to disrupt the economy. When you grow up, the appreciation of the rose does have more appeal, especially if you enjoy the cultivation of a garden, or receive a bunch of roses from the person you love most. In the same way, there is an appropriateness to each realm of happiness.

The whole nature of the aesthetic is the appreciation of each thing in itself. The Elizabethan playwright, Ben

Jonson, challenges us to see that it is appropriate to appreciate everything:

> *Have you seen but a white lily grow before rude*
> *    hands had touched it?*
> *Have you seen but the fall of snow before the earth*
> *    hath smutched it?*
> *Have you felt the wool of the beaver, or swan's down*
> *    ever?*
> *Have you smelt of the bud of the briar or the nard in*
> *    the fire?*
> *Have you tasted the bag of the bee?*

These are good questions. Have we seen, felt, smelt or tasted the beauty of the world? And if happiness opens up to us such vast caverns of the soul, have we in a much greater sense been sufficiently aware of the greatness and the mystery of God? Even popular magazine articles recognize that there are appropriate steps necessary to being happy. These include the following pieces of advice.

*Form close relationships with other human beings.* Of all the circumstances that happy people share, loving relationships are the most important. So the first priority is to spend time in cultivating friendships.

*Aim for durability and frequency in relationships, but not in intensity.* There can be high peaks of pleasure, but these cannot last, whereas steady, constant relationships are more likely to sustain and deepen the qualities of true happiness. So work consistently and faithfully in your personal relationships.

*Do good, by seeking the well-being of others.* This relieves the stress of being selfish and competitive with others, in recognizing that relating is far more important than selfishly achieving within society. This enhances a true sense of personal integrity and self-worth. It also creates an atmosphere of harmony with friends.

*Develop an emotional interest in other people.* It has been proved that when people are not emotionally involved with other people, and have no interest in the world around them, they cannot be happy. We get much more happiness in investing in other people's lives than we do in self-isolation.

*Strive to see things in proportion.* This gives us space for others, allowing us to show kindness and understanding and helping us to live appropriately with others. So we can mourn with those who mourn as well as rejoice with those who rejoice.

*Keep your body fit.* Exercise your mind by reading widely and reflecting on life. Cultivate the affairs of the heart and of the soul. Be open to God in all of your existence, as the highest good in all of life.

All these pieces of advice contain a certain amount of wisdom. How much further do we need to explore to discover happiness in God? The answer is clearly stated in the New Testament. When Jesus Christ becomes the focus of our emotions as well as of our minds, then the Christian life is essentially a joyful life. In ancient Greek literature, joy was seen only as the delight of the gods, who alone were the lords of joy. But in the New Testament joy becomes an essential element in the life of the ordinary Christian. This joy is not questioned or limited in any way. We simply 'rejoice in God through our Lord Jesus Christ'.

Christian joy expresses a fullness of life that is infinite, everlasting, and incorruptible. It is like the enormous energy of the sun's radiation, of which a fraction of less than one per cent is absorbed by all the life-systems of the Earth. The potential of joy is vastly greater than our capacity to absorb it all. God's love is able to sustain human happiness beyond our wildest desires. How can we enter into this happiness and make it part of our lives?

## Joy accepts the rule of God

Jesus came as the messenger of joy. At the heart of his message was a call to belong to the 'kingdom of God', which means to submit to the rule of God as king. Jesus said that God's kingdom would come in the future, at the end of time, when all evil would be destroyed. But he also spoke of the kingdom being present on earth now, in a way that pointed forward to the fullness of its coming in the future. The kingdom of God, he said, could be seen in the hearts of all who love and obey God now. Accepting his teaching and following him as a disciple means to live in that kingdom now.

To belong to God's kingdom is to experience the reality of joy. For Christians who live closely with God, life is like a festival, and with each new believer brought into reality there is joy for all believers. In Jesus' parables, this was the joy experienced when the lost son returned to his father, or when the lost sheep was found, or when the lost coin was pulled from its hiding-place. The presence of Jesus within our hearts, as we submit to his rule, brings the greatest joy. This is why we pray, 'Your kingdom come, your will be done on earth as it is in heaven.'

The evidence of belonging to God's kingdom is that our character changes and is re-formed. As we saw in chapter ten, the beatitudes of Jesus express the radicalism of living under the rule of God's own character. Happiness only comes about when we live within the disciplines of life, given to us by God. The Book of Proverbs makes it clear that happiness and discipline go hand in hand from the beginning of our lives: 'He who spares the rod hates his son, but he who loves him is careful to discipline him.' Another passage says, 'My son, do not despise the Lord's discipline and do not resent his rebuke, because the Lord disciplines those whom he loves, as a father the son he delights in.' These Old Testament sayings are re-echoed in the New

Testament. The writer of the letter to the Hebrews tells us
what God's love for us means:

*My son, do not make light of the Lord's discipline,*
*and do not lose heart when he rebukes you,*
*because the Lord disciplines those he loves,*
*and he punishes everyone he accepts as a son.*

*Endure hardship as discipline; God is treating you as*
*sons. For what son is not disciplined by his father? If you*
*are not disciplined (and everyone undergoes discipline)*
*then you are illegitimate children and not true sons.*
*Moreover, we have all had human fathers who disci-*
*plined us and we respected them for it. How much more*
*should we submit to the Father of our spirits and live!*
*Our fathers disciplined us for a little while as they*
*thought best; but God disciplines us for our good, that we*
*may share in his holiness. No discipline seems pleasant at*
*the time, but painful. Later on, however, it produces a*
*harvest of righteousness and peace for those who have*
*been trained by it.*

We cannot enjoy a happy life with God unless we are willing to be disciplined—unhappy though that may appear at
first. We cannot receive the happiness of being sons and
daughters of God without the chastening education of our
Father's love. The uncomfortable truth is that our rebellion
against God has estranged us from him. This sin needs to be
uprooted from our hearts, which is a painful process.

The way of life which Jesus described in the beatitudes
appears at first sight to be a contradiction. How can we be
'blessed' or 'happy', if we have also to be humbled as 'the
poor in spirit', or to mourn, or to be meek, or to 'hunger and
thirst for righteousness'? This seems a very strange form of
happiness! But this shows how necessary it is for proud, independent, self-reliant people to be broken, re-educated, and

redirected to walk in the ways of the Lord. This process means that our characters have to be transformed. It is not simply a question of becoming nicer or trying harder to live a good life. We need the complete transformation of our inner selves that only God can achieve.

## Joy lies in repentance

The Bible's word for turning back to God is 'repentance'. This was the central message of the Old Testament prophets, as they called God's people to return to him. Jesus, too, called people to repentance. His parables are full of this message. The outcome of true repentance is always joy, pictured in several of Jesus' parables as a great feast. Because the transformation of repentance is always brought about by God's power, rather than our efforts, the images in these parables speak of God's generous giving. He provides the feast for rejoicing, as well as the fine clothes for the banquet guests to sit before him. The feast gives us a graphic picture of the character of God, showing how he loves to redeem those who have been lost, to restore the lives which have been wasted.

We might think that this change of life would bring joy primarily to the person who is redeemed. But Jesus' teaching shows us that repentance is God's joy. It is God who rejoices at the repentance of a sinner, just as the father rejoices at the return of the prodigal son. Jesus' parables, and his way of life, reveal some unusual features about the character of this merciful and forgiving God. Although God is holy and hates sin, yet Jesus had time for criminals, prostitutes and the men who exploited them. He encouraged them to turn back to God and accepted them with a forgiving spirit. He calls his followers to do the same in their relationships with others. In the Lord's Prayer, God's forgiveness of our sins is linked with our forgiveness of others. 'Forgive us our debts as we also forgive those that are indebted to us.'

To follow Jesus means to open ourselves to others. Jesus' parable of the Good Samaritan shows that a fully Christian life is one that is open to everyone who is in need. We live with a double command: to love God, and to love other people too. The joy that Jesus brings is the joy of sharing and receiving love in the mercy of God. This joy expresses unlimited trust in the power of God to transform the most stubborn aspects of our human nature.

## Joy experienced in Christian worship

The atmosphere of joy in the Gospels inspired the worship of the early church. Jesus, the man of joy, leads his followers to be filled with thanksgiving and praise to God.

Jesus is therefore the passport for fullness of joy. Jesus once told his disciples: 'So far you have asked nothing in my name. Ask and you will receive, that your joy may be complete.' Fullness of joy comes from entering into fellowship with the Father and the Son, through the Holy Spirit, each enjoying the company of the other. This is the heart of Christian worship, and the heart of our joy in God.

Christian joy is also founded on the historical events of the death, resurrection and ascension of Jesus Christ, the coming of his Holy Spirit, and the ongoing fellowship of God with Christian believers. Christian joy is the essential spark that gives vitality to true worship. Each service of worship should be an occasion for praise and rejoicing. The roots of this joy in worship can be seen in the psalms, the hymn book of the Old Testament. The psalms let us hear the exultant shouts of the worshippers, and allow us to join in imagination with the pilgrims who go up to Jerusalem to keep the festivals. In the psalms, the courts of the temple resound with praise and worship.

Christian worship on the first day of the week celebrates the whole life of the Christian. Just as bees scatter widely to collect nectar from many flowers, so the ideal of worship is to bring together our wide experiences of the goodness of God from the workaday world. In this way, every corner of our life is able to be brought in worship to God. The poet George Herbert expressed this truth:

> *Let all the world in ev'ry corner sing*
> *My God and King.*
> *The heav'ns are not too high,*
> *His praise may thither fly;*
> *The earth is not too low,*
> *His praises there may grow.*
> *Let all the world in ev'ry corner sing*
> *My God and King.*

While Sunday provides the flash-point for our worship, this can only happen when our Mondays to Saturdays are filled with praise for God as well. In a different poem, George Herbert says, 'Sev'n whole days, not one in seven, I will praise thee.' And he concludes that although hymns and songs of praise are a 'poore sort', they reflect the true worship of heaven, which itself cannot do full justice to God's greatness:

> *Small it is in this poore sort*
> *To enroll thee;*
> *Ev'n eternitie is too short*
> *To extoll thee.*

## Joy deepened through suffering

While we can appreciate that Christian worship is joy, it is harder to believe in what the poet George Matheson called

'Joy that seekest me through pain'. Experiencing joy through suffering is a paradox, and yet it was this that marked the life of Jesus. To follow Jesus as his disciples means that we too face opposition to living like him. One form of suffering which we can avoid is the surprise of being persecuted. In the New Testament, Peter wrote these words:

> *Dear friends, do not be surprised at the painful trial you are suffering, as though something strange were happening to you. But rejoice that you participate in the sufferings of Christ, so that you may be overjoyed when his glory is revealed. If you are insulted because of the name of Christ, you are blessed, because the Spirit of glory and of God rests on you.*

'Consider it pure joy,' says James in his letter, 'whenever you face trials of many kinds, because you know that the testing of your faith develops perseverance.'

This type of joy is not superficial, for it is a costly experience, gained only through suffering and sharing something of the crucifixion of Christ. The writer of the Book of Hebrews links the joy and suffering of Christ by saying: 'Let us fix our eyes on Jesus, the author and perfecter of our faith, who for the joy set before him endured the cross, scorning its shame, and sat down at the right hand of the throne of God.' This theme of joy won through suffering was especially powerful in the persecution faced by the early church, as it has been in times of persecution since. Paul understood his own sufferings as being a signal to unbelievers of the power of the crucified Jesus over suffering and death.

In a moving episode from the life of Francis of Assisi, Brother Leo asked Francis, 'What is perfect joy?'

> *Imagine, said Francis, that I returned to Perugia on the darkest of nights, a night so cold that everything is covered with snow, and the frost in the folds of my habit*

*hits my legs and makes them bleed. Shrouded in snow and shivering with cold, I arrive at the door of the friary, and after calling out for a long time, the brother porter gets up and asks: 'Who is it?'*

*And I respond: 'It is I, Brother Francis.'*

*The porter says: 'Be on your way. Now is not the time to arrive at the friary. I will not open the door for you.'*

*I insist and he answers: 'Be on your way right now. You are stupid and an idiot. We are already many here and we do not need you.'*

*I insist once more: 'For the love of God, let me in, just for tonight.'*

*And he answers: 'Not even to talk. Go to the leper colony that is nearby.'*

*'Well, Brother Leo, if after all this I do not lose patience and remain calm, believe me, that is perfect joy!'*

This is the nature of Christian joy through suffering, which reconciles the negative with the transcendent love of Christ, enabling us to say, like Paul the apostle: 'I can do all things through Christ, who strengthens me.' This is the absolute character of Christian joy, not in being supermen or women, but in receiving the gift of faith in Christ, who is able to do far above all that we can ask or think. To experience joy in suffering is to realize that Jesus stands with the poor, the underprivileged, and those, like Francis of Assisi, rejected by their own people. This is not a call to glorify suffering for its own sake, but to realize that nothing can separate us from the love of Christ, whatever it may be. It is to anticipate eternity, when death will be no more, and when God will wipe away all our tears, allowing us to behold his glory.

This chapter began with a quotation from Monica

Furlong. This passage from her writings gives us a sense of proportion about our joy through suffering:

> *Among the many other things that Easter means to the Christian, it must also mean a particular sense of proportion about our griefs and sufferings. They hurt, sometimes excruciatingly, but on the deepest level of all, it is somehow 'all right'; and out of the praise and gratitude and joy that spring from it when we can grasp it, I think that we may give ourselves permission for the more mundane, but wonderfully healing emotion of happiness.*

Yes, we do have a supernatural gift of joy in Christ that is quite baffling for those outside Christianity. Yet we remain human beings with quivering flesh and throbbing nerves who need the small delights of emotional well-being. Much of what we have just talked about may seem far beyond our reach or experience yet, but it comforts us to believe that no exigency of life can ever rob the believer of accepting its transcendence as well as its immanence.

## Joy sustained through prayer

Unlike our emotional highs and lows, which oscillate naturally, the quality of Christian happiness is sustained by the constant presence of Christ within us. Prayer is the celebration of this constant presence. Because prayer is the language of our hearts before God, it enables us to grow in our emotional life before God, so that these qualities of Christian joy become part of our very selves. This experience is very different from having merely a cold, distant belief in God. We no longer have 'beliefs' that are isolated from the way we live or from our emotions. Instead, we become integrated and whole persons, where faith, hope and love all play a part.

Prayer becomes a constant relating to God throughout our daily lives, as we depend on him in trust and love. This is because prayer is simply allowing ourselves to become new persons in Christ, reshaped in our attitudes and emotions. To believe and trust in God means to communicate constantly with him, as friend to friend. We allow our feelings to flow out towards him in adoration, confession, thanksgiving and praise. In this way, prayer gives new shape to our emotions and a new character to our attitudes. We acknowledge who we are in his sight, and we open ourselves to receive what he has to tell us.

Prayer is therefore another dimension of our whole lives. In one of his letters, Paul told his readers to 'pray without ceasing'. The early Christian leader Origen commented on these words in his book *On Prayer*:

> *The man who links together his prayer with deeds of duty, and fits seemly actions with his prayer, is the man who prays without ceasing, for his virtuous deeds or the commandments he has fulfilled are taken up as a part of his prayer. For only in this way can we take up the saying 'pray without ceasing' as being possible, if we can say that the whole life of the saint is one mighty, integrated prayer.*

Significantly, Paul links his command to 'pray without ceasing' with two other directions: 'Be joyful always' and 'give thanks in all circumstances'. Gratitude to God is the pulse beat of prayer and communion with God. To experience the true power of prayer, we need to do away with the indifference and moral complacency that so readily chill our feelings for God. We can do this by giving thanks to God in all our circumstances. This is obviously not always an easy thing to do, especially if we are in the darkness of suffering. But giving thanks to God, even in suffering, can be inspired by a radiance of hope that sees all things in the light of eternity. To praise God, says C. S. Lewis, 'not merely expresses but completes the enjoyment; it is its appointed consummation.' As we praise God for all our circumstances, seeing them in the light of his presence and love, then we become literally 'thankful persons', transfused by a new radiance of joy and thanksgiving. The more we understand of God, the more we long to praise him for who he is.

One of the psalms says, 'Happy are the people who know the Lord as their God.' This sums up well this chapter's exploration in search of happiness. We live today between the times. The blight of western civilization has been to divorce our thought from our emotions. Even many Christians have split lives, with a thinking faith that leaves their emotions untouched. They may believe in Jesus Christ, yet they do not enjoy him. They have a rational understanding of faith, but they do not live by faith. They have lots of theological notions in their heads, but little evidence of transformed feelings for God. This is why the search for true happiness will inevitably start to expose the shallowness of our lives. And hopefully it will lead us on to deepen and enrich ourselves, providing a strong foundation for a new way of life. This quest for happiness will not fail with prayer as our means of friendship with God.

> *Light that groweth not pale*
> *With day's decrease.*
> *Love that never can fail*
> *Till life shall cease.*
> *Joy no trial can mar,*
> *Hope that shineth afar,*
> *Faith serene as a star,*
> *And Christ's own peace.*

# 12

# Delighting in God

*There is a joy that is not given to those who do not love you (O God), but only to those who love you for your own sake. You, yourself, are their joy.*

**Augustine**

The search for happiness, as we have seen, has been the quest of western civilization, as well as for all of us as individuals. That is why we have pursued its progress in the changes of society, as well as through individual story-telling. The vivid emotions of childhood are vitally important to our growth as adults, and perhaps the stages of change in society can also be likened to the stages of childhood. The recent history of western culture certainly corresponds to the struggles of adolescence: the flower-children of the sixties, the rebels of the seventies, and the yuppies of the eighties.

We have also looked further back, to the roots of our culture in the classical period, when philosophers first interpreted happiness as peace of mind. This emphasis was developed during the renaissance, when happiness was interpreted as the search for Utopia. In the modern world, we looked at the findings of psychologists, with all their promises of self-knowledge—or at least, self-analysis.

And yet, despite our earnest desire for happiness, we persist in disregarding the spiritual depths of ourselves. If it is true that God made us for himself, then without God we are bound to live with an underlying frustration and unhappiness. What should we do about this?

## Power or love?

We first need to recognize that probably our most basic choice in life is between power and love. Either we choose power or we choose love as our first priority in living. If it is power we seek, then our grammar of living is to communicate the need of achievement. To achieve or succeed we have to climb over others in the struggle to rise to the top. In a remarkably candid expression of this issue of his faith, the American Secretary of State, James Baker, said: 'Power doesn't really bring the fulfilment that many think it does.' As a successful campaign manager of two presidents, Ronald Reagan and George Bush, James Baker has been a highly efficient operator of political power. But he confessed:

> *Power, of course, can be intoxicating. It can be addictive, for power tends to corrupt and absolute power corrupts absolutely. Over these last nine years, I have had opportunities to participate in the exercise of more power than I ever imagined I would have. I have felt the weight of responsibility that that brings, and I have to admit to you as well that I have felt the temptations that are attendant to it.*

James Baker said that he had always believed that a professional should never admit to hurt or personal problems. This changed when he became aware not only that he had a personal problem, but that he was that problem. Then he began to see that friendship and love, shown to our marriage partner, our friends and to God himself, are ultimately the most important dimensions of life. He learnt, he said, that he 'really needed to stop trying to play God, and to turn the matter over to him'.

This struggle is acted out at every level of society. Jesus, too, was tempted by the Devil in the wilderness. He had to choose whether to grasp power at every opportunity or to love others and to trust in God.

We also begin to realize that making such a choice is not merely a matter of changing habits, even habits of mind. We need a change of heart to become truly unpossessive in our love for God and each other. To love in this way implies the total surrender of self. In chapter two, we saw how Gloria struggled to see God as real and relevant in her life. She had to struggle to understand what she already knew about in her head, but not in her heart. In her journal, she wrote these words to God:

> *Self-surrender is simply giving back to you what you have given me. My possessions, my talents, my desires, my friends, my knowledge, my accumulated belongings—all of them belong to you. They all have their source in you, and you have allowed me to own them. But that is just half of the plan. If I stop there and clutch my possessions, they grow to possess me and I will be their slave. I must choose to give it all back to you and to feel the happy liberation of unpossessiveness. For true freedom lies not in holding, but in letting go; not in receiving, but in giving. This is all such old stuff. I've heard it many times before. But to fully relinquish myself and to trust you, O God, is a much deeper and wider experience than I can yet fully enter into. But I am going in that direction.*

Self-surrender also means to surrender the imprints of our childhood emotions. We give up seeing ourselves as 'the dream child', 'the shadow child', 'the rejected child', or any of the other wounded images that affect our relationships with others. Of course, these images of ourselves are deeply persistent. In an indifferent and often insensitive world, we so often feel alone and misunderstood. The words of a song by the group Supertramp express the feelings of many people:

> There are times when all the world's asleep,
> the questions run too deep
> for such a simple man.
> Won't you please, please tell me what we've learned,
> I know it sounds absurd
> but please tell me who I am.

The wisdom of the ancient world saw that it is in our points of greatest personal weakness that we are most defensive, and where we compensate addictively in our emotions. However, when we recognize that God is able to rule over our personal woundedness, then we begin to appreciate how profoundly indebted we are to him. He heals us, saves us from ourselves, and redeems us. In place of an animal existence, which trivializes the needs and desires of our hearts, we see that true happiness has a glory and majesty about it. As C. S. Lewis observed in his sermon, 'The Weight of Glory':

> Indeed, if we consider the unblushing promises of reward and the staggering nature of the rewards promised in the Gospels, it would seem that Our Lord finds our desires, not too strong, but too weak. We are half-hearted creatures, fooling about with drink and sex and ambition when infinite joy is offered us, like an ignorant child who wants to go on making mud pies in a slum because he cannot imagine what is meant by the offer of a holiday at the sea. We are far too easily pleased.

Certainly, in reading the biographies of popular

celebrities, we can see the truth of this. Their total lack of concern for any spiritual growth, other than what pleases the senses of the body, exhibits what medieval writers described as Animal Man.

Yet we are also familiar within ourselves with what we may call our rational streak. We are able to remain detached observers of life. We need to rise above the animal and rational levels in us, and seek to become spiritual men and women. We have to be prepared to sacrifice lesser values such as physical or rational pleasures, and search for happiness as the gift of God to us. In the words of a quotation from William of St Thierry, worth considering again and again:

> When the object of man's thought is God and the things that belong to God, then the will reaches the stage when it becomes love. Then the Holy Spirit, the Spirit of life, makes his presence felt by the way of love and gives life to all.

But he adds:

> This way of thinking does not lie at the disposal of the thinker. It is the gift of grace. It is bestowed by the Holy Spirit who breathes where he chooses, and upon whom he chooses. Man's part is simply to prepare his heart continually by ridding his will of foreign attachments, his reason of anxieties, and his memory of idle or absorbing business—even though that business appear to be so very necessary.

That is it. Instead of merely existing on the animal or rational level, we want to experience the fullness of life as truly spiritual men and women. Then our happiness will become authentic and secure. However, there is room for even more progress. While we have already had a taste of the true joy of the Christian life, how can we progress to delight in God as the source and fulfilment of all our happiness?

## Motives for delighting in God

The Christian experience is that in this life, as the Bible puts it, 'we have no continuing city', no permanence of abode. Instead 'we seek one to come.' This sense of being a stranger on earth is well expressed by Malcolm Muggeridge, who was an old hand at lampooning the foibles of the world:

> For me there has always been—and I count it the greatest of all blessings—a window never finally blacked out, a light never finally extinguished. I had a sense, sometimes enormously vivid, that I was a stranger in a strange land; a visitor, not a native, a displaced person. The feeling, I was surprised to find, gave me a great sense of satisfaction, almost of ecstasy. Days or weeks or months might pass. Would it ever return—the lostness? I strain my ears to hear it, like distant music; my eyes see it as a very bright light very far away. Has it gone forever? And then—ah! the relief. Like slipping away from a sleeping embrace, silently shutting the door behind one, tiptoeing off in the grey light of dawn—a stranger again. The only ultimate disaster that can befall us, I have come to realize, is to feel ourselves at home here on earth. As long as we are aliens, we cannot forget our true homeland.

It is only as we remain exiles, stay-behind agents, spies in enemy territory, that we can really learn to delight in God alone. As Thomas Aquinas observed, the state of ultimate happiness does not lie within ourselves, but in God alone. One of the psalms says: 'My soul, find rest in God alone.'

This then leads us to explore ultimate happiness in God's

own being. God delights in himself. Happiness is his essential nature. He is therefore the ground and source of all goodness and happiness. God's pleasure in himself is not a self-contained, self-satisfied pleasure, as we might imagine. God is a Trinity of three distinct persons, each loving and relating to the others within the unity of God. So the happiness of God—the happiness that is at the heart of the universe—is in the eternal relationship of the Father, Son and Holy Spirit.

It is in the descent of the Son to earth, and his return to the Father, that we learn how we too can relate to God's happiness. We renounce our own way of living and thinking to live the life of obedient faith—just as Jesus lived on earth. Our happiness lies, as Jesus said, in doing the things that please the Father. Only by the power of his Spirit can we see our lives oriented with his life; his will with our will.

It is God as Father who enables us to see the true essence of God. It is God as Son who reveals God to us in terms we can understand—by becoming a human being. It is God as Spirit who brings us the intimate presence of God to us, enabling us to be friends of God. It is no wonder that Christians throughout the ages have said that by contemplating the Trinity they have found the ultimate essence, expression and exercise of happiness. How does God communicate this happiness to us?

God's happiness generates new life within our hearts. It makes us more fully alive, like the sap in a vine that brings life to the branches. God's vitality and happiness produce the fruit of the Spirit that is 'love, joy and peace'. God's happiness also nourishes our inner life. It feeds the soul, so that we can grow spiritually and become more like Jesus Christ. God's happiness is contagious, producing delight in the lives of those who worship him. Out of the fullness of our hearts, praise flows out to God like a river in flood.

These are descriptions of a transformed, and transforming, happiness. The dazzling reality of God's happiness can only become a living experience in our lives when we discover the spiritual disciplines that keep us close to God.

The key to delighting in God is going through a constant process of sublimation. We exchange the things of lesser value for the things of greater value. This is what Paul meant when he said: 'I count all things but loss, for the excellence of the knowledge of Christ Jesus my Lord.' Jesus once told a parable about a merchant who sold everything that he had, in order to buy one single pearl of immense value. All growth of character implies this exchange of the lesser for the greater. There is the self-denial of the musician who devotes all her time and energy to mastering her musical instrument. We too are called to exchange the things that are important to us for the sake of the transformation God wishes to work in us.

How do we do this? We can simply summarize these ways as meditating on God's word, living a life of prayer and praise, and growing in our love for God.

## Meditating on God's word

Meditating on the Bible is a personalized way of thinking, reading, and learning from God. It is a homely way of doing your own theology. Meditation is habit-forming. It cultivates in us attitudes of obedience, humility before God, sensitivity to our conscience, spiritual discernment and moral wisdom. Meditation is a tacit way of acknowledging that truth does not live in us, but in God alone. It is a way of living 'under the shadow of the Almighty'. Meditation can bring us into the immediate presence of God. This is what the Deuteronomist meant, when he said: 'The word is near you; it is in your mouth and in your heart.'

The psalm par excellence for the practice of meditation is Psalm 119. At least nine times over the writer expresses his delight in meditating upon God and his word. Twice he says, 'I will delight myself in your statutes.' He also speaks of God's testimonies as being his delight. He compares himself with those whose hardened hearts are calloused and unfeeling, and then says: 'But I delight in your law.' By 'the law', the writer means a whole way of living. This is why no fewer than eight different terms are used to convey the richness of the law, which reveals God's own character. By spending each morning meditating on one verse and each week upon one stanza, we can happily fill half a year on this wonderful psalm alone.

Blaise Pascal has observed that 'a man's own need is the measure of his greatness'. This is certainly the case when we measure our intimate need of God before his word, in a constant life of meditation. Jesus is often described in the Gospels as 'having compassion' on people. This does not mean merely a general concern for others, but a unique perception of the precise needs of those who came to him. In meditation, we encounter the compassion of God for us. He knows the precise needs of our hearts, in such a unique and personal way that we experience the remarkable conviction that we are being personally and intimately addressed by his word. This is why meditation on God's word is of such vital and central significance for our personal and spiritual growth. We learn to delight in God alone.

In the meditative life, we exchange the worldly things that give us delight for the full commitment of loving God above all. The poet George Herbert knew this well, and expressed it best in his poem *The Pearl*:

> *I know all these, and have them in my hand:*
> *Therefore not sealed, but with open eyes*
> *I flie to thee, and fully understand*
> *Both the main sale, and the commodities;*
> *And at what rate and price I have thy love;*
> *With all the circumstances that may move:*
> *Yet through all these labyrinths, not my grovelling*
> *wit,*

*But thy silk twist let down from heav'n to me*
*Did both conduct and teach me, how by it*
*To climbe to thee.*

In the legend of Theseus, in Greek mythology, he prevented himself from getting lost in the Cretan labyrinth by holding on to a silken thread. The thread eventually led him out once more to safety. George Herbert took up this image by saying that God's 'silk twist' links earth to heaven. That thread is the word of God that guides us in our climb to God. Meditation is holding on to that silken thread throughout life. We make whatever sacrifices and exchanges we can for the 'pearl' of our objective, beyond the labyrinth of the world.

## Living a life of prayer and praise

Meditating on God's word leads us forward into contemplating God himself. These two motions of the heart towards desiring God are closely related and yet are quite distinct. They can be distinguished as desiring to know God's will, and delighting to live in God's presence. Desire for God prepares us for delight in God. The thought that prayer is ultimately about delighting in God helps us to stop seeing it as a 'technique' in which we are advancing. The purpose of praying is not prayer, but to delight in God, and commune with him for his own sake.

Of course, we also need to pray for the needs that others have, as well as for our own needs. We live exhausted, frustrated, perplexing lives that need the strength and clarity of purpose that God alone can give us. James, writing in the New Testament, focuses on the fact that we pray to the 'giving God', who enjoys giving to those who ask him. James calls him 'the Father of lights, who does not change like shifting shadows'. According to James, much of our unhappiness comes about by failing to ask God for what we need: 'You do not have, because you do not ask God. When you ask, you do not receive, because you ask with wrong motives.' The psalms help us to interpret this, by reminding us that we are given our heart's desires when we also delight in God:

> *O Lord, the king rejoices in your strength.*
> *How great are the victories you give!*
> *You have granted him the desire of his heart*
> *and have not withheld the request of his lips.*
> *He asked you for life, and you gave it to him—*
> *length of days for ever and ever.*

> *Delight yourself in the Lord*
> *and he will give you the desires of your heart.*

As we contemplate God in the beauty of his holiness, he shapes our hearts and our desires to what gives him delight. His happiness becomes our happiness, and his life becomes ours too. He gives us of himself, to be like him. This looking towards God is therefore the life of contemplation, which is at the heart of the truly Christian life. We can only experience God's happiness for ourselves when we grow in contemplative prayer. This is impossible without the Trinity, in which each person of the Godhead delights in the others. We live in the knowledge that 'the grace of our Lord Jesus Christ, and the love of God and the fellowship of the Holy Spirit' are indeed with us always.

A contemplative way of life can only grow gradually, because it implies the transformation of our natural, instinctual way of operating. Our emotional addictions need to be destroyed. Our inner wounds need to be healed. We have to learn to trust not in our own feelings, but in the God of our feelings. All this takes time. We discover that prayer grows as it keeps pace with the moral and emotional changes within us.

The essence of prayer is this: is our relationship with God characterized by the words of the psalm: 'My soul, find rest in God alone'? Resting and delighting in God is not confined to the mind, nor to the emotions, but brings our whole being into the presence of God. This means that we contemplate God in our many different moods and emotional conditions. We contemplate both the small things and the great realities, at times when it is very hard work, when we feel spiritually dry and unreceptive, or when we rejoice in God and receive his refreshment. Contemplation can mean watchfulness and moral vigilance, as well as quiet discernment and the pursuit of wisdom. Why is it so diverse, so varied in its character? Because the object of contemplation is God himself, who opens to us the infinite possibilities of himself and of our own lives.

It certainly makes a great difference to our lives when we see prayer as delighting in God. Prayer then becomes a way of living wholly before God. It becomes spontaneous, and is an intimate expression of our inner selves. We stop seeing prayer merely as a means of asking for things from God —important though that is. Instead, it is praise that begins to empower our prayer-filled lives. This is a praise that flows from superabundance, when 'our cup runs over'.

## Growing in our love for God

As we saw earlier in the book, our culture majors in rationality, while staying fearful and ignorant of human emotions. In contrast, the life of the Christian is a full-blooded existence. We are called to love the Lord our God with all our heart, and all our mind, and all our strength. Desiring and delighting in God express the fullness with which we love him. Miguel de Unamuno, the Spanish philosopher, made a point of this when he showed that it is impossible to separate belief from emotion:

*Those who say that they believe in God and yet neither love nor fear him, do not in fact believe in him but in those who have taught them that God exists. Those who believe that they believe in God, but without any passion in their heart, any anguish of mind, without uncertainty, without doubt, without an element of despair even in their consolation, believe only in the God-idea, not in God.*

True religious feelings clothe the nakedness of theory with practice. They give flesh to our desire for God and become lived expressions of our life in God's life. This does not mean that we all display the same feelings about God or become the same temperamental type. Some people are full of effervescence and spontaneity in their faith, while others are more quiet and reflective. We are not talking here about natural feelings, but a depth of desire which is given to us by God. This focuses on the effects of God's grace within our lives; the evidence of his Spirit at work in our spirits.

God has made us so that our affections are very much the spring of all our actions. Whatever affects us deeply will also take hold of our souls. This is why the Bible shows so much concern about the danger of having 'hardness of heart', or of being coldly indifferent in our thoughts towards God. It is much easier for us to disobey God when we have developed a calloused conscience, or have paralysed our desires for God.

The Bible is full of powerful imagery about the heart. The heart not only explains what we do, but why we do it. This inner focus is truly the compass of our lives, directing us in the ways we live and behave. This is why the Bible tells us that we need to have a 'new heart'—or, in modern terms, a heart transplant. This shows that faith, obedience, and belief are all intrinsically bound up with the cultivation of emotions that are appropriate to the truths we profess to believe. No one can believe in righteousness without living righteously. No one can love God or delight in God without having a passion for God. So the whole language of meditation, prayer, praise, contemplation and the love of God is interlocked with our emotions and commitment to God.

The New Testament is full of signs of the emotional engagement of its writers. They speak of having 'boldness', or the most intimate inner assurance, in their expressions of faith and worship. Godly sorrow, gratitude, humility, mercy, joy, thankfulness, love—all communicate the pulse beat of the believer's heart in the light of the good news of Jesus Christ. Desiring God is the essence of our response to God. This link between emotion and belief is beautifully expressed in the words of the Anglican Prayer Book:

*Almighty God, unto whom all hearts be open, all desires known, and from whom no secrets are hid. Cleanse the thoughts of our hearts by the inspiration of thy Holy Spirit, that we may perfectly love thee and worthily magnify thy holy name; through Jesus Christ our Lord.*

This is not simply to say that emotions are expressed, but that emotions are reformed, cleansed, redirected and redeemed. The practice of meditation and contemplation is life-long, reflecting this daily process of repentance and change at heart. We should never take for granted that we will find our happiness in God alone, as though it was ours by right to have. Instead, we need to live with discipline, persistence, and daily dependence upon God.

It is the mark of a truly human, and truly happy, life that we are ultimately contented in God alone. 'I have learned,' said Paul, 'in whatever state I am, to be content.' Paul had found all the resources for living, all the things that attracted him, all the relationships that mattered, in God alone. 'I have learnt the secret of being content,' he admitted, 'in any and every situation, whether well fed or hungry, whether living in plenty or in want.' Then he explained how he had found this incredible contentment: 'I can do all things through him who gives me strength.'

For all of us, happiness is the result of everything we have experienced and possessed in life. It is in a sense the balance sheet of our human existence, the closing of the accounts. A happy life is a good life, the mark of integrity. But, without contentment and happiness in God, it can be interpreted as a complacent, even smug, life. Blaise Pascal has the last word:

*Happiness is neither outside or inside us.*
*It is in God, both outside and inside us.*

# For Further Reading

Among the books quoted in the text, the following are particularly noteworthy:

Jonathan Edwards, *The Religious Affections*, Yale University, 1954.

T.S. Eliot, *The Family Reunion*, Faber and Faber, 1939.

E.N. Genovese, The Utopian Vision, San Diego State University, 1983.

Andre Gide, *Two Legends: Oedipus and Theseus*, A.A. Knopf, 1950.

Hermann Hesse, *Siddharta*, Picador, 1975.

C.F. Jung, *Psychological Reflections*, Harper and Row, 1961.

C.S. Lewis, *Miracles*, Macmillan, 1947.

C.S. Lewis, *The Screwtape Letters*, Collins, 1954.

Shirley MacLaine, *Dancing in the Light*, Bantam, 1985.

John MacMurray, *Reason and Emotion*, Faber and Faber, 1962.

John H. Schaar, *And the Pursuit of Happiness*, Virginia Quarterly Review, 1970.

Anthony Storr, *Solitude*, Fontana.

Theodore Tack, *If Augustine Were Alive Today*, Alba House, 1988.

Paul C. Vitz, *Psychology as Religion*, Lion, 1981.

Denis Wholey, *Are you Happy?* Houghton Mifflin, 1986.

# Index

# INDEX